INDENTURED SERVITUDE

STATES, PEOPLE, AND THE HISTORY OF SOCIAL CHANGE
Series editors: Rosalind Crone and Heather Shore

The States, People, and the History of Social Change series brings together
cutting-edge books written by academic historians on criminal justice, welfare,
education, health, and other areas of social change and social policy. The ways in
which states, governments, and local communities have responded to "social
problems" can be seen across many different temporal and geographical
contexts. From the early modern period to contemporary times, states have
attempted to shape the lives of their inhabitants in important ways. Books in
this series explore how groups and individuals have negotiated the use of state
power and policy to regulate, change, control, or improve peoples' lives and the
consequences of these processes. The series welcomes international scholars
whose research explores social policy (and its earlier equivalents) as well as
other responses to social need, in historical perspective.

Indentured Servitude

Unfree Labour and Citizenship in the British Colonies

ANNA SURANYI

McGill-Queen's University Press
Montreal & Kingston · London · Chicago

© McGill-Queen's University Press 2021

ISBN 978-0-2280-0667-1 (cloth)
ISBN 978-0-2280-0668-8 (paper)
ISBN 978-0-2280-0778-4 (ePDF)
ISBN 978-0-2280-0779-1 (ePUB)

Legal deposit third quarter 2021
Bibliothèque nationale du Québec

Printed in Canada on acid-free paper that is 100% ancient forest free
(100% post-consumer recycled), processed chlorine free

Library and Archives Canada Cataloguing in Publication

Title: Indentured servitude : unfree labor and citizenship in the British colonies /
    Anna Suranyi.
Names: Suranyi, Anna, 1967– author.
Series: States, people, and the history of social change ; 4.
Description: Series statement: States, people, and the history of social change ; 4
    | Includes bibliographical references and index.
Identifiers: Canadiana (print) 20210144653 | Canadiana (ebook) 20210144807
    | ISBN 9780228006688 (softcover) | ISBN 9780228006671 (hardcover)
    | ISBN 9780228007784 (PDF) | ISBN 9780228007791 (ePUB)
Subjects: LCSH: Indentured servants—Great Britain—History—17th century.
    | LCSH: Indentured servants—Great Britain—Social conditions—17th century.
    | LCSH: Contract labor—Great Britain—History—17th century. | LCSH: Slave
    labor—Great Britain—History—17th century.
Classification: LCC HD4875.G7 S87 2021 | DDC 303.3/63094109032—dc23

This book was typeset by True to Type in 10.5/13 Sabon

Contents

Figures

Notes on Spelling and Punctuation

In quoting from seventeenth- and eighteenth-century sources, I have mostly left spelling as is, except for the following changes: I have modernized capitalization and changed the anachronistic letters *u, f, i*, and *y* [the thorn] into their modern variants (as in "seruant" to "servant," "flaue" to "slave," "ffreedome" to "freedome," "Ione" to "Jone"[Joan], and "ye" to "the," while "gyuen" becomes "gyven"). For shorthand abbreviations, I have supplied the missing letters in brackets, clarifying that "plt" means "pl[ain]t[iff]" or "agst" means "ag[ain]st." If a word can be relatively easily deciphered, I have left it as is. For instance, I have not modified the historical spelling of the suffix "tion" in modern English, which was usually spelled "con" in the seventeenth century, as in "condicon" or "transportacon." For some idiosyncratically spelled words, I have supplied modern spellings in brackets while leaving the original in the text: "roage"[rogue]. Irregular spellings of first names and surnames, such as Margarett or Bradye, have remained. In some cases, I have added punctuation (mainly commas) to clarify meaning.

Preface

During the seventeenth century, hundreds of thousands of men, women, and children from Britain and Ireland journeyed across the Atlantic Ocean to populate England's new colonies in the Caribbean and on the American mainland. Most of them, about 70 per cent, were indentured servants, who undertook their odysseys for a variety of reasons. The majority were impoverished and searching for greater opportunity and sometimes adventure overseas. A significant proportion were captives, transported by government forces because they were seen as vagrants, criminals, or rebels, and some were trafficked by "spirits," professional kidnappers. Once servants arrived in the colonies, they were expected to work without wages for terms of four, seven, or more years, until receiving a payment of "freedom dues" at the end of their servitude. They often worked alongside enslaved labourers from Africa, who shared many of the labour conditions of the servants, but who remained captives for life. Indentured servants were frequently maltreated and exploited, but unlike enslaved people, servants possessed crucial rights of English and British subjects, not only to eventual freedom but also to certain standards of food, shelter, clothing, and care; to the final payment of freedom dues; and to defend their rights in court.

This book examines the role of indentured servitude in Britain and its colonies during the seventeenth and early eighteenth centuries, from the initial process of indenture in Britain and Ireland to the experience of living and working as an indentured servant in the North American and Caribbean colonies. In addition to establishing a population of white settlers in the British colonies, indentured servitude also shaped the way that settler communities envisioned themselves. The practice of indentured servitude was a crucial factor in shaping ideals of citizenship on both sides of the Atlantic. The condition of indentured servants in an undefined category between free English people and enslaved Africans compelled English and colonial societies to define the status of indentured servants and, by extension, the relationship of the subject to the state. By the time of the American Revolution, indentured servitude had had a significant role in shaping emerging ideals of citizenship.

In studying indentured servitude, I have examined a variety of documents, including indenture contracts; British and colonial government documents and legislation; political, moral, and economic treatises; autobiographical accounts; poetry, letters, wills, runaway ads, and other material. One of the most valuable of sources has been court cases from both Britain and the colonies, which described individuals being sentenced to servitude; servants being punished for misdeeds; servants taking their masters to court; merchants, sea captains, and government officials being penalized for illegal shipping of servants; disputes over freedom dues and indenture terms, and more. Together, these sources help to demonstrate the contemporary legal criteria defining indenture as well as the lived realities of indentured servants. They also show the resourcefulness of servants, who adapted to adverse circumstances, and strove for opportunity, agency, and better lives. Their struggle continues to resonate in our own time. We are still confronted with the fundamental problems of poverty and inequality, and there are similarities to the practices of the past in current official responses, which range from assistance and encouragement to exploitation, imprisonment, and forced labour. This book confines itself to the seventeenth and early eighteenth centuries, but readers will recognize some reflections of contemporary society.

Acknowledgments

In working on this book, I have benefited from conversations and encouragement from a number of colleagues and others who have supported my work in both large and small ways. I list them here: Semahagn Abebe, Sam Alexander, Katie Barnes, Steven Bruso, Arianne Chernock, Paul Deslandes, Charlotte Gordon, Mark Herlihy, Jerry Hunter, Brendan Kane, Krista Kesselring, Darryl Key, Ilham Khuri-Makdisi, Audrey Koke, Brian Lewis, Mel Manson, Liz Matelski, Muriel McClendon, Kelsey McNiff, Shannon McSheffrey, Maura O'Connor, Sharon Paradiso, Jen Purcell, Cindy Richard, Betty Roland, Laura Rossi-Le, Caroline Shaw, Jenny Shaw, Hilda Smith, Bob Tittler, Pamela Walker, Gab Watling, Elizabeth Winthrop, Gene Wong, and Elizabeth Wood, as well as many wonderful students. Additionally, I am grateful to the archivists and library staff at the Barbados National Archives, Boston Public Library, British Library, British National Archives, Brown University Library, Folger Shakespeare Library, Halle Library at Endicott College, Harvard University Libraries, London Metropolitan Archives, Maryland State Archives, Massachusetts Historical Society, Swem Library at the College of William and Mary, and University of Cincinnati library, for their help in procuring books and documents. I benefited from the use of a number of recently digitized collections, including British History Online, the Old Bailey Online, and the Archives of Maryland Online that have been of great usefulness. The team at McGill-Queen's University Press has been immensely helpful and supportive, especially acquisitions editor Richard Baggaley and managing editor Kathleen Fraser, as well as copy editor Eleanor Gasparik. I also appreciate the funding and leave time provided by Endicott College. In addition, I thank my husband, Tim Correll, and my children, Thalia and Jesse, for their support and patience in living with this manuscript for quite a long time.

INDENTURED SERVITUDE

1

Introduction

In 1661, Ricckett Mecane, an Irish indentured servant who had been "taken by force out of his native country" seven years earlier, appeared before a Maryland court, arguing that he had been held in indenture past the age of twenty-one, at which age a servant indentured in his youth should be released. He had been one of eight Irish boys kidnapped in 1654. Mecane's master, Thomas Gerrard, contended that Mecane had eight more years to serve. In order to be heard, Mecane first petitioned the court, which agreed "that the servant have the liberty to sue his master."[1] The local sheriff brought the case to the St Mary's County Court "to see justice done in the busines."[2] Once in court, Mecane argued that to remain in servitude for another eight years would be "contrary to the lawes of God and man that a Christian subject should be made a slave."[3] The court investigated, calling witnesses and checking archived records. The witnesses verified the dates of Mecane's arrival and expressed criticism of Gerrard's employing young children. Ultimately the court compromised between the two, but favoured the servant more than the master, and determined that Mecane had two more years to serve.[4] The following year, Mecane was sued by Gerrard to recover the court costs from the previous case and was temporarily arrested; yet by 1663, Mecane was a free man, and empanelled on a jury examining a case of suicide.[5] Mecane's suit illustrates many of the contradictory realities of indentured servitude. He had suffered from the initial abduction as a child and the many years of toil, but he had successfully established himself as a subject with rights and came to be acknowledged as a member of the settler community.

A similar case was that of Hester Nicholls, who was indentured at age ten or eleven in 1659 by her father John Nicholls, a poor Maryland farmer, to a wealthy planter, Thomas Cornwallis. In 1661, after Hester was resold by her master, her father sued for her freedom, arguing that Hester's indenture contract had specified that she be treated like her master's child and be taught to read and sew.[6] Although indentured women as well as children usually represented themselves in court, Hester Nicholls was somewhat unusual in that she had been indentured in the colonies and had family nearby. In general, unmarried daughters were usually represented in court by their fathers, if they were available.[7] After an initial victory in court, which found Hester's contract "illegall deceitfull and voyd," the Nicholls family ultimately lost the case on appeal, as the superior wealth and status of her master prevailed, aided by the fact that Hester's indenture contract, when produced, did not promise anything other than that Hester would "serve the said Thomas" and his wife, who were to provide Hester with "meate [food], drinke, apparrell and lodging."[8] As in Mecane's case, John Nicholls described Hester's condition as "slavery," and countered that his daughter, by then about fourteen, was "a free woman borne in this province." Nicholls referred to Hester's sale as "contrary to equity and justice," and asked for a court order "for her freedome soe that yo[u]r poore pet[itione]rs daughter may not be made a slave."[9]

Cornwallis's defence demonstrated concern not only about this particular lawsuit but also about the impact on his own business. He was a prominent merchant who described himself as a pillar of the community. He was also a shipper of servants. Cornwallis claimed "att his greate cost and charges ... for the space of twenty eight yeares [he had] been one of the greatest propagators & increasers thereof by the yearely transportacon of servants." He vehemently rebutted Nicholls's claim of slavery, objecting that the use of the word "slave" would deter potential future British servants from engaging in indenture contracts: it was "a tearme soe scandalous that if admitted to be the condicon or title" of indentured servants, then "noe free borne Christians will ever be induced to come over [as] servants." Cornwallis insisted that he was a responsible master of servants and had always kept his obligations toward them: "he hath always been soe carefull to discharge a good conscience in the true p[er]formance of his promises and obligacons, that he was never taxed with any breach thereof."[10]

Cornwallis tried to diminish the credibility of the Nicholls family by claiming that a witness from the initial trial, Edward West, had lied because he was Hester's fiancé.[11] He described himself as a good judge of servants, "whereof divers have been of very good ranck and quality" whereas Hester was a "rude, rawe, ill bred childe" and "useles" servant.[12] Finally, Cornwallis sanctimoniously concluded that negating Hester's father's claim about slavery would see "the abused serv[an]ts and apprentices of this province righted," shrewdly transforming Nicholls's claim of abuse into a slur toward other servants.[13] Although Cornwallis's statements were shaped by a self-righteous legal defence, his emphasis on his conscientiousness and aversion to the term "slave" delineated the official position that indentured servitude was a separate category of labour bondage from slavery. While in this case the defendant's privilege prevailed over the impoverished plaintiff's, the dispute also demonstrates, like the Mecane case, the obligations pertaining to the masters of servants, the right of servants to litigate against their masters, and the serious attention paid by the authorities to the rights and subjecthood of servants.

The lawsuits brought by Ricckett Mecane and John Nicholls on behalf of his daughter Hester highlight the legal, economic, moral, social, and even political complexities of the practice of indentured servitude.

Indentured servitude had a significant impact on both British and colonial societies, affecting labour economics, early capitalism, and discourses about poverty and labour as well as race and gender and citizenship. The two cases, which are addressed further in this book, touch upon many of the issues pertaining to servitude, including legal protections for servants, Irish servitude, kidnapping, the status of women and child servants, and justifications for servitude. The existence of indentured servitude and the debates about its validity shaped the development of societal attitudes about slavery, race, and citizenship, and influenced the creation of economic structures that developed into slavery. For individual indentured servants themselves, servitude led to a diversity of outcomes, ranging from increased social standing and economic opportunity to exploitation, poverty, and death.

The nature of indentured servitude was influenced at every level by the ambiguousness of the status of servants, positioned between "freeborn" English men and woman, and enslaved people. Inconsistencies were rife at every level, from official regulations in Britain and the colonies to legal encounters on both sides of the Atlantic to personal relationships between servants and their masters and mistresses. Servitude, for all of its injustice and exploitation, was distinct from slavery, yet the two forms of unfree labour had many attributes in common. During the seventeenth century, evolving social norms resulted in an increasing desire to sustain the distinction between the two through legislation. Ultimately, the need for more precise demarcation was a factor in the development of a nascent sense of citizenship, encompassing white colonists, that was to transform the relationship of colonial subjects to their government.

INDENTURED SERVITUDE COMPARED TO SLAVERY

During the eighteenth century, the servant trade began diminishing in scope because of the rise of an even more exploitative labour arrangement: African slavery. The two institutions shared many similarities, but they were also substantively different. Servants petitioning against their masters in court, like Ricckett Mecane or Hester Nicholls's father on his daughter's behalf, claimed that their experiences were tantamount to enslavement, but their very presence in court, as well as the arguments and verdicts in their cases delineated the differences. Perhaps the most important distinctions were the assurance of legal rights and the expectation of eventual freedom that were the due of indentured servants, who remained subjects of the British state. According to historian Betty Wood, it was "the legally binding guarantee of eventual freedom that differentiated indentured servitude from chattel slavery."[14] Although the language often remained ambiguous, from the 1620s, colonial laws in the Caribbean and on the mainland differentiated between "whites" or "Christians" and "blacks" or "Negroes," designating the former as temporary servants, the latter as enslaved for life.[15]

Both servitude and slavery were forms of bondage that deprived people of freedom and violated human rights. But to elide the differences between the two forms of exploitation is to flatten the ways in which the exploitation of the enslaved was more severe than that of indentured servants. There are two prevalent false narratives that persistently appear in popular culture: first, that indentured servitude was tantamount to slavery and, second, that the Irish made up the majority of indentured servants and were treated differently from other nationalities (this second theme is addressed in chapter 3).[16] The "white slavery" and "Irish slavery" myths have been contested by

Jerome Handler and other historians.[17] Works that promote these ideas are not only historically problematic but also racist, aiming to detract from condemnations of African slavery. Some of the promoters are affiliated with white supremacist groups. Unfortunately, there are increasing numbers of books, websites, pseudo-documentaries, blogs, and other media sources "replete with historical inaccuracies" that are reaching ever-wider audiences.[18]

There is no question that indentured servitude was a brutal and exploitative form of coerced labour. Like the enslaved, newly arrived indentured servants were typically sold from the decks of ships for the period of their indenture. Servants were purchased more cheaply than enslaved Africans because they served for limited periods, but also because the inherent rights that they possessed decreased the labour value that could be extracted from them. Servants did share some conditions with the enslaved: they were expected to be humble, loyal, and deferential toward their masters and mistresses, and to serve without pay. Masters and mistresses could physically punish servants deemed to have misbehaved by striking or beating them, yet they were not permitted by either law or custom to cause permanent harm or incapacity; they were not entitled to kill, rape, or maim servants, or to whip them naked.[19] On the other hand, there were few restraints on violence toward the enslaved, or even toward free people of colour.[20]

Children born to indentured women could be taken from their mothers and indentured until age twenty-one, but they would then obtain their freedom. Separation of a child from its indentured mother happened frequently, but required a court decision and usually court oversight of the child's care. By contrast, the children of enslaved women remained enslaved for perpetuity and could be separated from their mothers at any time with impunity. Masters and mistresses of indentured servants had a legal obligation to provide their servants with adequate clothing, food, and shelter, and to pay freedom dues. There was no obligation to care for enslaved people according to any kind of standard.

Indentured servants had recognized legal rights; one of the most important, as shown in Christine Daniels's "Liberty to Complaine," was the right to testify and petition in court if they were mistreated.[21] Servant plaintiffs frequently won their cases in court.[22] The many thousands of such cases, some of which are examined in this book, show that this right was taken seriously by the courts, and understood by servants. Some colonial courts appointed free legal counsel to servants, in accordance with English common law, as I discuss in chapter 4. In contrast, those who were enslaved were unable to petition nor lawfully testify as witnesses in court. They "had no legally recognized rights."[23]

Cultural norms also protected indentured servants to some degree. For example, in 1639, John Winter of Richmond Island, Maine, defended his wife in a letter to Richard Trelawny, the organizer of his fishing settlement, in response to criticisms that had reached Trelawny in England – "some yll reports" made against Mrs Winter "for beatinge the maid," Pricilla Bickford, who had been punished for idleness and running away. Winter's defensive letter demonstrates the disapproval of his community, leading him to protest that the beatings "hath never hurt her body."[24] Such objections were not made to the routine whipping of the enslaved.

Enslaved people could and did resist their bondage in both small and more substantial ways, but the opportunities to do so were fewer and the consequences more dire than for indentured servants. While indentured servants also endured brutality and a loss of self-sovereignty, their circumstances provided greater autonomy and dignity, more personal safety, a recognition of their subjecthood, and the promise of eventual release, unlike the situation of enslaved Africans.

It is questionable whether there was a real choice involved for the majority of servants, even those who voluntarily entered indentured servitude – they were constrained by poverty and lack of opportunity, and were deceived by false advertising about the benefits of indenture. Nonetheless, the numbers of servants who survived their terms of servitude and joined colonial society, or even prospered, increased greatly during the seventeenth century.

Indentured servitude could be a death sentence, especially during the early days of servitude in the 1620s. This was a function of the high mortality rates in the colonies, which resulted in casualties among a large percentage of the settler population – higher than they would have experienced in England.[25] Virginia, for example, experienced very high mortality rates until the 1640s, after which the population began to increase sharply; of indentured servants, about 40 per cent died while in servitude in the early seventeenth century, dropping to 5 per cent fifty years later.[26] In 1670, Virginia governor Berkeley stated that new people "both whites and blacks" rarely died after arrival in the colony, whereas in the first year of the colony, "not one of five scaped."[27] Indentured servants were more likely to die, in part because there were significantly higher death rates for new migrants than for creoles.[28] It is difficult to disaggregate mortality rates for indentured servants specifically, but the figures given above for Virginia essentially accorded to general mortality rates for both servants and the general population in the mainland colonies over the seventeenth century.[29] Mortality rates were higher in the Caribbean for all populations: white and black, free, indentured and enslaved. Indentured servants in Barbados were more likely to die there than they would have been on the other side of the Atlantic, especially if they were serving the long terms given to criminals and rebels.[30] In Jamaica, about 15 per cent of the white settler population died annually in the late seventeenth and early eighteenth centuries.[31] Yet while death in indenture effectively made servitude a fatal sentence, slavery *always* comprised condemnation to a lifetime of inescapable cruelty and denial of humanity.

Scholars have frequently argued that it was Bacon's Rebellion in Virginia in 1676 that led the British colonies to seek ways to legally distinguish those in servitude from the enslaved.[32] The armed conflict involved collusion between indentured servants, enslaved labourers, and free white settlers seeking to seize Native American lands against the will of the English authorities, and demonstrated the dangers of cohesion among bound labourers.[33] However, I argue that from the beginning of the seventeenth century, colonial governments as well as settler communities strove to delineate servants and enslaved people, not only to define divergent forms of labour bondage but also to define different categories of people. While the rebellion did serve as a catalyst in this regard, earlier legislation as well as practices on the ground were already moving in that direction well before the 1670s. By mid-century, the population of the enslaved was becoming equal to the population of servants, and would soon supersede it.[34] Thus control over enslaved people, who had evident incentives for rebellion, had rapidly become an important concern for colonial governments. Indentured servants participated in Bacon's Rebellion under the perception that the promise of landownership through freedom dues was their right as they took their place in American society as freemen, but that this right had been unfairly limited by the British government's treaties with Native American nations. Enslaved individuals joined the rebellion because they hoped for individual freedom, but there was no expectation of wholesale abolition of slavery.

English law made sharp distinctions between servitude and slavery quite early on. These ideals were established based on precedents from the ancient world, Iberian Atlantic slavery, the English common law, and references in the Bible.[35] In England, the common law distinguished between slavery and servitude even before African slavery or indentured servitude existed in practice. In 1628, jurist Edward Coke's summation of the common laws explained that the relationship of apprentices and servants to their masters was similar to that of enslaved people to slaveholders, but also "more mild and limited," with the master of a servant only "entitled to their personal labour during the term stipulated ... consequently the master cannot claim any other acquisitions."[36] In England, a 1660 Council of Foreign Plantations report ambiguously stated that "servants are either blacks or whites," but went on to specify that blacks were "perpetual servants" while whites "after certain years (which are usually four or five years) are free to plant themselves, or to take wages for their service." The same report recommended government roundups of "felons and sturdy beggars" but condemned "spirits" or professional kidnappers who were involved in "forcing, tempting and seducing" servants into indenture.[37]

Colonial laws made sure to clarify that enslaved people and servants occupied separate categories. Even early colonial laws and informal texts employed the term "Negroes" in contrast to "Christians" or "servants."[38] These terms themselves are enlightening, because for seventeenth-century Englishmen, they delineated indisputable inborn classifications, distinguishing between Christian European servants and African "Negro" slaves, rather than merely designations of categories of bound labour. Even as early as the 1620s, prior to the formal legal codification of servant and slave status, there were already well-established informal customary norms that reflected differences in practices.[39] Arms were restricted from "Negroes," even if they were free people, as opposed to servants, who in some cases from as early as the 1630s were expected to carry guns.[40] The earliest colonial slave law was a 1636 code from Barbados that specified that "Negroes and Indians" would serve for life, unless they previously possessed a contract, but no such contractual agreements have been recorded.[41] Such laws prevailed on the mainland as well. A 1638 Maryland act limiting terms of indentured servitude to four years for adults specified that it applied to "all persons being Christians (slaves excepted)."[42] A 1664 Maryland law defined the length of indentured servitude, "provided that this acte nor anything there in conteyned shall not give or be construed to give any benefitt to any slave whatsoever."[43] This phrase was repeated in a 1676 elaboration of the law.[44] The 1661 Barbados slave code, one of the earlier surviving law codes from the island, referred to "Negroes" by nature as "heathenish, brutish and an uncertain dangerous kind of people." It ordered harsh punishments for a "Negro" or slave who harmed a "Christian," clarified that the enslaved had no right to be heard in court, and gave masters impunity to enact any kind of harm on enslaved people. This law and subsequent laws also made certain to codify the status of the "Negroes" as "chattel."[45] Meanwhile, in 1676, but before Bacon's Rebellion was well underway, the Lords of Trade and Plantations, a body supporting the colonial administration, reprimanded the Jamaican Assembly for referring to the "servitude" of white servants, because it was "a mark of bondage and slavery," inappropriate for people who were "only apprentices for years."[46]

The fact that servants were subjects of the British commonwealth was also acknowledged in early colonial laws. As white servants were inherently "Christians," colonial assemblies mandated that servants had a right to religious participation. From the 1630s, the Virginia assembly repeatedly reiterated that servants, as members of the household, should be taught the rudiments of Christian doctrine: "And all fathers, mothers, maysters and mistrisses shall cause theire children, servants or apprentizes which have not learned the catechism to come to the church at the tyme appointed, obedientlie to heare, and be ordered by the mynister until they have learned the same." To induce compliance, if any masters were to "neglect their duties," then "they shall be censured by the corts."[47] In contrast, that duty was not obligatory for enslaved persons – instead, a 1667 law stated that slaveholders, of their own "charity and piety," could "permit" their slaves to be baptized but should be "freed from this doubt" that doing so would free their slaves.[48]

While violence toward servants was punishable by the courts, masters essentially had impunity to inflict any punishment or to murder their slaves.[49] In Virginia, An Act About the Casuall Killing of Slaves (1669) established that the death of an enslaved person during punishment was not murder.[50] The 1705 Virginia slave and servant code specified that masters should not give indentured servants "immoderate" punishment nor whip them on their bare backs, but that if a master killed a slave while "correcting" him or her, then he "shall be free and acquit of all punishment and accusation for the same, as if such incident had never happened." If anyone apprehended a run-away slave, they had impunity "to order such punishment to the said slave, either by dismembering, or any other way, not touching his life," the intent of the latter provision being to allow the enslaved person to be returned to the slaveholder, because the next section stated that if the captive was indeed killed, the master would be reimbursed at public expense.[51] Maryland's 1716 Act of the Assembly ordered that "all Negroes and other slaves already imported or hereafter to be imported in this province and all children now born or hereafter to be born of such Negroes and slaves shall be slaves dureing their naturall lives."[52]

The differences between the lives of indentured servants and the enslaved is cogently shown in Jenny Shaw's book detailing relations of servitude in seventeenth-century Barbados. Shaw traces the life of Cornelius Bryan, an Irish-Catholic former-indentured servant in Barbados during the 1650s. He first appeared in the records suffering a whipping for threatening to drink the blood of English settlers, but his life showed a continuous upward trajectory from that point. By the time he died, he had become the owner of a small plantation, with a household that included his wife, several children, indentured servants, and slaves. Bryan began his career at the very bottom of the Barbados hierarchy for whites, but by the end of his life, he was moderately prosperous. Shaw compares his life to the more severe limitations, greater exposure to violence, and permanent vulnerability suffered by Pegg, an enslaved woman living on Bryan's estate.[53] Barbados was one of the most brutal locations for white servants in the English Atlantic, but Bryan's 1656 whipping can be contrasted to the 1654 torture of an enslaved man in Barbados by an Irish overseer for stealing a pig. The punishment, which was ended through the intercession of Father Biet, a visiting French cleric, had already involved a week of severe daily beatings, and severing the man's ear and forcing him to consume it. Had it continued, the man would have suffered further whipping, and also lost his nose and other ear.[54]

Although legally termed chattel, indentured servants were simultaneously British subjects and, as such, possessed certain inalienable rights, though legal language had not developed to the extent to describe them with those terms. Indeed, letters, government documents, and court records show servants' awareness of their rights, and resistance to exploitation: they wrote family members to ask for reimbursement of their contracts, sued masters for maltreatment or breach of contract, ran away, or even engaged in criminal activity. As shown in chapter 4 and elsewhere in this book, recourse to the law, including free court-appointed legal representation, possible only because indentured servants were seen as "freeborn" English subjects, presented a significant way for servants to resist violence and maltreatment outside of cultural norms – but this was a defence that by its nature was not available to the enslaved.

The practice of indentured servitude did provide a template for enslavement.[55] With slavery's growth as an alternative source of forced labour, it became necessary to define the distinctions between enslaved and indentured persons. In the earliest period of colonial settlement, the terminology was imprecise: Africans bound to servitude were sometimes described as servants and on occasion received indenture contracts; some were even expected to receive their freedom after a term of servitude, although the terms were much longer – usually fourteen to twenty years. Very quickly, however, the colonies developed the legal distinctions that described slavery as a permanent condition. Native Americans, too, were considered enslaved if brought in from the Caribbean, and often on the mainland as well if "taken in warre," though they were sometimes treated as indentured servants, with longer terms than whites.[56]

One important reason for the increasing distinction between servants and slaves over the seventeenth century was economic: because slaves had no rights and were trapped in bondage for life, more labour and, thus, more wealth could be extracted from them, a fact recognized by contemporaries. For example, in 1680, at a time when the numbers of enslaved people were overtaking the numbers of servants, the governor of Barbados wrote that "since people have found out the convenience and cheapness of slave-labour, they no longer keep white men, who used to do all the work on the plantations."[57] Over the course of the seventeenth century, the value of the enslaved as labourers rose compared to the value of servants.[58]

A further basis for the developing divergence between the status of servant and slave was a change in ethical norms and new expectations of social community and citizenship. During the seventeenth century, the British public as well as Parliament grew increasingly uncomfortable with the servitude of whites. This was reflected in the colonies by legislation defining the treatment of servants, and more strongly in Britain by disputes about whether freeborn white British persons

should undergo servitude at all, which are addressed in chapter 3. Ultimately, indentured servitude prepared the ground for slavery, but was
superseded by it as a form of coerced labour for two reasons: slavery
was more economically profitable and slaves did not possess the civil
and contractual protections in English law that British subjects were
increasingly expected to possess.

SHARED CITIZENSHIP IN THE COLONIES

English and British subjects did not regard themselves as participatory
citizens in the more developed sense of the late eighteenth century
and after. However, it is clear that they did think of themselves as
rights-bearing individuals who had an obligation to uphold societal
solidarity as well as an expectation of certain cultural privileges. This
perception of citizenship remained vague and inchoate when compared to later articulations of citizenship, but it was nonetheless real.
Although it is conventional to think of the ideals of citizenship aris-
ing from the eighteenth-century Enlightenment, more recently,
scholars have shown that like nationalism, it evolved gradually from
earlier ideals. The term "citizen," referring to an inhabitant of a state
with "rights, privileges, or duties," has been used since at least the sixteenth century.[59] For instance, the early lexicographer, Thomas
Thomas wrote in his Latin and English dictionary that "cīvīlĭtās" was
"the honesty, curtesie, and equallitie, which citizens use one to
another," while "cīvĭs" is "a citizen, both the man and woman," not only
"of the same citie" but also the same "countrie: our countrieman."[60]
However, the question of citizenship is obscured by the contemporary
use of the ambiguous term "subject," to explain the relationship of an
individual to the monarch and to the state. "Subject" implies a subordinate individual within a hierarchical political pyramid. Yet some
seventeenth-century usages of the word were not very distant from the
designation of "citizen," positing subjects who possessed specific indisputable rights. Indeed, the notion of subjects with rights intrinsically
begins to change the definition of subject. Much of the scholarship on
citizenship in the seventeenth century shows the frequent inter-
changeability of the two terms.[61]

Citizenship was fundamentally linked to the republican value of
equality, which was increasingly acknowledged during the seventeenth century. At least from the major political upheavals of the English Civil War of 1642–51 and the Revolution of 1688–89, republican

ideals were always present in the public sphere.[62] Many additional factors helped shape the nascent sense of citizenship: growing political participation, such as sitting on juries and voting, especially under semi-democratic colonial governments; a sense of common shared interest tied into the early growth of nationalism, which was deliberately fostered by the government to support the stability of outposts in a growing empire; and intellectual antecedents from Roman law and classical philosophers, particularly Cicero, that were increasingly promoted by humanist thinkers.[63]

Ideals of citizenship were not always articulated in ways that included everyone. The fact that a sense of citizenship in the nation slowly arose from notions of subjecthood to an authoritarian monarch, who was necessarily limited to one nation, meant that the form of citizenship that arose also emphasized nationality, intrinsically excluding those outside the nation. While we usually laud the progression of democratic ideals, an ugly component of the advance of ideals of citizenship was the increasing need to explain the exclusion of some groups, and especially to justify slavery. As enslaved populations grew and justificatory racist ideas developed in the seventeenth century, it became increasingly urgent to ensure that the status of white servants was clearly distinct from that of black slaves.[64] Although the delineation between indentured servants and enslaved people was initially vague, as the above discussion of legislation pertaining to slavery shows, very early in the colonial project, colonial assemblies strove to separate the two categories of people, an effort that became more urgent as the population of the enslaved grew.[65] For indentured servants, these developments meant an expanding sense of being participatory members of their society, with inalienable rights. But tragically, the increasing sense of citizenship and republican participation among British subjects in the Americas was an inherent complement to racism and the validation of slavery.

2

Justifications of Servitude

Thousands of British and Irish indentured servants crossed the Atlantic during the seventeenth and eighteenth centuries. Most had willingly contracted to serve overseas, but some were forcibly transported by government agents and some, like Ricckett Mecane, were "spirited away" by professional traffickers or "spirits."[1] Indeed, the word "kidnap" – the nabbing of kids – entered the English language at this time.[2] Some servants were "barbadosed," or sent forcibly to the Caribbean, or "trapanned" (conned) into signing away their freedom by unscrupulous contractors who employed enticing images of service, plied potential servants with drink, or took advantage of illiteracy.[3] The new practice of indentured servitude provided labour for England's new Atlantic colonies, and from the point of view of the government, removed troublesome paupers, criminals, vagrants, and rebels from Britain and Ireland. But from the beginning, state policies incurred significant criticism, which the government rebutted by political, legal, and literary justifications for servitude. That said, although forcible indenture continued, the seventeenth century was characterized by increasing uneasiness about the servitude of white colonists.

DEMOGRAPHICS OF SERVITUDE

Shortly after the initial establishment of English colonists at Jamestown in 1607, and continuing until the American Revolution, a flow of population commenced across the Atlantic Ocean that, by the mid-eighteenth century, included approximately 400,000 people from Britain and Ireland. Comprised of about 350,000 English and some Welsh, about 40,000 Irish, and 7,000 Scots, as well as some continental

Europeans, most sailed from the British ports in Bristol, Liverpool, and London. The majority of white people entering the colonies in this period were servants: about 320,000, approximately one-quarter of whom were female. More than half of all indentured servants went to the Chesapeake colonies of Virginia and Maryland, while 6 per cent travelled to Pennsylvania, 2 per cent to other mainland colonies, and about 35 per cent to the colonies in the Caribbean, especially Barbados and Jamaica, which received 17 per cent and 11 per cent respectively. During the same period, over 1 million enslaved Africans were brought across the ocean; by 1800, they made up 69 per cent of total migrants.[4] The majority of indentured servants were indigent youths from their mid-teens to mid-twenties, but some were older adults (the oldest I have seen recorded was fifty years old) and some, perhaps 5 to 10 per cent, were children under the age of fourteen.[5]

Servants crossed the Atlantic for a variety of reasons. The majority had agreed to serve for a specified number of years. They may have hoped for land or better economic prospects in general, or may have fled destitution or the lack of opportunity. Others were forcibly indentured, kidnapped by spirits, or "transported" by licensed government contractors. Although the records regarding the activities of spirits are scanty, it appears that professional human traffickers were responsible for kidnapping or tricking thousands of people into servitude.[6] It was illegal to force servants into indenture, but the laws were poorly enforced and widely evaded.[7] Those transported by the government comprised individuals deemed undesirables, such as criminals, vagrants, and political or military rebels. The latter group included English, Scottish, and Irish Royalist soldiers during the Interregnum, as well as Jacobites, other political rebels, and, at various times, Irish-Catholic priests, Quakers, and other religious nonconformists.[8] For example, in 1715, the slave ship *Elizabeth & Anne* was used to transport 112 Jacobite rebels to Virginia, 29 with indenture contracts and 83 without, to be indentured upon disembarking.[9]

There were four major types of indentured servant recruitment, as identified by historian John Wareing: "consigned" servants, a relatively small group, who travelled alongside their masters, and possessed an indenture contract; redemptioners, also a small group, who owed the ship's master for their passage, and had a short period of time after arrival, usually two weeks, to obtain funds or make a service arrangement to pay for their travel; "exchanged" servants, the majority, who possessed a contract and were sold from the deck of ships upon arrival

Figure 2.1   Detail of "The world, according to the latest discoveries," map by
Thomas Jeffries, showing Britain, Ireland, and England's Atlantic colonies, 1760.

in the colonies; and "customary" servants, who travelled without a
contract and were sold "at the custom of the country," or local custom.[10] There were also hired servants in the colonies who worked in
exchange for regular pay. All indentured servants served for specific

terms of servitude: usually four years for servants with contracts, and seven for those without contracts serving at the custom of the country, a group which included voluntary servants as well as convicts and others who had been tricked or forcibly indentured by either the government or professional kidnappers.[11] Underage servants like Ricckett Mecane who travelled without contracts would typically be expected to serve until age twenty-one.

PRECURSORS TO INDENTURED SERVITUDE

Various forms of bound labour, including paid servants and apprentices, had been part of the English economic landscape since the Middle Ages. Indentured servitude, however, was a new practice that arose in the colonial environment, combining features from apprenticeships and pre-existing forms of servitude as well as the stipulations of the Statute of Artificers (1563) and Poor Law (1601). This Elizabethan legislation, which included coercive measures to forcibly bind ablebodied poor persons to labour, was devised to address the problems of poverty within Britain.[12]

Domestic and rural servitude were common forms of bound labour for poor youths in early modern England.[13] In 1700, one-third of the English population was under the age of fifteen, and most people were poor, so the need for poor youths to labour was a significant factor in the English economy.[14] Most poor youths left the households of their parents to work in another home.[15] Rural agricultural servitude was the most common occupation for English youths during the early modern period. Rural servants were hired through informal verbal arrangements, usually for the period of a year, during which they laboured for a master, receiving some form of payment at the year's end. This was different from adult rural labourers, usually men, who were paid by the day.[16] Urban youths often were hired for domestic service. Work obligations were significantly influenced by gender, and domestic servants were more likely to be girls and women, while rural servants and urban apprentices were typically male youths in their teens and early twenties.[17] Early modern servants were seen as household dependents who owed deference and subservience to the head of the household – usually a patriarchal father who was seen as a parental figure toward the youth.[18] The term "servant" was imprecise and often used interchangeably to refer to anyone living and working in a master's household, including domestics and rural labourers.[19]

Apprenticeships represented another tradition of bound labour for youths. These occurred in an urban setting and focused on formal training in a craft. The arrangement involved a written contract that obligated both master and apprentice to a relationship, usually of seven years, during which the master housed, fed, cared for, and trained the apprentice in a trade.[20] The parents of an apprentice paid for this opportunity, sometimes a considerable amount.[21] The seven-year span for craft and parish apprenticeships and later indentured servitude was in accordance with Deuteronomy 15:12 of the Old Testament, which stated that if "thy brother ... be sold unto thee," then "in the seventh year ... thou shalt let him go free."[22] The youths engaged in these arrangements were not expected to remain in apprenticeships for life, only during a temporary period of extended adolescence until they were able to form households of their own.[23] Similarly, their counterparts in farm or domestic service had expectations of independent adulthoods.

Youthful servants and apprentices were more likely to travel than other people in their society, with rural servants moving up to five miles from their birthplace, but apprentices sometimes going twenty to thirty miles away to enter big cities such as London.[24] High mortality rates insured that there would always be fresh opportunities for youths looking for employment. Service and apprenticeships were an important stage of youth in a society in which the nuclear family was the main household unit.[25] Since most people were poor and young engaged couples needed to assemble the wherewithal to form a new household before marrying, marriage typically occurred at a later age in western Europe than in other parts of the world – in the late twenties for men and mid-twenties for women.[26]

From the fourteenth century, various English statutes addressed the relationship between masters and servants.[27] By the seventeenth century, these labour practices were also adapted into legislation crafted to address societal anxiety about the increasing numbers of poor individuals in England, especially the Statute of Artificers (1563) and Poor Law (1601), which forced able-bodied poor persons into binding "apprenticeships."[28] Like traditional craft apprenticeships, these individuals were bound to a master for a term, commonly of seven years, during which they were fed and housed but usually not paid. However, pauper apprentices were not necessarily taught a skilled trade. Instead, similar to rural and domestic servants, they did whatever work was set to them. If they did receive training, it was to be a low-level labourer. The Poor Law in particular was a reaction to problems such as vagrancy, crime, and the large populations of "masterless" men and women. It aimed to penalize and punish those whom it considered the "undeserving" or "able-bodied" poor – those who were physically capable of working – despite the reality that sufficient work was not available.[29] As England acquired colonies, these practices would evolve into indenture contracts in overseas settlements.[30]

The forcible indenture of "surplus populations" was a novel practice that combined parish apprenticeships with another traditional way for ridding a parish of undesirables: banishment. Banishment had been established in law from before the fifteenth century to expel prostitutes and beggars from the parish.[31] By the late sixteenth and early seventeenth centuries, legislation specifically referred to deportation to overseas territories, those controlled by England as well as to foreign countries, for transients and lawbreakers.[32] For example, in 1631, the city of London, displaying some geographical confusion, sent "fifty vagrants" as "bound apprentices to merchants to serve in the islands of Barbadoes and Virginia."[33]

Parish apprenticeships and banishment were precursors to indentured servitude, yet there were significant differences from the new colonial labour practice. Indentured servants were usually youths from their mid-teens to mid-twenties who were contractually obligated to work in a master's household for a period of years. Their masters or mistresses were responsible for housing, feeding, and clothing them. Voluntary servants may have sought opportunity or were fleeing destitution, and their travel across the Atlantic can be seen as an extreme form of the mobility seen among poor youths within Britain. Servants who travelled without a contract, even if they had agreed to enter indentured servitude, usually served a seven-year term, consistent with the Elizabethan statutes. Instead of receiving training like apprentices or pay like hired servants, the labour of indentured servants paid for their passage across the ocean and for the "freedom dues" provided by their master at the end of their servitude. Rarely, the passage across the ocean might itself be the incentive for entering indenture, as it was for Elizabeth Gardenier, who sought to travel as an indentured servant to Virginia in 1691 because "she has a daughter there whom she has a great desire to see."[34] Freedom dues likely originated from the tradition of paying rural servants after their year of service, but also, like the seven-year length of indentured servitude, came from the Book of Deuteronomy's promise of payment after completing servitude: "And when thou sendest him out free from

thee, thou shalt not let him go away empty: Thou shalt furnish him
liberally out of thy flock, and out of thy floor, and out of thy wine-
press: of that wherewith the Lord thy God hath blessed thee thou
shalt give unto him."[35]

Indentured servitude was distinct from hired servitude in England
in significant ways. Traditionally hired English servants either
received a regular wage or were paid at the end of an informally
arranged one-year term. Unlike servants in England, indentured servants could be sold – or have their contracts sold – from one master
to another, usually without consent.[36] Once in the colonies, labour
norms were altered, and both women and men did farm labour such
as cultivating, planting, and harvesting, typically men's work in England, though domestic service remained mainly women's sphere.[37]
Living conditions in the colonies were harsher than in Britain, with a
much higher mortality rate and greater impunity for abusive masters
and mistresses.[38] Historical sources demonstrate considerable variation in the treatment of indentured servants, from by-the-book labour
arrangements to physical and sexual abuse, and illegal attempts to
extend the length of service.

Indentured servants were intrinsically vulnerable to maltreatment
because of the structural conditions of their labour. Their contracts
legally bound them to serve their masters or mistresses. Fleeing a master was a crime. Freedom dues diminished in value over the seventeenth and eighteenth centuries, while the colonial masters who
purchased servants' contracts increasingly saw servanthood as the consequence of undesirable traits such as criminality, indebtedness, and
idleness. Women servants additionally faced sexual double standards
that restricted their autonomy and placed more stringent standards on
their behaviour. Nonetheless, indentured servants both voluntary and
involuntary continued to stream across the Atlantic until the American Revolution.

POVERTY IN EARLY MODERN ENGLAND

One pressing incentive for the rise of indentured servitude was the
sharp increase in poverty during the early modern period, coupled
with a significant rise in population. The growth of destitution,
hunger, and unemployment presented a serious concern for the government.[39] These developments coincided with increasing centraliza-
tion of power in the English state, which was intent upon limiting

public disorder, but was unable to fully adapt to the increasingly capitalist economy. The early modern state lacked resources to effectively
dole out poor relief, although it did provide some relief through
parishes and workhouses. Additionally, in the early modern period,
poor, jobless, or vagrant individuals were usually perceived as lazy and
morally deficient. Cultural and social norms dictated that inferiors
owed deference to their betters and should be enfolded within a patriarchal household, yet the burgeoning population of the poor defied
these ideals.[40] The state was forced to develop new models to address
what it perceived to be a growing crisis.

Fears of crime and social disorder led seventeenth-century commentators to pursue political solutions. For instance, in the early
seventeenth century, writer Gervase Markham urged that jobs in husbandry be found for "waste persons."[41] In 1610, Thomas Blenerhasset,
a leading planter in Ireland, proposed that England, "overcharged
with much people," should find room for its "overplus" population in
Ulster.[42] By 1621, colonial entrepreneur Edwin Sandys encouraged
plantations in Virginia as a way to allow the "nation to disburden
itself" of "the abundance of people."[43]

The establishment of overseas indentured servitude provided a resolution for many of these problems. The state adapted older practices
to contractually bind servants to colonial masters in a way that had
never been practised in the British Isles. Criminals and rebels presented similar problems, leaving government officials grasping at
solutions for resolving financially and politically costly incarcera-
tions and executions. Like indigents, these groups could often be
managed more cheaply and effectively as forcibly indentured servants. These policies initially faced little opposition in a political climate in which innate human rights were not recognized, though, as
will be seen, they still aroused disquiet among both commoners and
political elites.

In addition, poverty provided a strong incentive for the enlistment
of voluntary servants, who were the vast majority of indentured servants. It is worth questioning whether a decision shaped by economic
constraints was a true choice, especially since mortality rates were
much higher in the colonies than in Britain. Yet the colonies, particularly on the mainland, also offered real opportunities for economic
and social advancement. Servants travelling overseas risked much, but
had the potentiality of obtaining land, economic independence, and
civic participation unavailable to them in England.[44]

A caveat: I have used the term "voluntary" to refer to servants who gave verbal or written consent to indenture, but self-evidently there was a formidable element of compulsion in their decision to enter servitude. Even when servants were not deceived by recruiters about the terms of their contracts, few servants had any understanding of the hardships and dangers that awaited them during servitude. Historians have debated the varying degrees of volition, constraint, deception, and market forces, but it should be clarified that while most "voluntary" servants faced severe economic hardship in England, it appears that most were choosing between alternatives.[45] Their choice was a precarious and risky one between two poor outcomes, but for most, there was not an obligation to enter indenture. Ultimately, however, it is questionable whether indenture was a better choice.

WRITING ABOUT SERVITUDE

In addition to a body of legislation dating back to the Middle Ages regulating labour relations, there was an extensive literature that addressed the moral duties and obligations of both masters and servants, within both the colonial and the English context.[46] Typically, these works focused on hired servants who worked for a wage, but they were applicable to indentured servants by virtue of concentrating on the dependent nature of the servant's role within a patriarchal household rather than delineating the specific contractual nature of servitude. These sources can tell us much about the expectations and beliefs about servitude from a variety of perspectives. They range from moral and philosophical tracts that rationalized the practice of servitude and explained its role in the social hierarchy; to promotional tracts that promoted migration and servitude as ways to people the new colonies and find employment for the abundant labouring population; to political petitions protesting against servitude, autobiographies that touched on the authors' time of servitude or described observations of the colonies, a few letters from indentured servants, and literary works such as ballads and poems purporting to describe the lives of indentured authors.

Cotton Mather

One American treatise was Puritan Cotton Mather's short yet meandering *A Good Master Well Served* (1696): in examining how to obtain and oversee a servant, it constructed an analogy of a Christian's relationship to God.[47] In a sermon peppered with biblical quotes almost to the point of incomprehensibility, Mather emphasized the hierarchical nature of society, in which "there must be some who are to command, and there must be some who are to obey," such as "wives, children, and servants," the latter the "lowest of all" the categories.[48] Mather urged that servants could "sanctify" their "servile employments" by seeing them as obedience to the commandments of God.[49] He also emphasized the value of work in itself, as a guard against idleness.[50]

At the same time, Mather exhorted masters to "lay no sinful commands" upon their servants, "nor appoint them any evil work." A servant was not to be "handled like a beast," and masters were not to be tyrannical: "Let not your servants have their lives embittered, healths impaired, their bodies macerated" by the dictates of a despotic master. In addition, eliding apprenticeship with servitude, he asserted that masters were obliged, if servants were "with you" in order "to learn any mystery in your occupation," to convey this knowledge. It would "be a most complicated cousenage [cozenage, i.e., deceit] and robbery in you to conceal that mystery from them," he wrote. Masters, he asserted, owed their servants nourishing food, medicine when needed, and clothing that was "neat, warm, and modest," and most importantly, they were obligated to provide spiritual guidance.[51]

Mather had little sympathy for disobedience by servants, however. Masters "owed" their servants "discipline," and lest it be doubted what was meant by the term, he specified "some servants are so refractory as to come under [the] lash."[52] Runaway servants were "driven" by the devil.[53] Overall, Mather emphasized that obedience was a central component of society, an implicit theme of his sermon. He also addressed slaves in this sermon, but rather than urging them in the way he had servants — to subordinate their will to their masters because it was a component of Christian humility — he condescendingly advised them that they were "better fed & and better clothed, & better managed by far" than they would have been if free. Their reward would come in the afterlife when their souls would be liberated.[54]

William Fleetwood

In England, the sermons of prominent Anglican divine William Fleetwood, first published in 1705, more clearly exemplified the early modern conceptualization of the appropriate relationship between servants and masters.[55] Fleetwood did not explicitly distinguish between indentured and hired servants working for regular wages. However, he clearly appears to have been addressing the former in some cases, as well as referring to the colonial context.

Although only a few years removed from Mather's tract, Fleetwood offered a much stronger emphasis on the contractual nature of master-servant relations. Like other authors, Fleetwood associated master-servant relations with the patriarchal familial relationships between husbands and wives and parents and children, and explicitly situated servants as dependents. He defined obedience to servitude as a religious duty, but he also saw servitude as a legal compact between masters and servants. He explained the relationship by combined evangelical religious and capitalistic justifications that were emerging in the late seventeenth century as well as older notions of deference and patriarchy. Fleetwood urged servants to "obey their masters according to the flesh in all things," remaining "exactly diligent and faithful in their service, whether their masters were absent or present," and to "serve sincerely and without dissimulation." He rationalized that while "paying all obedience and due service to their masters," servants should consider themselves to be undertaking a religious devotion, "in obedience to the Lord," and expecting a heavenly reward, even if "their earthly masters" did "over-look, neglect, or evilly intreat" them. Servants should see their labour itself as sanctifying.[56] He also articulated the capitalist expectations of the transaction: "a servant, when he enters into service, gives up his time and labour by agreement to his master ... And therefore he would be unjust to wast[e] that time, and spare that labour, that is truly none of his; they are his masters by his contract, and his master ought to have the advantage of them; it is defrauding people of what is their due, it is keeping back part of what is already sold them, and agreed for."[57]

Only in cases where a master ordered a servant to contravene "the laws of God" or "the laws of the land," such as if a master ordered a servant "to set upon another, and take away either his money or his life," were a master's orders to be disobeyed. Regardless of any orders, servants had an obligation "to be just and honest, and do no hurt or violence, or lesser injury to any one."[58]

Masters also, Fleetwood specified, had obligations to servants, on religious, moral, and contractual grounds. They had the right to correct servants, presumably even physically, but could not abuse them excessively: "masters must not be over-rigorous in their punishments when servants are faulty, but should inflict them with deliberation, good intention and compassion." In addition, they could not overwork servants: "they must not oppress them with immoderate tasks and labour, but are to have a merciful respect to the capacity, ability and strength of servants." Masters had the obligation to provide for their servants and, "in the case of sickness," to see that "they want not what is fitting their condition."[59] Also, they must be fair in contractual dealings with servants: "if a servant contract with a master to give him all his time and labour, for such a space of days or weeks, or months, or years, and he is as good as his word, and stand to his bargain, he has an undoubted right to whatever wages or advantage his master agreed to let him have, and his master would be a very wicked and unjust man to deny him it, because he earn'd it and deserv'd it, and it was his due, by contract and agreement."[60] Fleetwood expressed concern that sometimes servants could be cheated of their final wages, writing "there is reason to think this part of justice is very ill practis'd by many masters," encouraged by laws that "put the servant so much into the hands and power of their masters."[61] It is not fit, he averred, that "the laws should make the masters judges."[62] Masters must remember their religious duty, and quoting St Paul, as had Mather, he asserted, they "should give to their servants that which is just and equal," including "what is theirs by contract and agreement, that which is due in law," and "to deal fairly, honestly, and kindly with them," even if "they have not formally contracted with them."[63] "The reason and benefit of a contract," he emphasized, was that it created additional constraint upon masters to uphold their obligations to their servants.[64] These obligations could include "instruction, wages, maintenance, or cloathing, or whatever else is bargain'd for." A master who denied these things was "faithless and unjust."[65] Like servants, who were enjoined to serve their masters because they were in reality serving God, masters were exhorted to "give to your servants that which is just and equal, knowing … that ye also have a master in heaven." Indeed, "the meanest servant is as dear" to God "as the most honorable master."[66]

However, having laid out the limits of masters' authority, Fleetwood qualified that "the authority of masters over servants is very useful to the good and order of mankind." The value of obedience was such that even though masters should not order servants to commit serious crimes, servants should obey their masters' orders in the case of lesser infractions; it was accounted "reasonable that a great many small offences are excus'd in servants under authority and acting by command, because they are under some constraint and awe, and because a great many inconveniences would follow upon the scrupulous dispute of servants weighing and examining the orders and injunctions of their masters." In such "indifferent" cases, "submission and obedience" was the appropriate role for servants. Fleetwood seemed to be referring specifically to servitude in the colonies when he specified that "the state of servitude is very different in one country from what it is in another" and that servants "of different sorts and degrees are not alike oblig'd to obey their masters in all things, but are at liberty in some particulars, according to their contracts and agreements." He maintained, nonetheless, that servants, and even "downright slaves," had an obligation to uphold obedience toward their masters, even to endure exhausting labour, encouraging them to "obey your masters in all things, as becomes your sad condition, and make your chains as easie as you can, by your compliance and submission," to gain an eventual heavenly reward.[67]

These exhortations were clearly gendered. Fleetwood always referred to both masters and servants as masculine, perhaps in part reflecting the greater preponderance of males in both these roles, but also because he presented a patriarchal justification for servitude. Mather's treatise likewise emphasized the patriarchal hierarchy but, in contrast, briefly addressed "handmaids" who ought to cause their mistresses "to count you [as] their children" through the servants' obedient devotion.[68] However, Fleetwood was more concerned about the hierarchy within the family. A servant, he wrote, was responsible only for himself, having "themselves alone to provide for," but "their masters have wives and children and relations." In addition, masters had to involve themselves with the cares of everyday political and economic participation in public life, including "what-ever publick mischiefs oppress a nation" such as "changes of government," while servants "contribute little to the supporting of the publick, pay no rates nor taxes … suffer nothing by the malice or indolence of parties, undergoe no odium calumny, or slander," thus possessing a set of "conveniences" that accrued to them by virtue of being in a household under the protection of a master.[69] As part of their patriarchal obligation, masters had the responsibility to provide servants with "a good example"; to give them "good advice" and by "instructing them … in the common rules of honesty and justice, truth and faithfulness, exciting them to diligence and industry"; and "to make them virtuous and religious."[70]

Servitude was actually beneficial for servants, Fleetwood claimed. Masters had an obligation to ensure that servants laboured, as masters who were "too indulgent and remiss" would create lazy servants, and labouring for a master trained a servant to overcome obstacles in later life. After servitude was over, when the former servant required "industry and labour" as a result of "unusual urgencies" or "the necessity of their condition," they would be "at a loss what to do" if they had not previously been accustomed to labour. Indeed, Fleetwood argued that the deferred gratification inherent in servitude trained servants to become hard-working individuals who could eventually become self-sustaining members of their society: "They who have serv'd their masters with the greatest industry and diligence will certainly serve themselves the best when they come to it."[71] Fleetwood, like most of his contemporaries, saw servitude, with its temporary and transitional nature, as a bridge to success for the labouring classes.

Fleetwood's situation of servitude within conventional relations of patriarchal relations was popular, and his book came out in several additional editions. It was followed by a number of other works on the appropriate conditions and obligations for both servants and masters, even as the relations of servitude began to change in the eighteenth century with emerging ideals of human rights, citizenship, and spiritual participation.[72]

PROMOTION OF COLONIZATION

Indentured servitude was interwoven with many aspects of British colonial policy, including both political necessity and expediency, as well as economic gain. One pressing problem of the early modern state was the prevalence of poverty, but another was retaining and peopling the colonial territories. From the sixteenth century, English commentators began promoting the benefits of overseas colonies. In his 1584 book, *A Discourse on Western Planting*, Richard Hakluyt, one of the earliest advocates of colonization, suggested that "idle" people in Britain might be sent to people the colonies. His fourth chapter focused on the "manifolde imploymente of numbers of idle men" and the "many thousands of idle persons" who "having no way to be sett on worke, be either mutinous and seeke alteration

in the state, or at leaste very burdensome to the commonwealth, and
often fall to pilfering and thevinge and other lewdness, whereby all
the prisons of the lande are daily pest[e]red and stuffed full of them,
where either they pitifully pine awaye, or els[e] at lengthe are
miserably hanged."[73] Unlike many early modern commentators, he
understood that a major cause of vagrancy was insufficient work – a
"wante of sufficient occasion of honest employment" – and thus the
"sharpe execution" of the laws against "idle and lazye persons" and
"loiterers and idle vagabondes" would not be enough to prevent the
numerous poor and unemployed men in England from engaging in
crime and political rebellion.[74] Hakluyt presented the transportation of indigents as a policy that fulfilled two aims simultaneously:
it alleviated the state's burden of dealing with the poor and it provided "employment of our idle people" in a venture of colonization
— becoming in itself one of the "many noble endes" of such a venture.[75] In 1622, poet and divine John Donne, in a sermon before the
Virginia Company, agreed that the Virginia plantation would
"sweep your streets, and wash your doors, from idle persons, and the
children of idle persons, and employ them." He further averred that
"truly, if the whole country" had only a single purpose, "to force idle
persons to work, it had a good use," acting as "a spleen to drain the
ill humours of the body."[76]

John Hammond

Most indentured servants agreed to enter servitude, and some
authors aimed to encourage such migration, publishing propagandistic works that encouraged travel to the colonies, especially on the
mainland. In 1655, Virginian John Hammond published his tract
Leah and Rachel, or the two fruitfull sisters, Virginia and Mary-land to
promote settlement of the colonies, especially Virginia. He also
aimed to redeem the reputation of the colonies, which had been criticized in discouraging stories by former indentured servants.[77] Like
Hakluyt, Hammond proclaimed that "it is the glory of every nation"
to expand trade and control overseas territories. The Virginia colony
exemplified this, while providing plentiful opportunities for new settlers such as indentured servants. In the early days of Virginia, he
conceded, disorder had prevailed. In addition to Indian attacks and
hunger, the martial law in existence did not dispense justice: with
"no redresse of grievances, complaints were repaied with stripes

[whippings], moneys with scoffes, tortures made delights, and in a word all and the worst that tyrany could inflict or act." Yet while this had been true at one time, and rumours asserted this "lye" was still true, things had changed, he argued. The original problems had been "complained of in England," and now "the bondage was taken care of, the people set free," and servants with legitimate complaints against masters were treated with respect in the courts. Hammond lamented that many potential servants had been misinformed about their prospects in the colonies, and so preferred to remain in England living a "base, slavish, penurious life," and choosing "rather to beg, steal, rot in prison, and come to shamefull deaths, then to better their being by going thither."[78]

Hammond lauded Virginia as a place "wherein is plenty of all things necessary for humane subsistance." He described how "the people … had lands asigned to each of them to live of themselves, and enjoy the benefit of their own industry; men then began to call what they laboured for their own." He praised the current productiveness of the colony and the "increasing stocks" and "great plenty" of agricultural produce. The land was "wholesome, healthy and fruitfull," and there was a climate of religious, moral, and political justice in the colony. This rosy picture would have been a powerful inducement to the poor of England or Ireland, where land, the basis of wealth and self-sufficiency in a largely agricultural society, was almost impossible to come by. Hammond did warn potential servants of possible pitfalls, such as "mercinary spirits," urging them to find legitimate merchants; to make sure that they possessed an indenture contract "in writing and under hand and seal"; and to make sure that land, in addition to the usual corn, clothing, and tools, was a part of their freedom dues. He brushed off fears of the sale of servants, claiming that they could adjust their contracts to give them a fortnight to choose their master, and averring that "if a time must be served, it is all one with whom it be served, provided they be people of honest repute, with which the country is well replenished." There was no real reason to fear, he continued: "the labour servants are put to, is not so hard nor of such continuance as husbandmen, nor handecraftmen are kept at in England," and there was plenty of opportunity for rest. Food was plentiful, rumours of inadequate lodging were untrue, and even before servitude ended, "those servants that will be industrious may in their time of service gain a competent estate before their freedome."[79] This tract, with some truth and much exaggeration, illustrates both the temptations and the negatives that potential servants weighed when deciding whether to sign an indenture agreement.

George Alsop

Another propagandist, George Alsop, had actually laboured as a servant himself in Maryland in the 1650s.[80] His reverential tract begins with a description of Maryland as a "fertile and pleasant piece of ground" with "green, spreading, and delightful woods," unparalleled by "any place under the heavenly altitude," where people could "dwell here, live plentifully, and be rich."[81] Food was plentiful, and there was no begging or hunger he wrote.[82] There was also little crime, and no need for "Newgates for pilfering felons, nor Ludgates for debters, nor any Bridewels"; in Maryland, "the merits of the country deserves none."[83] Life in the colony was characterized by peace and order: "here every man lives quietly, and follows his labour and imployment desiredly," assured of "the protection of the laws." The colony was well governed, with no rebellion (Alsop was an anti-Cromwell royalist), led by a governing assembly made up of "good ordinary householders of the severall counties" who with a "plain and honest conscience" made laws "for the general good of the people."[84]

Alsop justified the concept of servitude as necessary to societal stability and criticized the "levelling doctrine" present in England, but he argued that the subtle difference in Maryland was that after completing their time of indenture, servants had the opportunity to "become masters and mistresses of families themselves." He minimized the "small computation of years" of servitude, maintaining from his personal experience that it was not "so slavish" as the "two year servitude of a handicraft apprenticeship" that he had served in London. He recommended that "those whose abilities" were "capable [to] maintain themselves" remain in England, but that those "who are low and make bare shifts to buoy themselves up" would be better off by "removal" to Maryland – which would also reduce pressures on those of the poor who remained in England.[85]

Once servants arrived, he wrote, their four years of servitude would "advantage a man all the remainder of his days," and they would live "plentiously well." Women servants "had the best luck here as in any place of the world," obtaining marriage quickly. In a rare promotion of sexuality outside of marriage, intended as an enticement, Alsop wrote that male servants, if "they be good rhetoricians, and well vers'd in the art of perswasion" and their masters were "deficient" from age, might, in an innuendo-laden phrase, "rivet themselves into the private and reserved favour of their mistress." Like Hammond, Alsop incorrectly claimed that upon arrival servants "may choose whom they will serve their prefixed time with." In a rare acknowledgement of the perception that indentured servitude was exploitative, Alsop criticized the "damnable ... untruth" that servants "are sold in open market for slaves and draw in carts like horses." Instead, he claimed, servants had leisure time, were responsible for relatively light work, and were without much work in winter. "Every servant has a gun, powder, and shot allowed him," and after their allotted time was over, became "a freeman" whose master owed him 50 acres of land, three suits of clothing, and a year's supply of corn.[86] These propagandistic accounts, though acknowledging some hardships, painted a rosy picture of opportunity, prosperity, and fair treatment for servants.

AUTOBIOGRAPHICAL ACCOUNTS

In contrast to the idealized depictions of the colonies represented by promotional tracts, there were several more authentic accounts of servitude written by people who had endured servitude, or who had travelled to the colonies and observed conditions of servitude there. For most, the description of servitude was only a small part of a longer autobiography; nonetheless, these renderings provide powerful first-hand narratives of what it was like to be an indentured servant. These are supplemented by other works by individuals who possessed personal experiences of servitude, including letters home from indentured servants, and political prisoners petitioning against servitude.

One of the most poignant testaments to the perils of indentured servitude comes from the letters of Richard Frethorne, who was a servant in the Virginia colony during the early 1620s.[87] In letters to his parents and a parish official in England, Frethorne described the harsh early days of the colony, when it was threatened with starvation, disease, and attack by Native Americans. Although he described dearth of food and unremitting labour, he does not seem to have been physically abused. He pleaded for his "loving and kind father and mother" to pay off his indenture, writing "if you love me you will redeeme me suddenlie, for w[hi]ch I do intreate and begg," and if that was not possible, he beseeched them to send provisions. He wrote that he would have died had not an acquaintance of his parents living in the colony provided him with food and shelter, and that the former "much marvailed that you would send me a servaunt to the [Virginia] Companie, he saith I had beene better knocked on the head." Frethorne's lists of the dead in the colony testify to the precariousness of life in the early days of the colony.[88]

Another servant from the Chesapeake region was Charles Bayly. Kidnapped from England as a thirteen-year-old in the 1640s, he described violence and neglect during his servitude, "where I was sold as a bond-slave."[89] Bayly's description of his servitude is brief; as an adult, he converted to Quakerism and his narrative is mainly a spiritual autobiography. Bayly prospered in later life, and eventually rose to become the first overseas governor of the Hudson's Bay Company.

In the mid-seventeenth century, several transported rebels wrote negative accounts of their servitude in the Caribbean. Heinrich von Uchteritz, a German mercenary in the Royalist army during the English Civil War, was transported to Barbados in 1652. He described scant food and poor conditions, although servants, he wrote, were kept under better conditions than the enslaved. He complained of the unaccustomed work, writing "I had to sweep the plantation yard the first day; on another day I fed the pigs and thereafter I had to do the kind of work usually performed by the slaves." However, von Uchteritz was privileged by both his white skin and noble birth; after eighteen weeks of bondage, he informed his master of his social rank, and the latter discharged him after arrangements were made for reimbursement for his master's outlay of 800 pounds of sugar.[90]

Marcellus Rivers and Oxenbridge Foyle, former royalist rebels against the Interregnum government, were sentenced to indentured servitude in Barbados in 1656. In 1659, they challenged their detention in Parliament.[91] A similar petition was filed by Rowland Thomas, another royalist sent to Barbados.[92] Foyle and Rivers decried their poor conditions of food and housing, as well as hard labour, abuse which included whippings, and "many other ways" they were "made miserable." They eloquently criticized merchants "that deal in slaves and souls of men" and who had no "authority for the sale and slavery of your poor petitioners." The pair questioned "by what authority so great a breach is made upon the free people of England," and argued that their case represented not only the former rebels but also "all the free-born people of England." Ultimately, they gained a privilege denied to slaves: the right to petition Parliament, which debated their punishment extensively. They were not reprieved, although Rivers and Foyle were jailed rather than returned to Barbados. One year later, royalists were pardoned at the Restoration of Charles II in 1660.[93]

Henry Pitman, a surgeon arrested during the 1685 Monmouth Rebellion against James II, likewise described the cruel treatment, meagre food, and physical abuse that he received as an indentured servant in Barbados in 1685. Pitman and his brother, who was indentured with him, were rebellious, and their master's "more and more unkind" behaviour with "abuses and unkindnesses" intensified after the two men defiantly refused to follow orders. Pitman's time in servitude was short, as he soon escaped, but his brother died there.[94]

John Coad, another Monmouth rebel, was sent to Jamaica. He described much better treatment by his nonconformist masters, receiving ample food and experiencing "Christian conference, and mutual love, and affection"; not only his master but also "all the rest of the neighbourhood were very kind and courteous to me."[95] A later master was less amenable, but Coad's greatest complaint was that as a supervising carpenter "to worke with negroes I must submit," while "the rest of our white men had no imploy, but to lye in the plantation for little service but to eat and drink and spend the time in idleness."[96] The Monmouth rebels, sentenced to ten years, were pardoned at the accession of King William in 1688, but not freed until an English warship arrived to the island in 1690.[97]

These accounts of servitude are supplemented by second-hand accounts from observers who travelled to the English colonies as free men and wrote about what they had observed. The most famous of these is Richard Ligon. A royalist escaping England and residing in Barbados for a couple of years during the 1640s, he provided more detail than most in describing the conditions he saw.[98] Although he himself held a plantation briefly, employing both servants and slaves, he was horrified at the ill-treatment of servants, although less concerned about the enslaved. However, he also wrote that the treatment of servants varied considerably, depending on their masters: "the usage of the servants, it is much as the master is, merciful or cruel; Those that are merciful, treat their servants well, both in their meat [food], drink, and lodging, and give them such work, as is not unfit for Christians to do. But if the masters be cruel, the servants have very wearisome and miserable lives."[99] On the same page he described both having "seen such cruelty done to servants, as I did not think one Christian could have done to another" and also "different better natur'd men" who had "come to rule there," making "the servants lives ... much better'd," including one master who "got such love of his servants, as they thought all too little they could do for him."[100]

Father Antoine Biet, a French priest who visited Barbados in 1654, was critical of the conditions under which indentured servants, "who are native born English, Irish, or Scotch" lived, and was sickened by the treatment of the enslaved, against whom he described great brutality. He was angered that servants with families were separated "so as not to receive any solace from each other." While "masters were obliged to support servants," he wrote, they barely upheld this, treating indentured servants "not much better than slaves." Biet, from monarchical France, did not quite understand the recent political upheaval in England and "found it strange" that "they sent from England those persons who were suspected of being royalists."[101]

There are also some eighteenth-century autobiographical reports of indentured servitude that confirm much of what was written in the seventeenth-century works, though the eighteenth-century authors, if they were men, generally fared better than their seventeenth-century counterparts. Some brief mentions of indentured servitude also occur in Ebenezer Cooke's satiric poem, *The Sot-weed Factor* (1708), in which the author describes a voyage to Maryland during his youth, probably with significant poetic licence.[102] There are also two accounts by women, who experienced harsher terms of servitude.

William Moraley, a young artisan from a previously wealthy but economically diminished family, indentured himself to Pennsylvania in the 1730s after being overlooked in his father's will. "Not caring what be came of me, it enter'd into my head to leave England, and sell myself for a term of years into the American Plantations," he wrote. In 1743, Moraley published *The Infortunate: The Voyage And Adventures Of William Moraley, An Indentured Servant*, which detailed his misadventures, as well as describing Pennsylvania more generally. Moraley worked amicably for a clockmaker in Burlington, Pennsylvania, for a time, with a mild term of servitude under which he was treated more like a traditional apprentice. Nonetheless, he described the conditions of more typical "bought servants" as "very hard." His account is notable for its length, his frequent descriptions of carousing, and the sympathy he demonstrated toward the enslaved.[103]

Two Scottish authors also had relatively mild experiences in indenture during the eighteenth century. Peter Williamson was kidnapped in Aberdeen at the age of eight along with several other boys and shipped to Pennsylvania in the 1730s, at a time when Aberdeen merchants were noted for "stealing young children from their parents, and selling them as slaves."[104] But after experiencing this terrible cruelty, Williamson was comparatively fortunate. He was purchased in Philadelphia by a fellow Scot, who "had in youth been kidnapped like myself." Williamson's master was sympathetic to him, treating him almost as a son, assigning him only light work, sending him to school, and, in his will, leaving Williamson £200 (approximately £20,000 in today's currency), his clothing, and his best horse and tack.[105]

John Harrower, another Scot, was a schoolmaster who indentured himself to Virginia in the 1770s, leaving behind his wife and children, to whom he sent remittances. His period of indenture was relatively easy: he was treated as a professional tutor rather than as a servant, paid for freelance teaching, well fed and clothed, and accorded considerable personal freedom. His motivations for travelling are unknown, but appear to have economic roots.[106] In his letters to his wife, copied into his diary, he repeatedly urged her to immigrate with the children and wrote, "I yet hope ... to make you a Virginian Lady among the woods of America which is by far more pleasent than the roaring of the raging seas round about Zetland [Shetland], And yet to make you eat more wheat bread in your old age than what you have done in your youth."[107] His diary ended abruptly during the American Revolution.

There are two accounts by women describing indentured servitude. It is difficult to generalize from a sparsity of sources, but both describe severe ill-treatment while servants. Elizabeth Ashbridge's spiritual autobiography described her progress toward Quakerism, but began with her "wild" youth, when she was "light and airy" and full of "vivacity." She disobeyed her parents as a young teenager, eloping and, after the death of her husband, engaging in a journey to New York in 1732, thwarting her parents' attempt to bring her back home from the ship. During the voyage, she was forced to sign an indenture by the captain. While in servitude, Ashbridge was often hungry and ill-clothed, and suffered abuse by her master. But always independent and capable, she managed to buy off her time after three years, expressing pride that she was able to maintain herself

"handsomely" by her needle.[108] Her unusual life trajectory culminat-
ed as a Quaker minister in Pennsylvania.

Another woman's voice was heard in a 1756 letter from Elizabeth
Sprigs, indentured in Maryland, appealing to her father in London.
Sprigs described abysmal conditions under which she was "toiling
almost day and night," so severe that it was like "horses drudgery";
repeatedly belittled and abused, her master accusing: "bitch, you do
not [do] halfe enough"; and "then tied up and whipp'd to that degree
that you'd not serve an animal." She suffered from lack of food
and adequate clothing. Like Ashbridge, she was apologetic about a rift
with her family, occasioned by "my former bad conduct," but begged
her father to remember his former "care and tenderness" for her, to
forgive her, and to send clothing.[109] It is possible that to her family,
Sprig's big fault was engaging in an indenture contract without her
father's permission, like Elizabeth Ashbridge.

There are so few accounts from women that it is difficult to know
how representative these experiences were, but eighteenth-century
men like Moraley, Williamson, and Harrower served easier terms than
many who served in the seventeenth century. The scarcity of women's
writing was due to several factors: lower rates of literacy among
women; doubts about the propriety of women writing; and a lower
percentage of women among the indentured. It should be noted,
though, that even Sprigs and Ashbridge with their stories of deprivation and violence were more fortunate than enslaved people. Both
possessed family members in England who were potentially willing
to provide support, and Ashbridge ultimately achieved some success
and renown after completing her indenture.

LITERARY NARRATIVES

Most of the descriptions of indentured servitude available on English
streets were probably oral accounts. While these can't be traced, there
was also a tradition of literary narratives and humorous satires, often
involving convict transportation, in which "reality and fiction are
intertwined."[110] These tended to present a negative account of indentured servitude. Probably most of these popular accounts were largely
fictional, but they were inspired by the real dangers of surviving
spiriting and servitude, and reflected contemporary views about the
lives of indentured servants.[111] Most famous today is Daniel Defoe's

The Trappan'd MAIDEN:
OR,
The Distressed Damsel.

This Girl was cunningly trapann'd, | There is no Cure, it must be so:
Sent to *Virginny* from *England*, | But if she lives to cross the Main,
Where she doth Hardship under go, | She vows she'll ne'r go there again.

Listen'd and Enter'd according to Order.

GIve ear unto a Maid,
that lately was betray'd,
And sent into *Virginny*, O:
In brief I shall declare,
what I have suffered there,
When that I was weary,
weary, weary, O.

When that first I came
To this Land of fame,
Which is called *Virginny*, O,
The Axe and the Hoe
Have wrought my Overthrow,
When that, &c.

Five years served I,
Under Master Guy,
In the Land of *Virginny*, O,
Which made me for to know,
Sorrow, Grief and Woe,
When that, &c.

When my Dame says Go,
Then I must do so,
In the Land of *Virginny*, O;
When she sits at Meat,
Then I have none to eat,
When that, &c.

The Cloath that I brought in,
They are worn very thin,
In the Land of *Virginny*, O,
Which makes me for to say,
Alas, and Well-a-day,
When that, &c.

Instead of Beds of Ease,
To lye down when I please,
In the Land of *Virginny*, O;
Upon a bed of straw,
I lay down full of Woe,
When that I was weary,
weary, weary, O.

Then the Spider she,
Daily waits on me,
In the Land of *Virginny*, O;
Round about my Bed,
She fixes her tender web,
When that I am weary, O.

So soon as it is day,
To work I must away,
In the Land of *Virginny*, O;
Then my Dame she knocks,
With her tinder-box,
When that, &c.

I have play'd my part,
Both at Plow and Cart,
In the Land of *Virginny*, O;
Billats from the Wood,
Upon my back they load,
When that, &c.

Instead of drinking Beer,
I drink the Water clear,
In the Land of *Virginny*, O;
Which makes me pale and wan,
Do all that I can,
When that, &c.

If my Dame says Go,
I dare not say no,
In the Land of *Virginny*, O;
The Water from the Spring,
Upon my head I bring,
When that, &c.

When the Mill doth stand,
I'm ready at command,
In the Land of *Virginny*, O;
The Mortar for to make,
Which made my heart to ake,
When that, &c.

When the Child doth cry,
I must sing, By a by,
In the Land of *Virginny*, O;
No rest that I can have,
Whilst I am here a Slave,
When that, &c.

A thousand Woes beside,
That I do here abide,
In the Land of *Virginny*, O;
In misery I spend
My time that hath no end,
When that, &c.

Then let the Maids beware,
All by my ill-fare,
In the Land of *Virginny*, O;
Be sure that stay at home,
For if you do here come,
You all will be weary, &c.

But if it be my chance,
Homewards to advance,
From the Land of *Virginny*, O;
If that I once more,
Land on English Shore,
I'll no more be weary,
weary, weary, O.

Printed by and for W. O. and for A. M. and sold by C. Bates, in Py-corner.

Figure 2.2   *The Trappan'd Maiden* (c. 1700).

eighteenth-century novel *Moll Flanders*, which described the titular character's transportation to Virginia.[112] An older account is *The Trappan'd Maiden or Distressed Damsel*, an English ballad of the late seventeenth century that described the travails of a young woman "cunningly trappan'd," or deceived, and "sent to Virginny from England" where she served five years in "sorrow, grief, and woe" in farming and domestic service. The ballad described deprived conditions, ragged clothing, and relentless hard labour. The narrator complained, "No rest that I can have, / Whilst I am here a slave," and the ballad's ending alludes to the precariousness of survival: "But if she lives to cross the Main [the Atlantic], She vows she'll ne'r go there [Virginia] again."[113]

Another popular account was James Revel's verse chapbook, *The Poor Unhappy Transported Felon's Sorrowful Account of His Fourteen Years Transportation, at Virginia*.[114] The earliest extant version of this dates from the late eighteenth century, but the original text probably stems from the seventeenth century, and possibly depicts a genuine experience of indenture.[115] Revel described himself as a young apprentice who took to "wicked company" and lived a life of "vice" as a thief, until he was caught and transported to Virginia as an indentured servant, where he wrote, "I was a slave." He did back-breaking work in the tobacco fields with "my fellow slaves": "five transports [servants] more, with eighteen negroes." Servants and slaves, he wrote, were treated alike: "We and the negroes both alike did fare, / Of work and food we had an equal share." When he fell sick, yet was still forced to work in the fields, he received more sympathy from the "poor negro slaves" than from his master. When the latter died, Revel had two years left to serve, but despite quick sales of "the negroes, who for life are slaves," it was trickier to sell "transported felons." Yet Revel was purchased by a benign master, who "said he would not use me as a slave, / But as a servant if I'd well behave." Revel lived his remaining two years in Jamestown "in plenty, peace, and ease," his master even paying for his transport back to England. Revel concluded his ballad with a warning to those tempted by a life of crime – they risked being "forc'd from your country for to go / Among the negroes to work at the hoe … sold for a slave because you prov'd a thief." Despite Revel's sympathy for the enslaved, the implication of this work was that slavery was suitable for Africans, but not whites.

Fictional or semi-fictional accounts like these countered the more positive promotional pamphlets and would have provided a significant disincentive for individuals considering indenturing themselves. However, indentured servants continued to flow across the ocean, impelled by poverty and lack of opportunity in Britain and Ireland, and drawn by what they saw as potentially promising economic prospects in the colonies. Perhaps they were also drawn by what they had heard about more egalitarian prospects in social standing and political participation on the other side of the Atlantic Ocean.

3

The Political Economy of Indenture

For the English authorities, indentured servants supplied requirements for particular kinds of labour within the early British Empire;
indeed, colonies sent regular requests for shipments of servants. Colonial expansion also created a need for white subjects to populate the
Caribbean colonies to ward off the threat of French and Spanish
encroachment. In addition, the authorities viewed forcible indentured servitude as a way of reducing what they saw as "surplus populations," developing policies through which indigents, criminals, and
rebels were sent overseas to serve their sentences. Shipping vagrants
and beggars also reduced incarceration costs, with older English poor
laws employed as a justification. Moreover, government authorities
believed that indigents, and especially destitute children, benefited
morally from being placed in positions of indenture. Thus, indenture
of "undesirable" populations emerged as a practical tactic that supported the expansion of the early English empire, while resolving persistent problems at home.

The government's policies were also shaped by the intertwining
of public imperatives with private interests: many influential members of English and colonial administrations were also entrepreneurs who personally profited from the transportation of servants.
The system was prone to corruption as magistrates, shippers, and
captains were paid per head without too much notice of how they
obtained their cargoes of servants. Economic and political priorities
guaranteed that the policy of transporting purported undesirables
continued unabated through shifts between Royalist and Parliamentary governments. However, emerging discourses of race and
citizenship led to vehement political debate about the conditions

for indentured servants and about the ethics of indenture itself, as well as legislation aiming to curb the worst excesses of forcible servitude in both Britain and Ireland.

FORCED INDENTURE POLICIES

Almost as soon as Elizabethan legislation provided models for care and punishment of the poor, it was adapted for a policy of overseas transportation. The earliest example was the 1597 Vagrancy Act; though not implemented, it allowed the forcible transportation of able-bodied vagrants and beggars, and was followed by similar acts in 1603, 1609, and 1620.[1] The earliest large-scale transportation, of one hundred children, took place in 1619.[2] Parallel Parliamentary orders were established for detaining vagrants and indigents in England and Ireland. For example, in May 1653, the Commissioners of Ireland issued the following order: "all laws and statutes now in force in the Commonwealth of England for the correction and punishment of rogues, vagrants, sturdy beggars, idle and disorderly persons ... and for relieving and setting of the poor to work, be and are hereby declared to be in force in Ireland."[3] These ideals were reiterated in various descriptively titled pieces of legislation, including the Orders of the Council of State "Concerning the apprehending of lewd and dangerous persons, rogues, vagrants, and other idle persons, who have no way of livelihood and refuse to work, and treating with merchants and others for transporting them to the English plantations in America" from August 1656, and Instructions for the Council "To consider how the colonies might be best supplied with servants; that no persons may be forced or enticed away by unlawful or indirect ways; that those willing to be transported thither may be encouraged; and a course legally settled to send over vagrants and others who remain here noxious and unprofitable" in December 1660, and others.[4]

Once begun, the policy of transportation was continued through several government administrations of diverse political persuasions. As it took office in 1649, the Interregnum administration reiterated the previous government's right to apprehend, punish, and put to work English vagrants, beggars, rogues, and poor children.[5] In addition, it transported rebel soldiers from England, Scotland, and Ireland as well as Irish civilians to the colonies, especially the Caribbean.[6] In 1652 and 1654, Parliamentary acts recommended shipments of the poor away from Britain, a policy reiterated by the Interregnum Council of State in 1656 and by the Restoration government in 1662–64, 1667, and 1670, with a term of labour usually set at seven years for involuntary servants.[7] In 1670, an act of the Scottish Parliament established transportation for those who refused to disclose evidence about rebels against the state or Presbyterian conventicles, an ever-present issue in culturally fractious and religiously divided Scotland.[8]

CRIMINAL SERVANTS

Convicts were another group forcibly transported by the English government. The perception of an escalation in crime resulted in increased numbers of criminal trials and higher conviction rates during the early modern era.[9] Convicts were always a small minority among servants, with fewer than 5,000 transported in the seventeenth century, increasing up to about 55,000, mainly during the eighteenth century, when they still made up less than 20 per cent of transported servants and about 30 per cent of women servants.[10] However, conviction records provide valuable sources for historians. Penal transportation was not an official punishment until the passage of the 1718 Transportation Act, which gave magistrates the power to sentence felons to seven- or fourteen-year terms, but from 1615, the government of James I allowed judges to reprieve criminals from death sentences by substituting transportation to "parts abroad."[11] Reprieves offered a conditional pardon during the seven-year sentence of transportation, which allowed felons to escape capital punishment for certain crimes, though not serious crimes like murder. This policy expanded considerably after the Restoration in 1660. In addition, convicts retained in prison, for example, for debt, could also agree to overseas indentured servitude. Shippers were induced to carry criminals with a stipend of about £5 per person.[12]

The ruthlessness of early modern criminal justice created an opportunity and even a desire among juries and magistrates to mitigate capital punishment. In addition to violent assaults and murder, lesser felonies such as robbery, negligent manslaughter, assault, and poaching, and even slighter crimes such as counterfeiting or the theft of small amounts of property, cash, clothing, or food, could incur sentences of death. It was recognized that many of these crimes were opportunistic, born of desperation, rather than the activity of hardened criminals. Sympathetic juries and magistrates sometimes convicted felons on lighter charges to save them from execution.[13] In 1622, John Donne deplored the fact that many convicts were sentenced to "ignominious death" for "perchance a small fault, or perchance a first fault, or perchance a fault heartily and sincerely repented," or had been accused through "perchance no fault, but malice," and countered that transportation reprieves would "redeem many a wretch from the jawes of death, from the hands of the executioner."[14] In 1656, even Oliver Cromwell criticized the practice of executing criminals for "petty matters" and "trifle[s]," specifically pinpointing execution for theft as "wicked and abominable" and an "ill framing" of the law.[15]

Mercy was seen as a virtue of governance, tied to the role of the monarch as a personification of state power, and in the case of transportation reprieves, probably also served to mitigate what was seen as excessively harsh penalties according to community consensus.[16] Thus, the stated aim of the 1615 legislation allowing reprieves of capital sentences was that "justice be tempered with mercie," as well as that convicts might "yield a profitable service."[17] By the 1630s, the practice of remitting sentences to transportation appears to have been standard.[18]

Both magistrates and the general public tended to regard felons as lawless dregs of society in both the colonies and Britain.[19] However, convicts themselves did not necessarily accept this assessment, and the records show them actively involved in negotiating for their lives against the power of the state, including bargaining for reduced punishments for crimes.[20] Strategies differed depending on the felon's sex. Men might plead the benefit of the clergy, a legal fiction that involved reading (or memorizing) a biblical verse to prove one was a clergyman, usually Psalm 51, the "neck verse," which saved one's neck. Rarely, an uncompromising judge could ask for another verse, eliminating the uneducated who had memorized the lines. Women were ineligible for this, but might plead the belly, involving a legal determination that the convicted woman was pregnant, established by a "jury of women" who exercised a kind of judicial judgment often based on their perception of the culpability of the accused.[21] For those for whom neither of these chances was possible, reprieves were another possibility. In some cases, reprieve from a capital sentence involved whipping, branding, or mutilation; some convicts or magistrates preferred transportation as a penalty. The existence of transportation as a form of respite for punishment also allowed judicial authorities to impose harsh penalties with the knowledge that they would likely be remitted. Transportation could also be perceived as a form of rehabilitation: hard labour as an appropriate consequence of punishment.[22]

In some cases, despite the letter of the law, convicted criminals appear to have been immediately sentenced to transportation even before 1718, especially if they were first-time or non-violent offenders. For example, in 1674, a woman in Newgate who had stolen a silver cup from a "victualling house": the cup was discovered on her person when she was later arrested for prostitution, and she was sentenced to transportation.[23] More typical was Mary Harris, imprisoned in Newgate after being respited from capital punishment in 1682: it was ordered she be sent "without delay … out of this kingdom of England" for a seven-year indenture in the colonies.[24] Another case demonstrates the ruthlessness of early modern criminal law: in 1676, Thomas Moore and James Parker were convicted of theft and agreed to transportation as a respite from punishment – the court records state they were "sent aboard a ship by their consent." However, they ran away before the ship sailed and were sentenced to execution. Parker had actually been transported five years before and had returned early. He refused to plead, which meant that he was subjected to the torture of being pressed to force him to "recant his obstinacy," an ordeal that injured him so much that "it was much doubted whether he would have survived" had his sentence been less than execution.[25] Returning early from transportation was considered evading punishment and had been added to his list of misdeeds, although it was not usually sufficient for a death sentence on its own.[26]

Transportation was obviously preferable to a death sentence. In 1676, when two women were arrested for "stealing a considerable parcel of linnen and other things," one of them, who had already been transported in the past, "begg'd for [it] heartily now again," although it appears without success.[27] Indeed, some politicians felt that transportation was excessively merciful. When a bill for transporting thieves who had not committed burglary or murder to the American

Figure 3.1 A group of convicts being marched from Newgate Prison, to be transported to the colonies.

plantations was debated in 1667, some Members of Parliament criticized it on the grounds that "it would be an incouragement to theeves and robbers" to commit crimes in order to obtain free passage to the colonies.[28] This theory was of dubious accuracy, but it did reflect the opinions of some politicians that transportation was an advantageous prospect for the poor.

On 18 June 1635, John Haydon, a prisoner in Bridewell, petitioned the Court of High Commission to be freed if he voluntarily went to Virginia. He appears to have been a member of a dissenting sect, as his crimes included "preaching abroad." He was also a security risk, who had escaped prison previously.[29] Haydon may have gone as a freeman, but many in the same situation agreed to have their passage paid for by their servitude. Two weeks after Haydon's petition, a warrant was issued to send nine women and five men from Newgate to Virginia.[30] Mall Floyd's plea for transportation as a respite from a capital sentence was granted on 17 July 1674.[31] Relatives, friends, or patrons could intercede on behalf of a prisoner, as when John Throgmorten's grandmother, in the second decade of the seventeenth century, begged that her grandson, perhaps an adolescent, be transported to Virginia rather than executed.[32] In 1619, Lord Russell requested that Harry Reade, a highwayman, receive clemency by being sent to Virginia.[33] In 1633, the king granted mercy to Thomas Brice, a condemned prisoner in Newgate, at the request of his father, commanding that Brice be transported to Virginia.[34] In some cases, an influential patron might even be able to help a convict escape punishment altogether. In 1663, Isabell Langley was reprieved from death by a sentence of transportation, but she was dissatisfied with this verdict and petitioned to obtain an unconditional release. She wrote to the Earl of Craven, who appears to have facilitated her initial pardon from the more severe penalty, thanking him but complaining that, "instead of my being in a free pardon, I am crowded into the transportation pardon ... and next week to be carried on board some merchant's ship to be sold into some of the plantations as a slave, which would be worse than the untimely death I was doomed to." She pleaded that her "age and impotency be not exposed to so much unbecoming misery," and she solicited him to try to influence the king ("move his Majesty") to grant "a warrant to stop my sudden transportation and [to include] me in the next general pardon for poor convicts without proviso of transportation."[35] Langley's connection with the earl, who had already bestowed "many undeserved favours" on her, was unclear, but it is quite apparent that she was ready to employ every ounce of influence she possessed and had likely initiated the earl's earlier activity on her behalf. Somewhat similar was the situation of Jane Steele, who was sentenced to death in 1691. Her mother, also Jane Steele, sought to have her sentence discharged rather than respited for transportation, because the younger Jane apparently had a learning disability and was "very foolish in all her actions" and "not having sense."[36]

Sometimes transportation was employed as an alternative to keeping petty criminals in prison. In 1638, Elizabeth Cotterell, who was still imprisoned in the Marshalsea prison eight months after she had been reprieved, likely for nonpayment of prison expenses, which prisoners were responsible for, successfully petitioned to be transported to Virginia.[37] For individuals like Cotterell, service overseas might have presented an opportunity, particularly when the fees for the passage across the ocean were paid through her service agreement. Similarly, 300 "malefactors" who had been made "free of fees from the gaols" were sent to St Christopher in 1676.[38] It is evident in these cases that a sentence of transportation was not intended to be a death sentence. In addition, transportation should also be contrasted with the prospect of remaining in prison, as typically prisoners were held in insanitary group cells without adequate food, and many did not survive there even for a few months.[39]

Yet, as in many transportation schemes, there was a disjunction between the needs and desires of English and colonial authorities. Although the government in England was eager to remove felons from Britain, colonial societies were hesitant to receive them. They feared that convicts would be troublesome servants and might corrupt voluntary servants.[40] For example, in 1663, the Virginia General Court complained of the "danger to the colony caused by the great number of Virginia felons and other desperate villains being sent over from the prisons in England," citing a "horror" of "the subversion of our religion, laws, liberties, rights, and privileges." It passed a resolution "prohibiting the landing of any jail birds."[41] Maryland passed an act in 1723 to regulate the importation of convict servants, who "of late years imported into this province have not only comitted severall murders burglarys and other felonies" but also "debauched the minds and principles of severall of the ignorant and formerly innocent inhabitants," made "honest people ... very insecure in their lives or properties," and had taken up the "greatest part of the magistrates time" in the "prosecution of the said convicts and their proselytes." In legislation that must have acted as a significant disincentive to those who hoped to save money by employing convict servants, those who purchased them had to henceforth provide £30 surety for the first year.[42]

REBELS

Another group with a reduced value on the labour market were enemy military combatants and rebels. Beginning in 1649, transportation was used to punish and remove military forces that had opposed the Interregnum government, following the precedents established for convicts.[43] Such men were considered a threat to order and might be transported if they seemed of no use in prisoner exchanges, were not charged with capital crimes, and were expensive to keep incarcerated. After the fall of the Royalist garrison at Drogheda in 1649, Oliver Cromwell infamously wrote to Parliament that "when they submitted, their officers were knock'd on the head, and every tenth man of the soldiers kill'd, and the rest shipped for the Barbadoes. The soldiers in the other town were all spared as to their lives only, and shipped likewise for the Barbadoes."[44] It should be pointed out that this policy did not inherently demonstrate retaliation against the Irish since most of the soldiers in this rebel army would have been English. However, such soldiers were seen as traitorous for aiding the Royalist and Catholic cause.[45] There were also a number of instances in which such troops were exiled to continental armies, a policy that acted as a double-edged sword: it removed rebel soldiers from Britain but meant they might be deployed in French or Spanish armies supporting non-British interests.[46] In 1654 then, the Irish Commissioners overturned plans to send a group of Irish Catholic military prisoners to the Spanish army on the continent, altering their destination to the West Indies and easing their servitude by stipulating "they will have as good condition as any English or other servants there," with terms of "four years" rather than the usual criminal term of seven to ten years, after which they were "to be free men to act for their advantage." Soldiers and male civilians who travelled voluntarily would be offered a fourteen shilling stipend. Women volunteers were to be given clothing.[47] A substantial number of the Royalist Salisbury rebels of 1654, many of whom were gentlemen, were also sent to work in the fields in Bar-

bados.[48] In September 1655, the Council of State ordered that the
English, Scottish, Irish, and Dutch sailors held in the Castle of Ply-
mouth and "not fit to be tried for their lives" were likewise to be sent
to Barbados.[49]

Although the Interregnum Parliament had initiated the practice of
transporting rebels, Restoration governments continued to employ
transportation to punish and remove military forces that had
opposed the government. The Scottish rebels of 1667, the 1685 Ar-
gyll rebels, and many of the 1685 Monmouth rebels were also sent to
Barbados, sentenced to ten-year terms of servitude.[50] It should be
noted that even captured rebels were not sent to permanent servitude. Rebels were normally sentenced to capital punishment, which
was respited to ten years' servitude. While conditions of servitude
were extremely harsh, there is also evidence that some survived to the
end of their terms. Numbers of former political prisoners in Barbados were freed at the accessions of both Charles II in 1660 and
William of Orange in 1688.[51]

COLONIAL NEEDS FOR LABOUR

The perception that work was available in the colonies was accurate.
Colonial economies were chronically short of labour, especially
before the expansion of the slave trade during the later seventeenth
century, and colonial assemblies sent many requests to Parliament
asking for cargoes of servants, even convicted criminals.[52] There was
a disjunction between the needs of the colonies, which mostly
desired adult non-criminal English men, and those of the government, which sent a much more heterogenous population of individuals, including women, children, criminals, and military rebels.
However, a significant portion of the labour needs of the colonies
were generally fulfilled by the servant trade during the first two-
thirds of the seventeenth century. The bulk of servants went to
colonies with plantation economies: Virginia, Maryland, Barbados,
and Jamaica.

As the British expanded their overseas colonies, there was an
increasing need to lay claim to them by expanding the settler population. After the settlement of Virginia in the late sixteenth century
and gradual settlement of the other mainland American colonies, the
British settled St Kitts (1624), Barbados (1627), Nevis (1628),
Montserrat (1632), and Antigua (1630s), and in 1655, seized Jamaica

from the Spanish. In addition, they developed the relatively sparsely settled colonies in Central and South America, such as Belize and British Guiana, as well as Canada. The acquisition of territories incentivized the shipping of servants, both to labour to make the colonies viable and to populate the territories with English subjects who could defend them if necessary. In some cases, likely men received a remission of their criminal sentences if they agreed to serve as soldiers in the Caribbean.[53]

The Caribbean territories were particularly vulnerable to encroachment by other imperial powers such as the Spanish, French, and Dutch.[54] The government aimed to send indentured servants in order to swell the island population of freemen once they had completed their indentures.[55] This aim was clearly indicated in a proposal to secure Antigua in April 1656, which lamented that as "no supplies of servants have of late arrived from England; [the] number of fighting men [was] very inconsiderable," and in the Antiguan governor's request for "a garrison of 500 soldiers be kept upon the island, or a supply sent of English and Scotch servants" with arms and ammunition. The plea expressed a preference for "prisoners and the like," but if not available, "Scots and Irish."[56]

In 1655, after the English seized Jamaica from the Spanish, they attempted to encourage settlement there as rapidly as possible, offering considerable incentives for New Englanders to transplant themselves to the new Caribbean colony and shipping servants there who, when they had served their time of indenture, would become colonists.[57] The ostensible reason was to increase the English presence, but Irish servants were seen as an acceptable alternative. On 3 October 1655, the Council of State ordered that 1,000 Irish girls and 1,000 Irish boys under fourteen be sent to Jamaica, presumably as servants, with a small stipulated compensation of cash, 20 shillings, perhaps to be given after completing servitude at the age of twenty-one.[58] The council also issued a proclamation more generally throughout Britain "for the encouragement of persons who will transport themselves to Jamaica" and provided for "an allotment of lands to officers and soldiers in Jamaica" as an inducement.[59]

These initiatives blended many of the government's goals in encouraging transportation. Contemporaries could actually, if unrealistically, define this proposal as beneficial to the youths involved.

Henry Cromwell, Oliver Cromwell's son and at that time de facto leader of Ireland, wrote of the girls requested by the Council of State that "concerninge the younge women, although we must use force in takeinge them up, yet it beinge so much for their owne goode, and likely to be of soe great advantage to the publique" that it would be a worthwhile endeavour. Cromwell continued that for the girls "it will be necessarye, that care be taken for the clotheinge of them," possibly a reference to the usual freedom dues of clothing for indentured women.[60] In reference to the boys, Cromwell continued that "it may be a meanes to make them English-men, I meane rather, Christianes." Unlike the women or girls, Cromwell believed that the "recruite" of men or boys would travel voluntarily, attracted by "encouragements" such as freedom dues: "if provision bee made for their pay and accommodation," he wrote, there "will be noe dificulty to engage 1000 or 1500 men, or perhapes more."[61] Notably this scheme assumed that the Catholic Irish would readily give up any prior national or religious affiliations and accept an identity as British subjects.

An obstacle to this plan was that the government was short of ready cash, "haveinge much exhausted our treasure" by keeping soldiers on the payroll. This meant that "we are not any waies able" to provide the pay that Cromwell wished. Nonetheless, Cromwell hoped that former soldiers might be recruited to go to Jamaica. While his letters are somewhat unclear, he appears to have been considering the possibility of recruiting soldiers from the English army in Ireland, which had not yet been disbanded. In the end though, the plan of a large-scale shipment of settlers from Ireland, whether former soldiers or as servants, seems not to have been implemented.[62] Twelve hundred soldiers – from government forces, not defeated royalists – were sent to Jamaica in 1656 from Carrickfergus.[63]

In addition to populating Jamaica, the undisguised underlying policy incentive was the desire to reduce the ranks of the Irish poor while supplying labour for the colonies; Cromwell acknowledged this, adding "we could well spare them, and they would be of use."[64] In addition, servant women were sometimes transported as potential wives for the colonists, which may have been an additional motivation to ship 1,000 Irish girls. A year later, over 1,000 poor English women, possibly including prostitutes and criminals, were sent to Barbados.[65]

The Caribbean continued to actively recruit white men as servants. As the dangers of French or Spanish invasions receded, a new imperative was to maintain populations of white men because of fears of slave revolts or collusion of the enslaved with foreign invasions. This was acknowledged by a scheme to send 300 convicts to St Christopher "for the better supply of white men in the island."[66] During the mid-seventeenth century, most Caribbean colonies adopted rules mandating that planters employ one white man for every ten slaves, although this was hard to enforce because of the reluctance of servants to go to the islands.[67]

CAPITALIST ENTREPRENEURS AND THE SERVANT TRADE

The actual task of shipping of servants under government auspices was done by independent contractors. The economic aspects of the servant trade illustrate the complex and ethically compromised interaction of public and private interests. The government-sponsored servant trade, involving the transportation of vagrants, criminals, or rebels, was immensely profitable, and largely controlled by politically influential merchant capitalists. Merchants who carried large numbers of servants had an advantage since the individual profit per servant was relatively small. Outlays could include £3–6 to pay off jail fees, £5–6 to an independent ship's captain for passage across the ocean, about £1 for food, £3 for clothing, and potentially £2 for medical costs.[68] Sale prices for servants were unpredictable, ranging from £12–18 for men and £10–12 for women, in some cases incurring a capital loss. In contrast, a slave sold for approximately £20. Merchants and independent captains who dealt in spirited servants could avoid paying jail fees but had to advance similar sums to kidnappers. However, government contractors were subsidized by up to £7 per head, which allowed for a significant profit margin.[69] In 1656, for example, shipper Martin Noell received a stipend of £5 10s per head for shipping Irish rebels.[70]

Martin Noell was one of the most prominent of government contractors; he regularly received subsidies for shipping coerced servants as well as profits from selling their contracts. However, Noell was not only a merchant. He exerted significant influence in political circles and served in the Boards of Trade and the Council of State, seamlessly remaining in the government through several opposing

regimes, including the royal administration of Charles I, the Interregnum Parliament, and the Restoration government of Charles II.
Noell was involved in many political endeavours, and controlled
excise farms in a number of colonial and domestic projects, held military contracts, and helped bankroll Cromwell's expedition against
Jamaica. He likely was one of the authors of the Navigation Act of
1651, an attempt to restrict foreign shipping. He received a knight-
hood during the Restoration period. In addition, Noell was a sugar
merchant and a colonial planter, owning estates in Jamaica, Barbados, Montserrat, and Ireland. He controlled a firm involved in a
number of shipping ventures to the West Indies, including human
cargoes of slaves and indentured servants as well as sugar, shoes,
horses, and other goods.[71] Noell exemplified the tangled incentives
and conflicts of interest inherent in the policy of transporting
unwilling indentured servants. His public and private roles intertwined, allowing him enormous influence over government economic policies to his personal benefit.

Although probably the most powerful of such capitalist entrepreneurs, Noell was by no means unique. There were many others,
such as Thomas Povey, who also exercised significant political
power, probably helped Noell write the Navigation Act of 1651,
and likely suggested the Council for Trade in the Americas, serving
as one of its more active members. He too held key government
offices and controlled excise farms and Atlantic shipping ventures.
Like Noell, Povey had a career spanning the administrations of
Charles I, the Interregnum, and Charles II.[72] Along with Noell and
Povey, several other entrepreneurs – among them, Maurice Thomson, Andrew Riccard, and Robert Rich, Earl of Warwick – were
simultaneously active in colonization, human trafficking, military
contracting, and government office-holding.[73] Such men retained
influence through three government administrations that held supposedly disparate political principles but were united by an interest
in the capitalistic exploitation of resources, whether colonial or
human as well as by a disinclination to separate the private interests
of their members from the will of the state. At a lower economic
level, merchants such as William Haveland openly employed spirits
to bring them servants.[74]

The interests of capitalist entrepreneurs and government policies
contradicted each other to some extent. For example, there is evidence that impoverished but self-supporting individuals were

swept up with some regularity when servant cargos were assem-
bled.[75] This was disadvantageous for the government because it
meant paying for the transportation of individuals who had not
previously been the recipients of government funds. However,
although there were instances of administrative strictures against
this practice, they were rarely enforced. This can be explained in
two ways. In part, the perceived need to rid society of certain populations – the poor, disreputable, and disorderly – led local and
national governments to turn a blind eye to their disappearance, or
even to encourage it. But a further factor that enabled this practice
was that interests of national and local governments, local officials,
shippers, and contractors did not always coincide. From a purely
economic perspective, governments might favour sending only
people enrolled in poor relief out of the country. Yet those who
profited through commissions or direct profits obtained by amass-
ing or shipping individuals were less fastidious about which individuals they chose to ship. In fact, the shippers themselves preferred
strong and healthy servants who would bring a greater price upon
the sale of their contracts, and fit individuals were perhaps less likely
to come from the destitute poor. The very system of government-
sanctioned indenture thus bred corruption.[76] In the eighteenth
century, the necessity of convincing contractors to ship criminal
servants resulted in increases to the length of the criminal sentences assigned to convicts, regardless of the magnitude of the
crime committed, as the government sought to make convicts desirable to shippers who were primarily interested in profits.[77] In addition, the financial obligation incurred in providing poor relief or in
maintaining poorhouses was considerably higher than the one-
time shipping cost for servants.[78] Thus, equality of justice under the
law was undermined in favour of capitalist concerns, which encouraged the commercialization of criminal justice.[79]

   And yet, even these merchant entrepreneurs were not able to fully
control English transportation policy. Whether in England or Ireland, implementation of the state's commitment to the policy of
shifting particular populations abroad often proceeded in a haphazard manner, like many policy initiatives of the early modern state.
One difficulty involved disjunctions between the English government's desire to remove certain populations that were seen as
unwanted and actual colonial desires for labour. Another was political uneasiness about the restrictions on rights of freeborn English-

men, causing even Martin Noell to defend himself against charges of enslaving Englishmen, as is discussed later in this chapter.

SPIRITING:
THE ILLEGAL TRAFFICKING OF SERVANTS

In addition to persons transported unwillingly but legally by the government, a considerable illegal trade in servants persisted. The sporadic attempts to regulate this trade reveal most of what we know about it. Fear of the spirits was very real, even as early as the beginning of the seventeenth century: in 1618 a warrant was issued against Owen Evans, Messenger of the Chamber, because he had "pretended a commission to press maidens to be sent to the Bermudas and Virginia, and raised money thereby." Evans's "undue proceedings breed such terror to the poor maidens, that forty have fled from one parish [in Somersetshire] to obscure places, and their parents do not know what has become of them."[80] While this case, in which the offender was not actually engaged in spiriting but in fundraising under the pretext of a government contract, shows prosecution of an influential member of society, such repercussions were infrequent, and enforcement of the laws against spiriting in Britain was rare.

When spirits were prosecuted, it was often piecemeal, a result of tips or the resolve of determined individuals: if children were kidnapped, it was often their fathers who traced them and then brought in magistrates to rescue their offspring. Ships' masters typically refused to release a kidnapped servant without a signed warrant and a public official present, so that when the father of Bart Broome traced his son to a docked ship in 1653 or the father of John Brookes demanded his kidnapped son in 1668, they were initially refused their sons. While eventually successful in rescuing them, many other unclaimed children were left on board the ships. The captain detaining Bart Broome had to be threatened that he would resist the warrant "at his peril."[81] Because of Thomas Vernon's diligent search for his stolen son, the spirit Edward Harrison and Captain Azariah Daniel were prosecuted, and 150 children were rescued. Nonetheless, other parents who had "lost their children" still required "the Lords of the Admiralty's warrant in order to search all outward bound ships for the recovery of 'em."[82] In the 1730s, Elizabeth Ashbridge's family still required the "water bailiff" to procure her release.[83]

Likewise in August 1657, a tip led to a search of the *Conquer*, about to embark for the West Indies. Of the twenty-seven servants on board, fourteen were willing to go into service overseas, with another two women willing to continue "if they had their clothes," seemingly negotiating contracts including the typical freedom dues of clothing, despite being originally coerced. Eleven more had been spirited and wanted to leave. The ship was only allowed to continue after the eleven people "unduly enticed" were freed. This investigation was taken seriously, sending the Lieutenant of the Tower to investigate, seize the captives, and report to the Council of State.[84] In none of these incidents were the merchants or ships' masters prosecuted, but in 1634, Henry Deane, a Greenwich fisherman, was prosecuted for "receiving" men and women, and in 1638, two men were arrested for "taking up of men and selling them like cattle," to be shipped by "such as have no licence to levy."[85] In 1670, William Haveland, John Steward, William Thiene, Robert Bayley, and Mark Collins were each individually charged with spiriting hundreds of people yearly (up to the astonishing number of 800) to Barbados, Jamaica, and Virginia.[86] John Wareing has identified 249 cases in which 353 spirits, both male and female, were accused, mainly for deceiving rather than kidnapping servants. However, prosecutions did not always result, in part because often "the victim was 4,000 miles away in America."[87]

Policy regarding spiriting was fraught with ambiguity. While the idea of kidnapping was regarded as abhorrent, it coexisted with a genuine need for labour in the colonies, the worry that England was overpopulated, and the belief that most vagrants were shiftless and lazy. Sometimes when kidnappers were apprehended, they were allowed to continue with their cargoes of captive servants because of the belief that vagabonds would be better kept in custody.[88] Such competing imperatives led to simultaneous condemnation of spiriting and disinclination to remedy it.[89] There was also substantial government collusion in kidnapping, as is shown by the activities of the spirit William Haveland, a career magistrate.[90]

Spiriting, especially of children, remained an emotionally resonant issue. There were a number of legislative initiatives meant to limit the practice, although most failed to pass in Parliament and child-stealing remained a misdemeanour.[91] The first ordinance to have ships leaving London searched for kidnapped servants before embarking was enacted in 1643.[92] In 1645, Parliament published a broadside ordering "the strict and diligent search of all ships" to apprehend any "lewd persons," who "in a most barbarous and wicked manner" endeavoured to "steale, sell, buy, inveigle, purloyne, convey, or receive any little children" so that the kidnappers might "be brought to severe and exemplary punishment." Magistrates were to be "very diligent in apprehending such persons."[93] In 1647, while encouraging "adventurers" to colonize, Parliament stipulated that all servants being transported be registered as willing, uncoerced, and adult.[94] In 1654, a Bristol ordinance reacting to people "carried away, stolen and sold" mandated that all servants be registered by officials before being taken onto ships, and that ships "from time to time" be searched for unwilling servants.[95] In 1660, there was an attempt to establish a registry "for all servants and children to be transported to Virginia and Barbadoes, to declare their willingness to go."[96] The Privy Council referred to the kidnapping of children as "a thing so barbarous and inhumane that Nature itself, much more Christians, cannot but abhorre," but the latest bill failed to pass.[97] In 1682, the spiriting of servants who had been "seized and carried by force to His Majesties plantations in America" by "evil-disposed persons," as well as the aim to regularize the servant trade, inspired a law mandating documentation and validation of indenture contracts.[98] Political commentator Narcissus Luttrell reported on the Privy Council orders of 1682 and 1686 as part of an increasing emphasis by the authorities on "putting a stop to so prodigious a villany" of child kidnapping.[99] There were at least nineteen attempts in Parliament to restrict illicit kidnapping and to ensure that servants being transported were "willing to serve," including mandates to inspect all ships and register all servants leaving British ports. However, most attempts to authorize legislation faltered and a considerable illegal trade in servants persisted.[100]

A hint as to why may be found in the July 1664 petition of a number of merchants involved in the servant trade. Although claiming that they "abominate[d] the very thoughts of" spiriting youths, they alleged that preventative legislation gave "the opportunity to many evil-minded persons to enlist themselves voluntarily to go the voyage, and having received money, clothes, diet, &c., to pretend they were betrayed or carried away without their consents."[101] Although presenting itself as a disavowal of spiriting, this petition in fact undermined the idea that it was occurring, or that kidnapped individuals could be reliably identified, implying instead that poverty-stricken individuals were exploiting the supposed benefits of an indenture contract and then claiming to have been spirited in order to take advantage of innocent merchants. This argument was taken seriously, which led to the evisceration of the bill then being debated, which in itself was relatively weak since it only recommended but did not mandate that shippers register their cargoes of servants.[102]

At journey's end, there do not seem to have been systematic safeguards in the colonies, such as officials charged with inspecting all cargoes of servants to ensure that they were voluntary. It would have been difficult to enforce given the laxity of the early modern state and, of course, would also have been detrimental to colonial interests. One example of an attempt to alleviate criticism can be found in a 1661 Barbados masters and servants act, which included a provision for kidnapped servants to complain to magistrates. However, this relief was limited to the first month of arrival, which must have prevented most servants from regaining their freedom because of lack of knowledge, difficulty of travel, inability to prove arrival dates, or fear of reprisals.[103]

CRITICISM OF GOVERNMENT INDENTURE POLICIES

The practice of legal but compulsory indenture by the government also caused disquiet, both among government officials and members of the public. The critique touched on two issues: firstly, whether the forcible indenture of vagrants was tantamount to spiriting, especially in the case of children, and secondly, whether the government was entitled to indenture freeborn Englishmen, even if they had been rebels against the government itself. This touched on the evolving ideal of citizenship and the rights of all English people. Criminal indenture, although criticized by servants themselves, was less prominent in public discourse because until 1718 it was widely seen as reprieve from even harsher punishment.

A 1650 broadsheet from the Office of Admiralty, the government body in charge of maritime policy, clearly illustrates administrative intent to deflect criticism that there was little effort to prevent spiriting.[104] The document was meant to be posted in the Royal Exchange and "other publique places" in order "to take off that most false aspersion," the "complaint and rumour, that there were diverse little children taken up, and shipped aboard of some ship or ships to be transported for the plantations." The Admiralty Court, the text declared, had made "strict search and inquirie," ordering the "stay of all such ships as should have any such children aboard." The lack of such ships – with one exception – showed the rumours "to be most false and scandalous." The one ship with children on board, the *Victory*, was on its way to Barbados and carried twelve "poore boyes and youths, who were for the most part, begger boyes," aged twelve to twenty, but the broadside claimed that "all of them [were] very desirous and willing to goe the voyage." The text maintained that the boys were orphans, and concluded with a listing of the names, ages, original parishes, and fathers' names and occupations.

This piece of propaganda is full of lacunae that divulge more than what is simply printed on the page. It reveals the government's responsiveness to allegations of inaction about spiriting and its desire to portray itself as a protector of the public. The text clearly delineates even "begger boyes" as valuable subjects possessing rights within the English commonweal. Yet the broadsheet also implies that the search of the ship was a one-time event rather than a systematic policy to counter what was an entrenched practice of kidnapping and coercing servants. The document neglects to explain how the determination of willingness to travel was made, but by noting the boys were destitute orphans, it provided a plausible explanation for their voluntary servitude, their fathers' deaths having left them without the protection of a household or employment. This was in truth a common reason for youths to sign indenture contracts.[105] The document's self-conscious listing of the theoretically verifiable list of names and parishes "to give notice to their parents, friends, and masters, if they have any," and its mandate to be displayed prominently aimed to reassure the public that kidnapping was rare and also that the government was ready to take immediate action if it occurred, while ignoring the possibly of coercive practices used for other cargoes of servants. Whether or not the youths on the *Victory* were actually travelling voluntarily or as a result of force (and misrepresentations about the conditions of servitude must be considered as a form of coercion), many servants were indeed unwilling.

Concern about the government's transportation of vagrants was a recurrent theme. For example, in 1645, Henry Whalley wrote in the Interregnum newsbook *The True Informer* that the poor should be placed in workhouses rather than "to send the children of the freeborn subjects of the kingdom to be … slaves in foreign part."[106] The similarity of indentured servitude to slavery led to denunciation of the practice by many contemporaries; they objected not to slavery itself, but to the maltreatment of English subjects by placing them in a slave-like status.[107]

Even more remarkably, the question of whether it was legitimate for the government to transport rebels was vigorously contested in Parliament, especially during the Interregnum period. The disputes centred on whether the government was overreaching by limiting the rights of the "freeborn people of England," a particularly striking reservation because the individuals being forcibly transported were considered criminals, rebels, and vagrants. There were several rounds of discussions about the legality of shipping "felons and prisoners" overseas, including in 1649, 1651, 1657.[108] Bills to outlaw the transportation of English prisoners were unsuccessfully introduced in 1670, 1674, 1675, 1676, and 1679.[109]

One of the most remarkable debates occurred in 1659, in response to the Parliamentary petition of Marcellus Rivers and Oxenbridge Foyle on the behalf of seventy Cavaliers (Royalists) who had been sentenced to ten-year terms of servitude in Barbados by the Interregnum government and the petition filed by Rowland Thomas, another royalist indentured in Barbados.[110] The three men had been permitted to travel to England to pursue their case.[111] Their petitions condemned the merchants who sold the indentured rebels as "their pretended owners, merchants that deal in slaves and souls of men," who "enslave[d] those of their own country and religion" in denial of their obligation to the "free-born people of England by whose suffrages they sit in Parliament."[112] Both complaints pinpointed Martin Noell as an exploitative profiteer. Thomas contended that he had been sold as a slave for £100 by Noell. Noell was forced to rebut this charge in Parliament, retorting that "he never sold anyone for money," and that "I abhor the thoughts of setting £100 upon any man's person. It is false and scandalous. I indent with all persons that I send over. Indeed, the work is hard, but none are sent without their consent. They were civilly used."[113] Noell continued that the prisoners had "four times of refreshing [daily breaks], and work but from six to six: so it is not so hard as is represented to you; not so much as the common husbandman here. The work is mostly carried on by the Negroes ... It is not so odious as is represented." He also reminded the MPs of the economic importance of Barbados: "It is a place as grateful to you for trade as any part of the world."[114] Noell's claim of "never" selling men was disingenuous since he typically shipped prisoners and convicts, but his defensiveness as well as the required deposition evidenced the necessity of emphasizing legality and fair practices. This case in particular, even though it ultimately led to little substantial change, was to have a real impact on Parliamentary consciousness.

Members of the Interregnum Parliament were powerfully affected by this discussion. Some members responded by defending the forced indenture of royalists on the grounds that they were serving a punishment for their crimes or by claiming that if the petitioners were reprieved, then all royalist prisoners – Scots were particularly mentioned – would clamour for release.[115] However, others thought like Sir Henry Vane: "I do not look on this business as a Cavalierish [royalist] business, but as a matter that concerns the liberty of the free-born people of England"; or like Sir John Lenthall: "I hope it is not the effect of our war to make merchandize of men. I consider them as Englishmen ... We are the freest people in the world."[116] Sir Arthur Haselrig was so affected that he could "hardly hold [from] weeping when I heard the petition." He maintained that without impartial application of the law regardless of faction, the rights of all Englishmen were endangered, leading to military rule: "That which is the Cavalier's case, to-day, may be the Roundhead's [Parliamentary supporter] a year hence ... we must be careful of suffering such precedents." Otherwise, he contended, "we are likely to be governed by an army ... I would have every man be careful how he acts any man's commands against law."[117] Haselrig continued that "no Englishman ought to be imprisoned but in order to a trial." While he would "never plead for a Cavalier" in Parliament, he would stand for "the liberty of an Englishman, and for the laws."[118] Likewise, MP Edward Boscawen stated: "I am as much against the Cavalierish party as any man within these walls," but "we are miserable slaves if we may not have this liberty secured to us."[119]

The debate on transportation centred on whether the government was overreaching by limiting the rights of free English subjects, specifically about whether it was legitimate for Parliament to authorize the imprisonment of Englishmen without trial, even if they had conspired treasonously against the state. Although not all MPs agreed, those who supported the right of the petitioners to be heard based their position on the rights of freeborn Englishmen, regardless of the rebels' political affiliations. The very terms of this debate seemingly excluded those who were not English – the Irish and other British nationalities were not mentioned, other than a brief reference to the

Scots. Yet they may implicitly have been included as subjects, a position for which there was some legal precedent.[120] At the same time, the speakers who condemned the servitude of royalist rebels explicitly indicated that they did not extend the same English rights to African slaves. MP Boscawen declared, for example, "I would have you consider the trade of buying and selling men," but specified that if the plaintiffs were ignored, "our lives will be as cheap as those negroes."[121] For Sir Arthur Haselrig, one of the hardships of servitude was that "these men are now sold into slavery among beasts" – that is, African slaves.[122] Slavery itself was not at issue – only the servitude of Englishmen, and perhaps other subjects of the English state. This question would not be resolved by Parliamentary debate, but Charles II was restored to the throne the following year, and most political prisoners in Barbados were freed.

In the end, this attempt at regulation failed, as did most others. However, the government continued to attempt, albeit inadequately, to ensure that the servant trade proceeded according to the law and included legal protections for individuals both in England and Ireland. This was consistent with the government's self-representation as a protector of freeborn Englishmen, which included a paternalistic interest in the welfare of servants, including servant children who were supposedly being shipped overseas for moral redemption. The debates about this practice centred on moral concerns – reforming the undesirable populations and removing negative influences from the commonwealth or, conversely, safeguarding the rights of the transported. Yet evidence suggests that another unspoken imperative was stronger in the end: the economic interests and political influence of capitalist entrepreneurs like Martin Noell outweighed the scant political will in elite circles to effectively curtail abuses in the servant trade.

Despite government assurances that it was protecting servants against kidnapping and inequitable indenture practices – even those shipped unwillingly – the validity of these claims was diluted by the weakness and endemic favouritism of the early modern state and the lack of will to implement impartiality. Within this framework, the rights of the poor or of adversaries of the government were recognized, as evidenced by debates in the government and the attempts to regulate, but ultimately were treated as almost negligible. Thus, the state's claim to protect its subjects was compromised by its willingness to countenance the intertwining of public and private aspirations. The violence of indenture demonstrates the complex and sometimes contradictory nature of state participation and intervention in unfree labour systems in the English Atlantic.

Despite the high-minded ideals expressed in the many discussions and written works detailed here, the practice of indenturing people, even through legal means, was inherently exploitative and abusive. Yet at the same time, by their very existence, these debates constituted an articulation of the nature of the rights of English, and to some extent British and Irish, subjects and citizens. They envisioned a polity in which beggar boys as well as rebels who had conspired to bring down the government possessed inalienable natural and legal rights, and re-emphasized a model of government that governed with the consent and in the interests of the people. It would take many generations for these ideals to solidify, but just as the existence of indentured servants in the colonies forced British settlers to define the rights of white subjects, critiques of the practices of indenturing individuals in Britain and Ireland pushed the English government along the path of delineating individual and corporate rights of citizenship.

IRISH SERVANTS

Irish servants comprised a special category. As a colonial territory, the Irish were conquered and in subjection to English law. Their rights might not seem to be encompassed within the rights of freeborn Englishmen, but legal and political theorists of the time were divided about whether the Irish were subject to English common law either by virtue of conquest or as a by-product of *Calvin's Case*, a 1608 legal determination that a Scot born after the 1603 union was an English subject.[123] Yet, as the case of Ricckett Mecane illuminates, the situation of Irish servants was remarkably similar to that of English servants in the practice of indenture and in the conditions of servitude, although there were also important differences.

Like the claims of "white slavery," there is a persistent pseudohistory of "Irish slavery" that must be addressed. Advocates argue that during the Interregnum period, the British government accomplished large-scale raids of Irish civilians who were sold into permanent slavery, mainly in the Caribbean. This contention has been effectively contested by Jerome Handler and others.[124] The narrative relies on a few grains of truth – there were indeed some raids on the Irish coast by spirits as well as some instances of forcible indenture by the

British government, but it ignores the bulk of the factual evidence. The vast majority of servants in British territories were English, with lesser numbers of Scottish, Irish, and Welsh servants. Despite the reality of virulent prejudice against the Irish by many of the English during the seventeenth century, there is little evidence that Irish servants were recruited differently from English servants, were treated differently while in servitude, or served longer terms. Conversely, there is evidence that former Irish indentured servants like Ricckett Mecane were integrated into colonial society once they had served out their terms of servitude, with free people of Irish descent making up part of the population in the Caribbean and mainland colonies.

As Mecane's case shows, forcible indenture of Irish civilians did exist during the Interregnum period in particular.[125] The seventeenth century was an era of tremendous English prejudice against the Irish and against Catholics, magnified by the Irish Rebellion of 1641 and Ireland's royalism during the English Civil War. Many in the English government viewed all Irish Catholics, including civilians, as dangerous and actively hostile to English rule. Sending the Irish to indenture overseas was a policy in concert with the forced migration of landowners to Connaught on the western side of Ireland, especially as those who refused to relocate were further threatened with "banish[ment]" overseas within six months if they remained.[126] The 1650s was a peak period for the forcible shipping of Irish indentured servants, and in 1660, approximately 20 per cent of the servants travelling across the Atlantic were Irish, though percentages ebbed and flowed.[127] Yet during the English Civil War and Interregnum periods, when defeated royalist soldiers from Ireland were sometimes "barbadosed," most of those soldiers were actually English in ethnicity, and few were in fact sent into indentured servitude.

During the Interregnum, the Council of State's vagrant removal legislation was applicable in both England and Ireland. For example, in 1653, a Bristol merchant applied to ship 250 Irish women to New England. This was turned down, but shipment of a cargo of male and female "beggars and vagabonds" from Cork was granted.[128] In 1654, local town governors were ordered by the Irish Commissioners to hand rogues and vagabonds to three Waterford merchants.[129] Just as in England, such schemes encouraged vice. Officials looking to rapidly fulfill quotas swept up non-vagrant individuals or shipping contractors pressured officials to ignore unhealthy indigents in favour of vigorous servants who would bring higher prices. These measures resulted in the transportation of many thousands of Irish civilians to the colonies, especially the Caribbean.

Yet the English government also established and enforced legislation to prevent spiriting in Ireland, possibly more stringently than within Britain, even during the Interregnum period. As early as 1636, Captain Anthony of the *Abraham*, recruiting servants in Kinsale, was briefly imprisoned by the city's mayor until two kidnapped servants in his hold were released.[130] In the 1654 roundup of vagrants, town governors in the south of Ireland were ordered to demonstrate that no persons of good repute or members of families were shipped.[131] During the 1650s, there were repeated attempts by the Commissioners General for Ireland to prevent non-vagrants from being transported unwillingly from Ireland and to enforce the search of all ships bound for Barbados. Vagrants were to be identified by warrants signed by two justices of the peace. By December 1654, the Irish Commissioners were ordering that all ships in Irish harbours bound for the colonies be searched to ensure that no persons on board had been detained without warrants.[132] In 1655, a ship in Dublin harbour was ordered to be searched on the suspicion that the servants within its holds had been taken forcibly.[133] That same year, the Irish Commissioners stopped issuing licences to contractors, and Irish vagrancy laws were temporarily put in abeyance because they had been misused "to delude poor people by false pretences into by places, and thence they force people on board their ships."[134] By 1657, widespread abuses of the vagrancy laws led to the transportation orders for Irish vagrants being repealed.[135] Such stringent measures never occurred in England, perhaps because rule breaking was less frequent, but these actions showed the rights of Irish civilians being taken seriously. It remains difficult to assess the government's level of assiduousness when many factors still remain unknown, including the extent of the government's knowledge about abuses and outcomes of servant transportation, accurate tallies of numbers of individuals spirited, and the degree of success of government initiatives against spiriting.

The largest numbers of forcibly indentured Irishmen were sent to Barbados, the most brutal and dangerous colony for indentured servants.[136] But even there, less than half of the indentured population during the mid-seventeenth century was Irish, and the Irish were a minority of settlers: there were about 2,000 Catholics, probably mainly Irish, among a population of 25,000 whites, with fewer than

3,000 currently in servitude.[137] By comparison, in Virginia, Governor
Berkeley stated in 1670 that about 1,500 servants arrived in the
colony yearly, of which "most are English, few Scotch, and fewer
Irish," as well as two or three ships carrying enslaved people in the
preceding seven years.[138]

Colonial planters themselves had distinct preferences regarding
servants and tried to influence the demographics of servant shipments, though sometimes their aims contrasted with government
desires to remove certain populations from Britain. Unsurprisingly,
planters favoured servants who were healthy young adults without
criminal records. Caribbean planters repeatedly expressed preferences for English or Scottish servants rather than Irish.[139] Protestant
colonists stereotyped the Catholic Irish as lazy and rebellious, while
Scots, in contrast, were seen as hard-working and diligent. Irish
Catholic servants were particularly believed to present a risk in
the Caribbean, where there was danger of conspiracy with Catholic
French or Spanish forces. These suspicions were not entirely unmer-
ited, as shown by the collusion of Irish servants with the French in
the Leeward Islands in the 1660s and 1680s. Irish servants had also
gained a rebellious reputation from their involvement in revolts in
Barbados in the 1630s, '40s, and '50s and their suspected participation in slave revolts in the 1670s, '80s, and '90s.[140] In 1655, Barbadian
planters sent a petition to Oliver Cromwell to ask for exemption
from military service because of the dangers of leaving potentially
rebellious African slaves and Irish and Scottish servants, the latter of
whom were "formerly prisoners of war and ready to rebel" on the
island. They concluded by asking for more English servants.[141]
Planters soon reconciled themselves to Scottish servants as well as to
slaves, but continued to try to eschew the Irish. In a 1675 petition by
Barbados planters asking for increased shipments of slaves, the
planters again requested English and Scottish servants, since "Irish
servants they find of small value."[142] In 1676, the English government
responded to similar concerns by discussing a plan to recruit Scots to
go to Jamaica "as being very good servants."[143] Meanwhile, Governor
Jonathan Atkins of Barbados was complaining that Irish servants
were "idle."[144]

In the mainland colonies as well, Irish servants were less desirable
as servants. In 1654–59, the height of Irish transportation, there were
instances of legal discrimination based on national origins of servants. In 1657, the Barbados governor, claiming that Irish servants

and free people were often involved in crime and rebellion, instituted measures to limit Irish mobility on the island and prevent their bearing arms. These were repealed by 1660 because of fears of slave rebellion, which were addressed in a 1661 master and servant act.[145] The Virginia legislature briefly increased the length of terms of servitude for Irish servants, as well as of other "aliens," who had come into the colony without indentures. Such servants would otherwise have served at the "custom of the country," but "notwithstanding the act for servants without indentures," the colony maintained that it was "only [for] the benefit of our owne nation." Irish servants without indentures were to serve six years, and if under sixteen, then until the age of twenty-four.[146] The previous 1642 law regarding servants without indentures had stated that servants older than twenty were to serve four years, those thirteen to nineteen were to serve five years, and those twelve and younger were to serve seven years.[147] The Virginia law may have aimed to make undesirable Irish servants more attractive for purchase or to retain Irish servants under indenture for a longer period of time because they were believed more disorderly, or both. Yet within five years, this law was repealed because the longer terms "discouraged" potential Irish servants from coming "and by that means the peopleing of the country" had been "retarded." Instead, all servants "of what Christian nation soever" (i.e., not Africans) would serve the same term of servitude as others of their age category.[148] Implicit in this later legislation was the idea that most Irish servants were migrating voluntarily into indenture. The initial law and its rapid repeal illustrate the fluctuating perceptions of Irish servants. On one hand, prejudice against Catholics, rebels, and people from a foreign "nation" meant the Irish were not seen as part of the commonwealth; on the other hand, the colonial need for workers, and the objective of delineating the rights of white people, increasingly placed the Irish in the category of British subjects. Claims that the Irish were particularly targeted for indentured servitude, universally treated more severely, kept in indenture longer than other indentured servants, or sold into permanent slavery are mainly untrue. This falsely magnified atrocity seeks to replace the real history of oppression of the Irish and the forcible indenture of both Irish and English civilians as well as of former soldiers.

Henry Cromwell's plan to ship 2,000 Irish youths to Jamaica is often cited as an example of the special malevolence of English indenture policies in Ireland.[149] However, as shown earlier in this chapter, the proposal, never enacted, would have provided the Irish servants the same indenture provisions of four-year terms and freedom dues that were available to English servants, and was intended to provide white British subjects to people the island. The implication of "conversion" to Christianity suggests a repellent intention of cultural obliteration but not enslavement. Like the life trajectories of Cornelius Bryan or Ricckett Mecane, Henry Cromwell's proposal shows the "malleable nature of social status in the early modern English Atlantic world" and how Irish Catholics, although the object of prejudice, were also seen from the earliest period as "white."[150] In addition, the many instances in this book of Irish indentured servants suing for the rights belonging to English subjects illustrate the participation of some of the Irish in a form of British citizenship well before it was clearly articulated in law or social ideology.

The practice of indentured servitude contained intrinsic contradictions that forced the English government as well as ordinary people in Britain, Ireland, and the Atlantic colonies to wrestle with questions that had often previously been confined to esoteric legal disputes. Indentured servitude compelled debate about the right of the government to confine and transport large segments of the population against their will, even criminals and traitors. It laid bare the influence of capitalist entrepreneurs like Martin Noell within the government, but also revealed Parliamentary attentiveness to the rights of subjects. The existence of white servitude compelled new conceptualizations of the limits to which English, Irish and other British subjects, in contrast to African slaves, could be regarded as chattel. It also helped establish the validity of legal precedents for representation in court, including, as shall be seen in the next chapter, the right to be represented by an attorney. While fluctuating and contradictory, the increasing consensus that indentured servants, the lowest rank of the white population, were freeborn subjects with rights was a formative step toward the idea of a rights-bearing citizen, which would be more fully articulated in the late eighteenth century.

4

Contracts and Rights

For many voluntary servants, the first experience of indentured servitude was signing a contract in London or Bristol. Contracts, as John Hammond had pointed out, could significantly better an indentured servant's experience. They usually limited the term of servitude to four years, compared to seven for servants indentured at the custom of the country, and provided crucial verification of the date of indenture, expectation of freedom dues, and sometimes other benefits. However, although most servants fell into the "voluntary" category, it appears that most also did not possess a paper contract, which would have required enlisting with a shipper who was relatively scrupulous in adhering to the letter of the law.

Contracts provide a revealing source for historians because they precisely delineate the responsibilities of both servants and masters. Contracts also demonstrate how the law viewed the parties engaged in a transaction. Indenture contracts shielded masters, including the merchant shippers who were usually the initial signatories, but also protected servants. Additionally, they intrinsically configured the contracting parties as voluntary and equal participants in a regulated exchange. To ensure validity, they typically required a magistrate or clerk to oversee the transaction and to sign, and often seal, the documents as well as signatures of both contracting parties and usually of witnesses. Illiterate servants signed with a mark, which was certified by the magistrate. The documents were produced in duplicate, one copy to the shipper and one to the servant, and also recorded in registers at the point of origin, usually London or Bristol.

In order to guard against counterfeiting, the two copies of the contract were often laid one on top of the other, and their top edges were
trimmed with matching patterns of ripples or zigzags, a crude way of
discouraging either party from making false claims. Indeed, the word
"indenture" was used in the seventeenth century for all contracts, not
just those involving servants, and originates from the indentations at
the top of contracts.[1] It might have been relatively easy for the holder
of a contract to imitate the other copy of the pair by trimming the
paper to match the original, but falsifying a contract was a crime that
would have required forging the signatures as well. In addition, the
archival record at the point of registration could also be turned to for
verification, though in practice would be difficult to obtain across
the ocean.

By modern conceptions, servants and masters were unequal parties
in the transaction. According to early modern law, however, the contract bound both participants, even in circumstances where one individual might be assumed to be under some constraint.[2] Indeed, early
modern legal courts and legal theorists accepted that subordinates
were able to actively consent, even under conditions of compulsion,
such as a wife fearful of her husband.[3] Indentured servants, typically
impoverished, and sometimes deceived, were inherently under some
compulsion. Yet nonetheless, by requiring consent, and construing
contracting parties as real participants, the law also constructed them
as active citizens. The development of contractual equality before the
law was a formative factor in the development of the seventeenth-
century political doctrine of contractual governance between a monarch and the people.[4]

It is worth looking at the details of actual contracts, and I examine
three in the course of this chapter.

OFFICIAL DOCUMENTS

During most of the seventeenth century, contracts were sometimes
printed, but often remained handwritten documents, though usually
upholding similar provisions. In 1682, the government passed an act
aiming to regularize the making and recording of indenture contracts, which specified that they be verified by a magistrate and
recorded by court clerks. There were further protections for children:
their contracts were required to certify parental consent and, if under
fourteen, the child was to be retained on shore for at least two weeks

while the local magistrate searched out their parents or the local parish overseer. Any expenses associate with this were to be compensated by the Crown.[5] Adults also possessed some protections. In an unusual case in 1698, an indentured servant who had already contracted to travel to Jamaica changed his mind, "not now being willing to go," and successfully sued the shipper to recover the value of his clothing already on the ship.[6]

Printed contracts were normally sold by printers in pairs, and after the servant was indentured, usually initially to the ship's master, both the master or captain and the servant retained one copy.[7] The earliest contract blanks were available from printers by 1635, and from 1685, they consisted of four basic types, two of which are shown in figures 4.1 and 4.2.[8] Each copy was signed by both participants. Illiterate servants scrawled an X or other mark, to be followed by the clerk's clarification: "The mark of William Smyth." Some individuals who signed with a mark might have been able to read if not write, but for most, the contract would have been read to them by the clerk or magistrate during the transaction.

Contracts included many options for individualizing the arrangements. They contained unfilled sections where specific items could be written in, such as dates, the names of the contracting parties, the age of the servant, the length of servitude, obligations or duties for both the servant and master, and the amount of freedom dues. Some contracts made provisions to use a pronoun that aligned with the servant's sex, with an *h* followed by a blank or underline to fill in "h[is]" or "h[er]," or simply gaps for the pronoun as in Mary Hillyard and Charles Oldridge's contracts (figures 4.2 and 4.3). Others, like William Smyth's (figure 4.1), defaulted to male pronouns, which were accurate for the majority of servants. Contracts specified the rights and duties of both masters and servants, and although these could be modified in the unfilled areas, they were usually laid out in standard terms in the pre-printed sections of the contract. They included measures to protect both contracting parties, including the rights of servants to food, clothing, and shelter, and the rights of the master to the loyalty and obedience of the servant. The contracts specified that the shipper paid for the passage across the ocean and that the servant signed voluntarily. There was usually a space at the bottom that allowed for further individual comments. The 1682 contract of William Smyth, for example, clarified that Smyth was to "serve in such employment" as his master assigned, while his master was to "pay for his passage ...

and to find and allow him meat [food], drink, apparel, lodging, and washing necessary." A crucial aspect of indenture contracts was that they represented the servant as an equal participant in a legal contractual proceeding. For example, in the language of the contract, William Smyth did "voluntarily covenantath, promiseth, and granteth" to serve his master, while Mary Hillyard and Charles Oldridge in their contracts did "hereby covenant, promise, and grant" to serve.

Some contracts might include more unusual arrangements, such as making the indenture more like a traditional apprenticeship. For example, in 1688 Virginia, there is a note in the Middlesex County Court order book that "Robert Jones servant to Mr William Churchill comes and acknowledges that he is freely willing to serve his master seaven years from his arrival, the said Churchill promising that he will imploy his said servant in the stoar [store] ... and not imploy him in common workeing in the ground."[9] In 1680, the court recorded servant John Talbert's agreement with his master, Richard Willis, to serve an extra year in exchange for Willis's promise "to keep the said Talbert constantly at the shoomakers trade and not to work in the ground" and also to provide extra freedom dues: "to give the said Talbert a new serge suite, shooes, stock, and hatt more than the law enjoynes att the time of his freedome."[10]

Most contracts, like the ones included here, were endorsed by the shipper, who would sell the servant upon arrival in the colonies, so the contracts also specified that servants could be handed over to the master's or mistress's assigns or heirs. This also meant that if the servant's master or mistress died before the term of the contract was completed, the heirs would gain possession of the servant for the remainder of the term, a provision that resulted in the frequent appraisals of servants' value in estates. If a contract did not include this provision, it could potentially be challenged. For example, in 1662, John Normand successfully claimed in the Arundell County Court in Maryland that he should be released from his indenture after his master John Hatton died because his contract specified that he was "to serve the s[ai]d Hatton, but noe assignes or any other p[e]r[son]s whatsoev[e]r."[11] When one of Hatton's heirs challenged the decision in the higher Provincial Court, it upheld the lower court's decision and Normand was declared free.[12] Similarly, Edward Jessop argued in Baltimore in 1665 that his indenture stated that he was to be freed upon the death of his mistress, but that her husband,

Colonel Nathaniel Utie, continued to retain him as an indentured servant. Jessop was able to produce his copy of his indenture to show the court. The court found in Jessop's favour, ordering that he "be free and acquitted from the service of the said Nathaniell Utie and to dispose of him selfe as he pleaseth."[13]

The existence of the contractual procedure, including the legal requirements for official records, the presence of government officials and witnesses, and the duplication of documents, indicates a genuine effort on the part of the government as well as of the parties involved in these transactions to ensure legitimate and fair interactions. These aimed to protect the rights of servants as well as those of employers, setting aside the reality that the employment of indentured servants was in itself intrinsically exploitative. Again, it should be emphasized that by employing provisions and language that bound both parties, the law was implicitly engaging in a leveling manoeuvre that recognized servants as rights-bearing subjects, even as paradoxically they were being locked into an unequal status. Both masters and servants recognized the power of contracts and safeguarded them. Those who were in possession of a corroborative contract in a legal dispute were more likely to prevail, like Thomas Cornwallis, the master of Hester Nicholls.

Examination of the contracts themselves provides a number of significant insights. William Smyth's indenture, signed in London in 1682, included the characteristic fluted top, witness signatures, and wax seal demonstrating that the contract was legitimate. Smyth himself had signed with a squiggly mark, possibly meant to be an S. Smyth, from Cambridge, was twenty-one years old and on his way to Barbados to serve as an indentured servant for a four-year term. The top of the print section of his contract emphasizes the voluntary nature of the transaction, summarizing the 1682 Privy Council Act stating "all servants that are any time free and willing to be retained in His Majesties plantations in America are to be duly examined by any of His Majesties Justices of the Peace and bound accordingly and recorded in the Court of Sessions." The text emphasized that Smyth had "voluntarily" engaged in a legal contractual procedure, agreeing to serve with the notorious merchant William Haveland or his "executors and assigns."[14] This language permitted Haveland to sell Smyth's contract once the ship arrived in Barbados. In exchange for indenturing himself, Smyth was to receive passage across the Atlantic, "meat, drink, apparel, lodging and washing necessary for the said term."

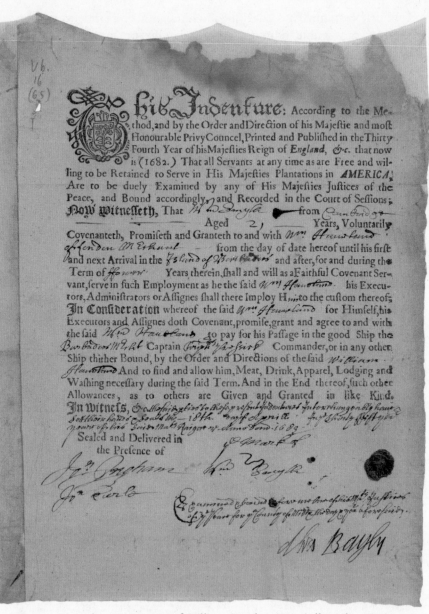

Figure 4.1   Indenture contract of William Smyth (1682), Call #: V.b.16 (65).

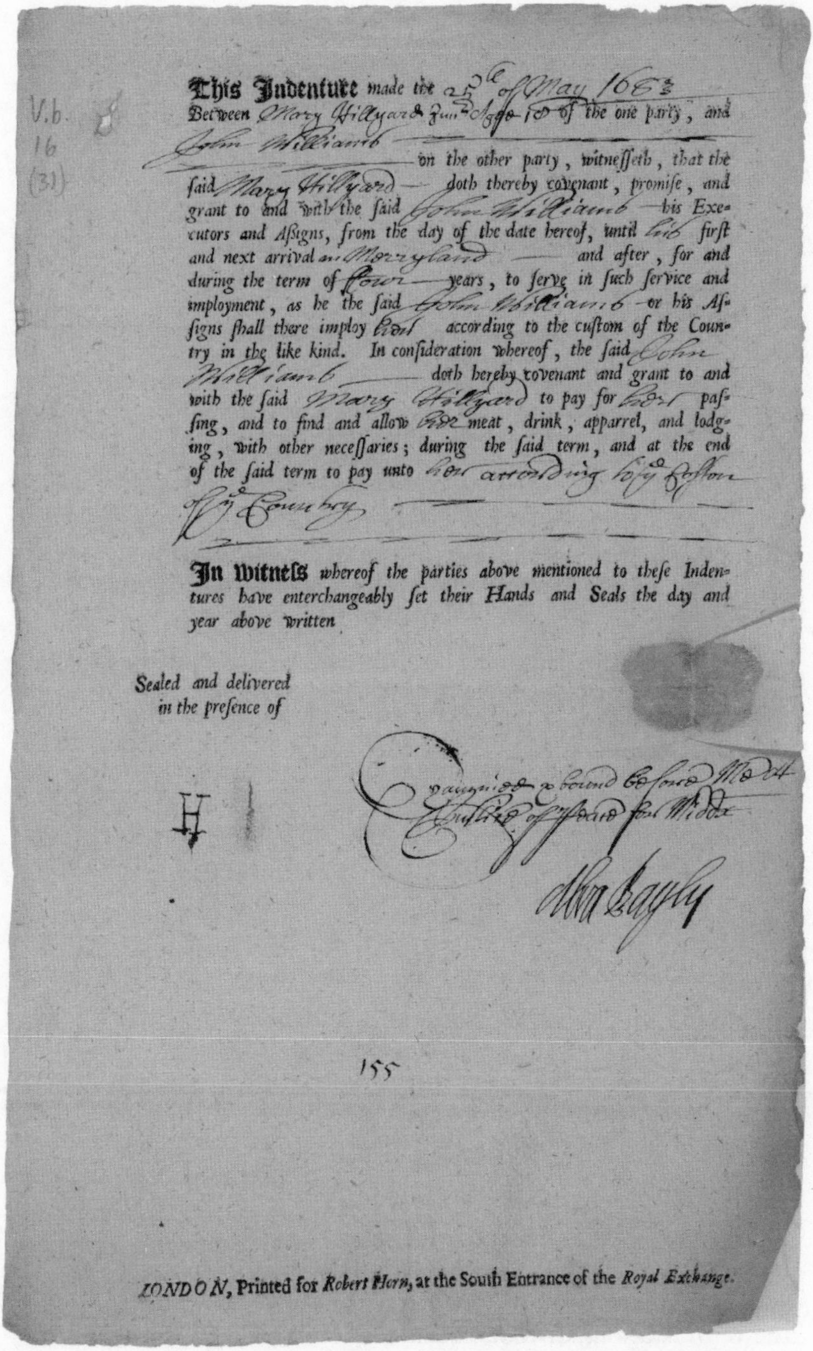

This Indenture made the 25ᵗʰ of May 1683 Between *Mary Hillyard* ~~Spinster~~ of the one party, and *John Williams* ———— on the other party, witnesseth, that the said *Mary Hillyard* —— doth thereby covenant, promise, and grant to and with the said *John Williams* his Executors and Assigns, from the day of the date hereof, until *her* first and next arrival in *Maryland* and after, for and during the term of *four* years, to serve in such service and imployment, as he the said *John Williams* or his Assigns shall there imploy *her* according to the custom of the Country in the like kind. In consideration whereof, the said *John Williams* —— doth hereby covenant and grant to and with the said *Mary Hillyard* to pay for *her* passing, and to find and allow *her* meat, drink, apparrel, and lodging, with other necessaries; during the said term, and at the end of the said term to pay unto *her according to the custom of the Country* ————

In Witness whereof the parties above mentioned to these Indentures have enterchangeably set their Hands and Seals the day and year above written

Sealed and delivered
in the presence of

*examined & bound before the Ma[...]
Justice of peace for Midd[...]*

John Bayly

155

LONDON, Printed for *Robert Horn*, at the South Entrance of the *Royal Exchange*.

Figure 4.2   Indenture contract of Mary Hillyard (1683), Call #: V.b.16 (31).

Specific freedom dues were not itemized, but the end of Smyth's contract notes that he was to receive "such other allowances, as to others are given and granted in like kind," which meant according to the custom of the country. Smyth's new master or mistress would have been obligated to pay his freedom dues at the end of his service or, if he were sold before that time, then his final master or mistress.

Mary Hillyard's 1683 contract is simpler in format and does not have a fluted top, but does include the magistrate's signature and seal. Hillyard was travelling to Maryland with a four-year contract. The bottom of the contract includes the publisher's information. Like Smyth, Hillyard's contract paid for her passage across the ocean and "meat, drink, apparrel, and lodging, with other necessaries," and at the end of her term, she would be paid freedom dues "according to the custom of the country." Unlike Smyth's contract, the last portion was handwritten, but it should be noted that in both contracts, the obligation to provide the servant with food, clothing, and lodging was in the print text, and therefore not negotiable – the implication was that the servant had certain rights that were not subject to compromise, unlike the freedom dues. Hillyard had signed her contract with a capital *H*.

An unusual aspect of Hillyard's indenture is that she was travelling with another woman, almost certainly her mother, also named Mary Hillyard.[15] Mary Hillyard senior had contracted on the same day with the same shipper, John Williams. She had also signed with an *H*, though in a less practiced hand than that of her daughter. Hillyard senior was thirty-five years of age, but the age inscribed for the daughter is very difficult to read; the second part of the number is an obscure scrawl, and she could have been ten, sixteen, or eighteen years of age. Poor women in this era tended to begin having children in their twenties, but it is possible that Mary Hillyard senior had given birth in her teens.[16] The fact that they were journeying together may make a younger age more likely.[17] Although the two were travelling as a pair, they were likely to experience an unwelcome shock when they reached Maryland since their contracts did not specify that they were to remain together, and they would probably have been sold separately.[18]

Charles Oldridge's contract was similar to Mary Hillyard's. Oldridge was also age thirty-five and had indentured himself in 1683 to serve in Virginia for four years. Oldridge's contract used the same blank form as the Hillyards' contracts. It shares the fluted top and

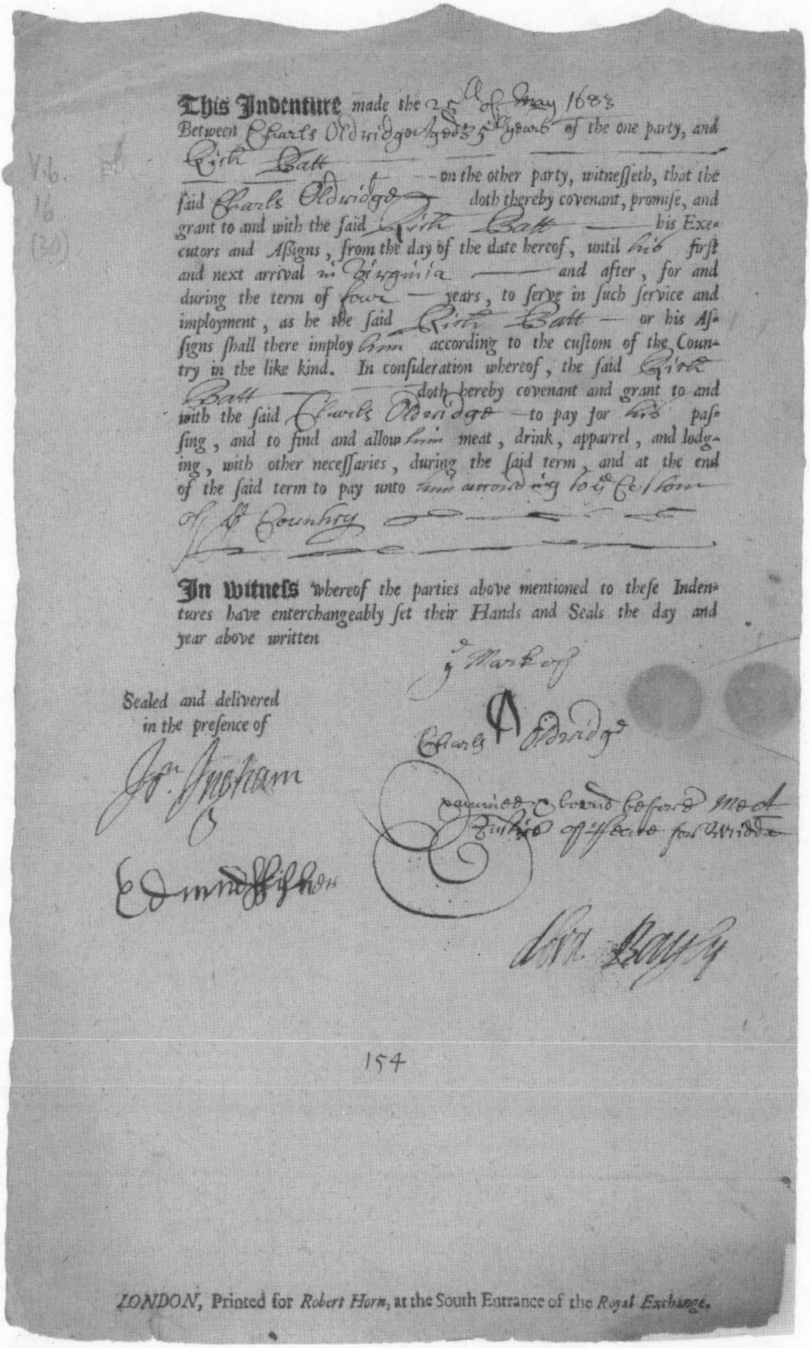

This Indenture made the 25 of May 1683 Between Charls Oldridge ... of the one party, and Rich Batt — on the other party, witnesseth, that the said Charls Oldridge doth thereby covenant, promise, and grant to and with the said Rich Batt his Executors and Assigns, from the day of the date hereof, until his first and next arrival in Virginia and after, for and during the term of fowre years, to serve in such service and imployment, as he the said Rich Batt or his Assigns shall there imploy him according to the custom of the Country in the like kind. In consideration whereof, the said Rich Batt doth hereby covenant and grant to and with the said Charls Oldridge to pay for his passing, and to find and allow him meat, drink, apparrel, and lodging, with other necessaries, during the said term, and at the end of the said term to pay unto him according to the custom of the Countrey

In Witness whereof the parties above mentioned to these Indentures have enterchangeably set their Hands and Seals the day and year above written

Sealed and delivered
in the presence of

154

LONDON, Printed for Robert Horn, at the South Entrance of the Royal Exchange.

Figure 4.3   Indenture contract of Charles Oldridge (1683), Call #: V.b.16 (30).

multiple witness signatures of Smyth's contract, while like the Hillyards' documents, it explicitly lists "the custom of the country" as the
specification for freedom dues. Oldridge had signed with an O with
two strokes through it. Like Mary Hillyard senior, Oldridge was unusually old for an indentured servant. While the Hillyards likely
travelled because of the difficulty for single women in London to sustain a living, we can't know what prompted Oldridge to make this
drastic move.

The contracts discussed here all established the typical four-year
term for the servants who engaged in them. They also established a
legal recognition of the servant's role and position. The substantial
segment of servants travelling across the ocean without contracts were
automatically in a weaker position regarding their rights and treatment once they arrived across the Atlantic. However, while servants
without contracts were more vulnerable to mistreatment, the custom
of the country also provided significant protections for servants, as
discussed below. For indentured servants who did not possess contracts, the custom of the country shaped not only what freedom dues
they were allocated but also how long a term they were to serve. For
adult servants without contracts, this was normally seven years, while
child or teenaged servants usually served until age twenty-one, which
could be a substantial number of years for a young child.

FREEDOM DUES

All indentured servants were entitled to freedom dues upon completing their servitude. The specific compensation was either noted in the
contract or paid to servants without contracts according to the custom of the country, which established uniform freedom dues for each
individual province or colony.[19] Even if a servant's master or mistress
died before a servant was freed, freedom dues were an obligation. For
example, in 1656 the Charles County Virginia court ordered that servant Tom Chappell's freedom dues be paid from the estate of John
Richards, lately deceased.[20]

In the earliest period of settlement, freedom dues included the
most valuable form of compensation: land. The opportunity to
become a landowner would have provided a powerful incentive to
voluntary servants because there was simply no way to earn land within Britain; the only way to obtain it was by purchase, an option
unavailable to the poor.[21] Land allotments were most generous in the

early seventeenth century, becoming progressively less so, and eventually disappearing from freedom dues by the end of the century as available land became scarce.

Legislation regulating the custom of the country was meant to ensure the fair distribution of freedom dues. When Virginia passed its first law regulating the term of servitude for the custom of the country, it specified that this was to protect masters and servants, who both "have often been prejudiced" about what they were entitled to.[22] In Maryland, a 1639 act of assembly dictated that servants would receive land, three barrels of corn, two hoes, an axe, and clothing. For a man, the latter comprised a suit, shirt, shoes, stockings, and a cap, all new. Women received a petticoat, waistcoat, smock, shoes, and stockings, as well as the right to keep their old clothing. But the most important dues were the acquisition of 50 acres of land, at least 5 of them arable.[23] In 1647, the Maryland Provincial Court verified that the freedom dues required by the custom of the country included "one cap or hatt, one new cloath or frize suite, one shirt one p[ai]r shooes & stockins, one axe, one broad & one narrow hoe, 50 acres land, & 3 barrells corne."[24] But by the time of Maryland's 1676 Act Relateing to Servants and Slaves, freedom dues for those serving at the custom of the country were defined for men as "a good cloath suite ... a shift of white linen ... one new paire of shews[shoes] & stockens, two hoes, one ax & three barrels of Indian corne," while for women, "the like provision of cloathes & corne," but no tools; more importantly, no land was included for either men or women.[25] From 1715, the custom of the country in Maryland dictated that male servants would obtain a new hat, good-quality suit, new shirt, shoes. and stockings, two hoes, an ax, and a gun, while women were to receive a new waistcoat, petticoat, shift, shoes and stockings, an apron, two caps, and three barrels of corn.[26]

In the Caribbean, Jamaica was the most desirable location, with shorter contracts than the norm, usually lasting two to four years, and freedom dues including up to 20 acres of land, while Barbados was the least desirable after 1660, where little land was available and dues were given in sugar.[27] As labour conditions and availability in England improved in the late seventeenth century, the Caribbean became even less desirable for voluntary servants. Caribbean planters tried to entice servants by shortening terms of servitude below those of the mainland, but the prospect of better freedom dues as well as information about harsher conditions for servants in the Caribbean led most servants to continue to choose the mainland.[28] In the late seventeenth century, the Carolinas, a less desirable location, were still offering "100 acres to any servant when out of his or her time to their own proper use," later reduced to 70 acres.[29] In colonial Pennsylvania, indentured servants who had finished their servitude received 50 acres in freedom dues.[30]

Land was available not only to servants but also to those who brought servants into the colonies, a practice known as "headright." For example, in 1636, Alice Bagwell claimed 200 acres for bringing herself, her son, and two servants to Virginia.[31] In 1638, Thomas Melton received a certificate for transporting four people, including himself, to Virginia in four separate ships between 1632 and 1637.[32] In 1650, William Mosely gained 550 acres for bringing himself, his wife, two sons, and seven servants to Virginia, and Johnathan Martin gained 100 acres for bringing in two men, but in 1652, Robert Wyard only received 10 acres for each of three manservants transported into Virginia.[33] In 1659, Henry Morgan claimed an unspecified number of acres for bringing servant Hanna Grinley to Maryland.[34] The typical amount in early Virginia was 50 acres per servant.[35] In the Carolinas in 1667, colonists were encouraged to bring indentured servants with promises that those who transported themselves would receive 150 acres for each member of their family and each male servant, and 100 acres for women servants and boys, later reduced to 100 and 50 acres respectively.[36] The practice of headright competed with land allotments for servants. Expending the master's newly acquired land on freedom dues disincentivized land headrights for shippers who might bring in more servants. In Maryland, for example, the dues of land for servants had been revoked by 1663, but masters who brought in servants continued to acquire 50 acres per servant to encourage them to bring servants into Maryland.[37]

SERVANTS AS COMMODITIES

Some individuals were contracted as servants within the colonies themselves. These were usually orphans and indigent children contracted by the courts or parish authorities, or poor children contracted by their parents, like Hester Nicholls, although there was a small subset of poor adults who entered servitude arrangements in their locality. As discussed earlier, indentured servitude did not exist as a practice within Britain or Ireland, but in the colonies the pattern of indenture of orphans generally followed the practice of "apprentice-ships" from the Elizabethan poor laws. The contracts of orphans were more likely than standard indenture contracts to specify some form of education for the child and were often overseen by the courts or parish authorities to ensure care for the child, an expectation that had been expressed by Hester Nicholls's father.

For example, in 1657, the Kent County Court in Maryland oversaw the indenture of Margrett Anderson for four years by her parents.[38] In June 1668, the same court indentured Christian Deare, orphan, to Robert Dunn for four years, unless she married earlier. She continued to possess some goods that were to be held in security by Dunn. On the same day, John Dabb indentured his daughter Sarah to Morgan Williams and his wife for a four-year term.[39] Although most of these cases do not mention a payment to parents, it is possible – and even likely – that some of the parents indenturing their children were receiving some form of compensation from the child's new master or mistress.

Children or adults could also be pledged as security in a loan. In 1658 Maryland, Thomas Mitchell pledged his own son as security in a future tobacco sale. When the other party in the transaction died, Mitchell successfully sued to have his son returned from the benefi-ciary of the estate, contingent upon the payment of 1,000 pounds of tobacco.[40] Likewise, in 1640 Barbados, merchant James Marshall engaged in a transaction involving the delivery of several thousand pounds of tobacco to three planters. As collateral, he bound "himself together with two saddle mares" and apparently also his son, while the planters, if they defaulted, likewise owed him two horses as well as the "bodye" of each to serve him.[41]

In addition, occasionally adults were indentured by the colonial courts, usually for nonpayment of debts. For instance, in 1670, the Maryland Provincial Court ordered that Charles Vincent pay his debt to the sheriff of Somerset County, Randall Revell, by serving him for a year "in discharge & accquittall from payinge of the said fees," presum-ably as an alternative to imprisonment for a possibly longer period until the debt was paid in cash.[42] As in Britain, the policy of making prisoners pay for court fees could result in long-term imprisonment for debt. In another case in 1669 Maryland, servant Joseph Thompson, together with his master Peter Bawcomb and Henry Gottney, another of Bawcomb's servants, was arrested for stealing and butchering a calf and two hogs. Bawcomb and Gottney pled not guilty, while Thompson pled guilty and "putt himselfe upon the mercy of the Court." Thompson was in a particularly unfair position because his master Bawcomb had ordered the servants to commit the thefts and had received the stolen meat. Bawcomb and Gottney were found not guilty, and Thompson's indictment "was quashed," despite his plea. Nonetheless, he was made to serve another master for three years to pay his imprisonment costs. After one year, he came before the Provincial Court again to petition for freedom, and he was released upon providing security for the remainder of his fees.[43]

Sometimes even more voluntary arrangements fell afoul of the law when masters attempted to take advantage of the servants in their power. In February 1667, William Oglethorp petitioned the Maryland Provincial Court about a breach of contract. He had at first voluntarily "hired himself" to Thomas Wynn for a period of eight months for 800 pounds of tobacco, but Thomas "would not let yor peticonr rest" until he had "inticed" Oglethorp to sign a contract to work for four years for "good sufficient diet, lodging, washing, and a cow, calfe, and clothing." Apparently, the latter were not freedom dues but were to be provided immediately. However, after two years and "many delayes," Wynn had not fulfilled the terms of the agreement. Oglethorp asked to be compensated for the two years of work and for the return of his contract. The court agreed, and ordered Wynn to pay him 950 pounds of tobacco and free him.[44] Servants who voluntarily contracted themselves in the colonies seem to have been a minor subset, however – perhaps because they could see with their own eyes the hardships of working as an indentured servants. which the servants who contracted themselves in Britain and Ireland could not.[45] In addition, there were potentially other economic opportunities aside from indenture for an impoverished individual already residing in the colonies.

A contract was a legal document and obligated both parties according to the law, but the hardest provisions often fell upon the servants, who were regarded as chattel in the valuation of estates or debts. In 1648, the appraisal of John Pille's Maryland estate included various goods, and also various servants and cattle. As if to emphasize the status of the servants as property, the servants' names – William Wenham, Cornelius Cormace, and Margarett Teresa – were listed together with the names of the cattle – Gent, Long Tayle, Black, Bobbe, Stiles, and New-Towne.[46] In the Maryland Provincial Court in 1658, a servant woman was used as collateral in a transaction involving the upcoming sale of a mare, with her master pledging, "In case I fayle

performance hereof, my servant Jane Witton is hereby engaged for satisfaction."[47] The productive labour of servants could also be enumerated as part of their value. In 1663 Maryland, George Marshall sued to
recover a portion of the profits from the sale of a tobacco crop because he possessed "an interest" in the servants who had produced the
crop, who had belonged to his father-in-law.[48] In a 1666 Maryland letter discussing financial obligations, one party was expected to deliver
to another "two able men serv[an]ts betweene the age of eighteene
and eight & twenty yeares," or if that was not possible, 5,000 pounds
of tobacco and five barrels of corn.[49]

Servants could be resold by their masters, but only for the time they
had yet to serve, as is shown by the following examples. A 1658 debt
in Maryland was satisfied by the transfer of "a servant boy th[a]t had
5 years to serve."[50] In Barbados in 1656, John and Margarett Lewis
received 8,000 pounds of muscavado sugar in exchange for two-thirds
of their plantation of 154 acres as well as "two thirds of all the servants, slaves, cattle, stock, houses," while merchant Seth Rowley, in
exchange for 6,500 pounds of sugar to Edward Benney, received one-
eighth of a plantation of 195 acres "with an eigth part of all houses,
coppers mills, stills, cattell, servants, negroes, and other appurte-
nances."[51] However, many Barbados deeds distinguished between
enslaved people and servants, listing "Christian servants" by a first
name and surname with time left to serve specified, and "negroes"
with only a first name.[52]

Servants also frequently appeared in wills as part of the estate. In
January 1664, an appraisal of a Maryland estate enumerated the value
of livestock, a number of household goods, and also human beings in
terms of their worth in pounds of tobacco. For servants as opposed to
slaves, the inventory specified their term yet to serve; the appraisal
included "two Nigro man, 5000; one Nigro woman, a childe, and a
girle, 4000; two men servants having two yeares and upwards to serve,
3200; two boyes having allmost 2 yeares ap[iece] to serve, 3200; three
boyes, 4000." The last three boys are not clearly delineated as servants
or slaves, but are likely the latter because of their place in the list.[53] A
1658 will from Maryland valued two servants at 300 pounds of tobacco,
as a form of chattel, but with limited terms, specifying that "one servant having one yeare to serve, & one having 2 yeares to serve."[54] In
1656, Thomas Haukins's will in Maryland included, among various
"items," "Mary Bally, 6 mounth to serve; Thomas Simons, 6 mounths
to serve; Henery Wharton, 1 yeare ½ to serve," and somewhat

aspirationally, the absent "Will Courttiour, runn away, w[hi]ch had 2 yeare to serve."[55] The 1664 appraisal of Humphrey Haggett's will gives insight into how servants' value was gauged. Initially, the sheriff ordered two men to determine the value of James Williams, who was appraised at 2,000 pounds of tobacco, and Daniel Russell, whose value was assessed at 3,000 pounds of tobacco. However, Johnathan Meekes, who had a lien against the estate, had heard that the two servants had been deliberately valued high and asked for a reappraisal by "indifferent men," which was ordered by the court. The new appraisal, taking into account the two servants' time left to serve, was set at 1,500 pounds tobacco for Williams and 2,000 pounds for Russell.[56] There were many similar cases.

RIGHTS TO A COURT HEARING

Indenture contracts were exploitative by modern standards, forcing servants to promise away their autonomy and years of their productive lives while offering little real protection against abuse and exploitation by their masters and mistresses. It is difficult to know how indentured servants perceived contracts. However, seventeenth-century magistrates and officials saw the contract as documentation of a fair transaction between master and servant. Nonetheless, simply possessing a contract was insufficient without legal support to back it up. By English law, servants were not free and independent, yet because their unfreedom was a temporary condition, they were regarded as covered by the protections in the English constitution, as embodied in the Magna Carta and common law.

As Christine Daniels has shown, one of the most important legal protections servants possessed was the right to be heard in court, unlike slaves.[57] Without this, the possession of a contract would have provided only precarious protection. The servants' "liberty to complaine" indicates that while indentured servants were bound in servitude, they had not surrendered all rights – retaining the right of protection against unjust or cruel masters, the rights of all subjects to be heard in court, and the rights of English liberty.[58]

Even Irish servants like Ricckett Mecane, as subjects of the British commonwealth, had the right to bring complaints against their masters in a court of law. Although servants, being dependents, could not officially "sue" in court, they could "petition" the court to hear their case, which was functionally the same as long as the courts were willing to hear servant cases.[59] In practice, these cases were conducted like other suits, in at least some cases with court-appointed attorneys who brought in witnesses to testify on behalf of their clients. There was some truth as well as exaggeration to John Hammond's claim that "servants complaints are freely harkened to, and (if not caus[e]les[s]ly made), there[their] masters are compelled either speedily to amend, or they are removed upon second complaint to another service; and often times not onely set free, (if the abuse merit it), but ordered to give reparation and damage to their servant."[60]

It appears that legal practices varied regionally. Maryland seems to have had a higher rate of favourable outcomes in court than other colonies. Servants rarely prevailed in Barbados, although they technically possessed the right to petition in court, as well as to complain to the Council; the lack of surviving records in Barbados means there are few sources.[61] In Maryland, servants whose complaints were deemed compelling by the courts – and there appear to be thousands – usually received remission of court fees and, most importantly, the right, in some cases at least, to court-appointed attorneys.

The right to counsel in misdemeanour cases had been established in the English common law from the thirteenth century and, from the late seventeenth century, for felonies as well. The practice, though not always followed, was to provide an attorney for indigent individuals, including plaintiffs, termed suit *in forma pauperis*, as a pauper. While this practice did not always prevail in the northern American colonies until the late eighteenth century, Rhode Island provided a right to legal counsel by 1647 and Pennsylvania by 1701; plaintiffs and defendants were entitled to attorneys in New York by the early eighteenth century; and in the southern colonies, defendants had a statutory right to counsel from the early eighteenth century, with some variation between colonies.[62] However, Maryland and Virginia lawsuits show court-appointed lawyers for indentured servant plaintiffs even during the seventeenth century. These lawyers argued on behalf of their clients, called witnesses, requested documentation, and frequently won their cases, which were decided by juries. Many trials in Maryland did favour the suits of servants against their masters, despite the pervasive cultural partiality against servants that tended to predispose magistrates and juries to support the claims of masters.

As today, local attorneys seem to have been eager to take up such cases, perhaps even frivolous ones, because they were sure of being paid by the court. In 1673, the Charles County Maryland Court cautioned lawyers not to independently take the cases of servants, but to wait until appointed by the court: "Whereas sev[er]all attorneyes have undertaken to manage serv[an]ts causes ag[ain]st their maisters & m[ist]r[esse]s to the m[aste]rs & m[ist]r[ese]ss greate charge & damage, it is ordered that no p[er]son act as attorney for any serv[an]t hereafter, but such as the court shall appointe."[63] While this ruling perhaps was meant to limit servants' access to suits, it also acknowledged that it was a routine practice to assign attorneys to servants that brought cases, though normally only when the courts decided that such cases had merit. Yet the courts appeared to recognize their responsibility to provide a venue for servants bringing concerns. In Maryland, with a population of under 30,000 people, there were hundreds, and perhaps thousands, of cases brought by servants during the seventeenth century.[64] Attorneys were not always mentioned in the court records, and so it is not certain whether all servants received them. Yet the very existence of court-appointed attorneys indicates that the Maryland and Virginia courts took servant complaints seriously. It indicates that servants were subjects with more than just standing in the body politic, because the ability of an individual to contend against authority, including the state, is a key aspect of citizenship. Servants were legally dependents, locked into an unequal relationship at the lowest-status category – yet local governments and judiciaries acted to ensure that their rights were defended against their masters.

Indentured servants also had little or no ready capital, so in most servant lawsuits, the plaintiffs not only obtained special permission by the court to allow a suit but also received remission of court fees. For example, in April 1674, the Provincial Court in Maryland issued a special provision of court fees and a court-appointed attorney to a poor woman servant: "upon the complaint of Mary Philips of St Maries County, spinster [i.e., a single woman] ... of several injuryes done unto her by some persons of this province, and she being a servant and not of capacity and ability to presente them at law, ordered that she be admitted *in forma pauperis* and that Kenelm Cheseldyne be appointed her attorny therein."[65] What became of this case was not clear, nor whether the "injuries" referred to were physical or other sorts of harm, such as theft or libel.

It appears that such attorneys provided a robust defence for their indentured clients. The attorneys who defended indentured plaintiffs were not public defenders, with either of the modern connotations of principled vocation or inadequate defence. Rather they were also involved in many other kinds of cases before the courts. For example, Mary Philips's attorney, Kenelm Cheseldyne, was not an obscure lawyer. In 1674, the year of Mary Philips's suit, he served as attorney in at least six other cases involving debts or disputes between executors.[66] Cheseldyne was born in England about 1640 and obtained his law degree there, arriving in Maryland around 1669 already relatively well off and marrying his first wife that year. By 1676, two years after defending Mary Philips, he was a member of the Maryland Assembly; he later became a member of the Maryland Council, the colony's Attorney General, Speaker of the House, a judge, and eventually a chief justice in St Mary's County.[67]

Likewise, Elizabeth Hasell, a runaway servant, was skillfully defended by her attorney, Richard Boughton, in Charles County, Maryland, in 1669.[68] In this case, Hasell was the defendant being sued by her master, Nicholas Emanson, who argued that she had run away several times and should remain in indenture for a longer period. Runaways were regarded as treacherous and disloyal and were treated sternly by the laws, which mandated that additional time be added to a servant's indenture.[69] Boughton, however, ably argued that since Hasell had received "corporall punishment" for running away, she could not in effect be punished twice by invoking the laws applying to runaways. He brought in several witnesses who testified to the severe abuse Hasell had endured from her master and mistress, including chaining in irons and severe beatings, emphasizing one instance that had opened "great wounds in her back" and left "a puddle of blood" on the floor. However, the witnesses disagreed about whether the beatings had been occasioned by running away or other misdeeds. Nonetheless, the jury, motivated by the brutality of Hasell's treatment, found in her behalf.[70] Boughton, like Cheseldyne, was a prominent member of the community who had already served as a judge of the Provincial Court.[71]

In a 1664 case, servant Jone Nicculgutt was ably defended by her attorney James Thompson before the Maryland Provincial Court. The case focused on a dispute over Nicculgutt's time to remain in indenture. Nicculgutt, who must have been transported as a child, had served twelve years in the household of Cuthbert Fenwick. After numerous court appearances, which included several witness depositions and the display by Fenwick of a misleading indenture that had been produced a year after Nicculgutt had arrived in the colony, she was found by the court to be free.[72] Thompson demanded not only Nicculgutt's freedom but also "sattisfacon for this unjust molestacon as justice and equity shall require." He admonished the court to consider larger issues of legal rights: "if orders of court bee soe weake and mens oathe so little available … noe man shall ever have either security for his debt or certainty of his cause" and the right of "courts to maintaine the right of lawes" would be "excluded and totally overthrown."[73] Nicculgutt was ultimately successful not only in gaining her freedom but also in her suit for both freedom dues and back wages in tobacco for the extra year she had been held in servitude.[74]

The eloquent defence by Thompson broached some of the larger issues in the legal rights of indentured servants. His assertion was that even a servant like Nicculgutt had a right to "justice and equity" and, further, that the colony had the obligation not only to recognize but also to defend such rights. If these were infringed upon, it would diminish the rights of any person in the colony as well as the very foundation of the courts and laws. Although Thompson appears to have focused entirely on the particular case he was involved in, the claims he made implicitly addressed the rights of both servants and women to claim citizenship in society.

Virginia records are terser about attorneys' arguments, but they do show them defending indentured clients. In an indication of the participants' relative statuses, the masters and attorneys in these cases, but not the indentured clients, were usually referred to by the honorific "Mr." In 1685, Richard Curtise sued his master Richard Davis for keeping him in indenture with an illegal contract. His attorney Richard Moore invoked a recent Act of Assembly to successfully convince the court that Curtise should be released and paid his freedom dues.[75] Likewise, when Sarah Maud sued her master for tricking her into signing "a fraudulent indenture," her attorney Orlando Jones was able to obtain her freedom, leaving her former master responsible for court costs.[76] Thomas Danford pleaded through his attorney Henry Holdcraft that he was being held illegally in indenture; his master was subpoenaed, but the outcome of the case is not recorded.[77] It should also be noted that while most servant lawsuits did not mention the presence of attorneys for the plaintiff, the formality of the language recorded in many of the cases suggests that many or perhaps most were in fact defended by an attorney, though this cannot be verified. An example of such language can be found in Ricckett Mecane's statements that it was "contrary to the lawes of God and man that a Christian subject should be made a slave" and "yo[u]r pet[itione]r most humbly desireth that yo[u]r honor will be pleased to grant yo[u]r peticon[e]r an order for his freedome."[78]

Most legal disputes involving servants also required the subpoe- naing of witnesses, who were paid compensation for their attendance by the day, even if servants. For example, several witnesses "having attended as evidence" did "crave order for attendance" in the 1688 Somerset County Maryland Court. The case involved a dispute about who was the legal master of Mary Maxwell, a servant woman; Maxwell herself had been deposed in court and was one of those compensated for her court attendance.[79] Servants might be asked to testify in court in cases unrelated to their servitude, such as in a seventeenth-century Maryland case in which servants testified about a disputed will.[80] In contrast, slaves were not allowed to petition in court nor allowed to serve as witnesses under any circumstances.[81]

Such trials also provide one of the most enlightening sources about the nature of indentured servants' lives and of their possession of inherent rights, although legal proceedings must be viewed with sev- eral caveats. Court cases inherently emphasize abusive and polarized relations between masters and servants and, thus, not necessarily the majority of circumstances. There must have been many instances of amicable or fair relationships, at least according to the letter of the law, and likewise, many occurrences of abuse in which servants did not resort to the courts and maltreatment was left unchallenged, or perhaps settled through informal negotiation. The significant attempts at fair dealing in legal disputes do, however, demonstrate the cognizance of the colonial courts that indentured servants, both men and women, were rights-bearing members of the commonweal.

CONTRACTS AND LEGAL DISPUTES

Indenture contracts were a valuable source of documentation in court. Both servants and masters retained them carefully, as can be seen in Thomas Cornwallis's successful rebuttal to Hester Nicholls's com- plaint by producing her ordinary contract. In response, Nicholls was reduced to the unsuccessful argument that the contract itself was invalid because it had not been overseen by a magistrate.[82] However, contracts were more often used as evidence in petitions by servants against their masters. For example, in 1673, Elizabeth Hiccoks came before the Maryland Provincial Court arguing that she had finished

her four-year indenture. Her master was attempting to keep her at the
custom of the country for seven years. She won her case because she
had a copy of her contract, originally signed in England.[83] In 1678,
an unnamed servant boy of about fourteen was sold in Dorchester
County, Maryland, under the custom of the country for what would
have been seven years. However, when he was presented before the
court for determination of his age – which would determine his number of years to serve until age twenty-one – the boy produced an
indenture stating that he had to serve only four years. The case was
heard by the Maryland Provincial Court when the purchaser sued the
seller for making false claims.[84]

Possession of a contract was not always a sufficient safeguard. In
1671, Seth Foster's servant William Hackett "demand[ed] his freedom" and produced a contract "under the seal of the Reggester Office
in London" stating that his indenture was to last four years. However,
his master claimed to have bought him at the custom of the country,
and the Talbot County Maryland Court ruled that the contract was
superseded by Maryland law, asserting the contract was "of noe effect
ag[ain]st the law of this province for the limittacon of sarvants
times."[85] In this case, the local court contravened the law in favour
of the master's interests, forcing Hackett to serve one further year.
Similarly, in the Kent County Court in 1669, Ellenor Huchins was initially ordered by the court to serve for six years, based on determination of her age. She produced an indenture showing that she was contracted for four years; nonetheless, the court ordered her to serve for
five.[86] Yet courts were also not sympathetic to contract fraud. When
illiterate servant John de Creyger agreed to serve a few months' extra
time to receive his freedom dues plus a share of a tobacco crop, his
devious master appended, "I will not performe this condicon" beside
his signature. The court saw this as deception and found for
de Creyger.[87] However, unsupported claims of a contract were insufficient in court. In 1689, John Lyme, "a poor servant" who had been
"spirited out his native country" four years earlier, claimed that he had
been in possession of a four-year contract,] but that it had been stolen
from him by "deceitfull meanes." He claimed in court that his ship-
mates could testify to the existence of the document, but the court
concluded that as "no indentures appearing nor could be proved by
any evidences," Lyme was obliged to serve the seven years of the custom of the country.[88]

The Maryland Provincial Court tended to be more cognizant of the legal pre-eminence of contracts over the custom of the country than the lower Maryland courts. An instructive case was brought by servant Francis Gunby in 1663. He had been indentured in Bristol to merchant Richard Deavor and transported to Arundel County, Maryland. Gunby claimed that he had originally possessed a contract, but that it had been stolen from him, "taken away by force or fraude during" his "late sicknes." This putative contract was said to specify a term of four years and also to contain some apprenticeship-like provisions, including that Gunby would work only at his skilled craft as a joiner and that, instead of freedom dues, he would keep a one-third part "of what hee should by his labour gaine" as well as two suits and four shirts annually.[89] Gunby's petition to the court claimed that during the voyage, Deavor had "assigned" Gunby to William Jennings, the ship's surgeon, who had then "reassigned" him to George Beckwith. While the term "assigned" is ambiguous, Gunby later referred to himself as having been "sould" to Beckwith. However, the contract was then breached – "George Beckwith doth deny to performe the condicons originally made" between Gunby and Deavor – that is, Beckwith held that he was not bound by the terms of the original contract. Gunby also accused Beckwith of having stolen the contract: "hee having fraudulently taken away his condicon."[90] Gunby wanted not only to have his contract verified but also to receive the "allowance" of "wages" and clothing that he was due. The court responded by summoning Deavor, Jennings, Beckwith, and two other men to testify "uppon oath."[91] Jennings, the first to testify, initally agreed that Gunby had had an "[o]bligatory writing, graunting and allowing" him "a third part of his labour" and "suites & shirts in the yeare." However, he demurred somewhat, saying that this was "according to the best of my knowledge" and he could not swear that the contract had been actually signed by Deavor. He declared that "what since became of it, I nayther directly nor indirectly know."[92] The second witness, Henry Sewall, a lawyer, stated that he had previously been asked by Mr Jennings whether a new master was obligated to hold to the contract made by a previous master, specifically referencing Gunby's right to the proceeds of one-third of his labour and yearly clothing allowance. Sewall had affirmed that even "if it were to five hund[re]d prsofls [pursefulls?], the last [master] must & should make good th[a]t former condicon."[93] This testimony makes one wonder whether the theft of the contract was perpetrated by Jennings rather than Beckwith. The final resolution of this case is not clear – Gunby was not present at two subsequent meetings of the court, perhaps because of illness, but Richard Deavor came in again as a defendant to testify "uppon what tearmes the said Gunby became bound to the said Deavor." The resolution of the case is marked "noe returne."[94] Whether or not Gunby received his dues, this case demonstrates a number of legal realities critical to the servant experience. The importance of a contract, and the fact that it was stolen, testifies to its binding power, as does the court's sustained attempt to discover whether a contract existed and, if so, what it said. In addition, the court's attention to Gunby's case, which was revisited over four separate occasions, demonstrates not only legal due diligence but also a determination to treat the servant plaintiff fairly. Finally, however, this case demonstrates the difficulty for a servant in verifying allegations against his master. Gunby was a particularly litigious sort who was later the plaintiff in many other lawsuits, and made a good effort toward receiving his compensation, but even he may have failed to achieve his aims in the end.[95] Other servants who were less confrontational in defending their rights, or less literate, were not likely to receive satisfaction against unscrupulous masters.

The case of Ricckett Mecane, the Irishman kidnapped as a child, had also hinged partially around the lack of a contract. During the hearings, Judith Love, one of the witnesses brought in to testify about Mecane's age, testified that she had seen "certaine writings a draweing" – some kind of document being written up. She had also seen Mecane and the three boys indentured with him at Gerrard's house threatened with a beating and told they would serve fifteen years.[96] George Colclough, another witness, stated, in ambiguous language that seems to suggest the signing of a contract, that he had seen most of the four boys agree to serve: the "said servants, or the greater parte of them, did give under their hands the very same time to serve the said Gerrard severally certaine yeares which was then computed by sev[er]all persons p[re]sent to be according to the custome of the country and did subscribe the same voluntarily without force or constrainte."[97] A third witness, James Salstceme, further testified that he had seen Mecane willingly comply "whereas Ricckett Mecane hath by peticon complained that he was forced to sett his hand to an indenture, it is falce for he was then p[re]sent and saw the contrary."[98] How-

ever, it appears that a copy of this dubious indenture was not produced in court, and the jury's determination appears to have been
based on their estimate of Mecane's age rather than the claims and
counterclaims of the opposing parties.

A 1661 Virginia law focusing on runaways specified extra penalties
for servants who ran away and entered a new master's service, having
stolen or forged their previous master's copy of the contract. The law,
which probably had little impact, mandated that upon the expiration
of their contracts, servants were to receive a certificate to prove that
they had completed their servitude. This was to be recorded by a clerk
so that if the certificate was lost, it could be reissued.[99] There were
some anemic legal attempts to protect servants' contracts. In 1672, the
Virginia Assembly mandated that if a servant arrived without a contract, they must be brought before the court, and if the servant
claimed that they actually possessed a contract, they had one month
to produce it, otherwise, "he shall be barred from his clayme by reason of any pretended indenture whatsoever."[100] There was an obvious
incentive for a servant to prefer an indenture contract to the custom
of the country, as the term of servitude was usually considerably shorter.
However, it is likely that few were able to take advantage of this law.
If their contract had been lost or stolen, then the only way to prove its
existence would be to produce records from the place of indenture –
usually England. It would have taken months – not to mention significant expense impossible for servants to pay – to obtain evidence of
such records.

While many of these cases demonstrate indentured servants' great vulnerability to exploitation, they also reveal their considerable legal
rights. Indenture contracts shielded employers but also protected servants, and if a servant was able to demonstrate contractual rights, their
side typically prevailed in the courtroom. Crucially, servants had the
right to have their complaints heard by a court, and this was not a pro
forma dispensation. To ensure due process, courts supplied remuner-
ated attorneys, remitted court fees, and engaged in sustained investigations involving the calling of witnesses, the search of archival
records, and multiple hearings. These practices show a real attempt by
colonial authorities to ensure that court dealings were conducted fairly
and that indentured servants, including women, were treated as
rights-bearing members of colonial society. In addition, although

many cases of maltreatment of servants probably went unreported, or were dealt with through informal means that left no records, the countless servants claiming justice in the courts demonstrate that many recognized themselves as individuals with standing and rights within the community – in other words, as citizens.

5

Living in Servitude

Notwithstanding legal protections, the lives of indentured servants were often brutal and short. Both the continental and Caribbean colonies presented a hazardous disease environment, in addition to the risk of Native American attack in some parts of the mainland. Beyond that, servitude itself was perilous. The labour could be exceedingly difficult and dangerous, particularly if servants were working on a plantation. In addition, servants were vulnerable to violence, overwork, and neglect by their masters. As shown in the previous chapter, servants did possess contractual protections and the right to defend themselves in court, and public opinion also provided some protection as neighbours stepped in to intervene or bear witness in court, but masters retained considerable impunity. This chapter follows the experience of indentured servants from their ocean passage through the term of their servitude. It examines both the brutality and exploitation that they met with as well as the commitments and caring relationships that some experienced. It also shows the complex intertwining of servitude into everyday life in colonial societies.

PASSAGE ACROSS THE OCEAN

The first risk to servants was the ocean voyage. This was less deadly than the Middle Passage for enslaved people sailing from Africa since indentured servants were usually not chained, physically abused, tremendously overcrowded, or deprived of food and clothing, but significant mortality rates might still be incurred.[1] John Hammond warned servants that "when ye go aboard, expect the ship somewhat troubled and in a hurliburly," while George Alsop described his own "long" and "blowing and dangerous passage," and saw the "roughness of the ocean" as a deterrent for servants.[2] For example, the *Seaflower*, which regularly plied the route between New England, the West Indies, and Britain carrying cargoes of servants, was notorious for the bad conditions on board.[3]

Rebels and criminals could suffer worse conditions. In 1688, Monmouth rebel John Coad experienced a voyage with ninety-nine other men shut up below decks "in a very small room where we could not lay ourselves down without lying one upon another." Food and water were insufficient and bad, and Coad, like others, was wounded and feverish. At night, the men were kept awake by the "cries and groning of sick and distracted persons." Soon, disease spread and twenty-two men died. However, it was a relatively smooth and quick voyage of five weeks, and despite the captain's cruelty and stinginess, free passengers on the ship shared their food and interceded to bring Coad and the other captives above decks.[4] Rowland Thomas's petition for freedom in 1659 mentioned how during the voyage the men were "put under hatches, to see no light" until they arrived in Barbados.[5] Ebenezer Cooke, though not a servant, described the transatlantic voyage to Maryland in the late seventeenth century in his satirical poem: "we arrived in dreadful pain, / Shock'd by the terrours of the main; / For full three months, our wavering boat, / Did thro' the surley ocean float, / And furious storms and threat'ning blasts, / Both tore our sails and sprung our masts."[6] John Harrower's journal of his eighteenth-century journey to servitude in Virginia described a rough sea voyage of sixteen and a half weeks (with a stop in the Caribbean), during which the servants on board almost rebelled over the poor provisions; two servants were briefly put in irons; several servants died; and a number, including Harrower himself, fell ill.[7] Also during the eighteenth century, William Moraley and the other servants on board a ship en route to Pennsylvania were ordered to take turns standing watch on deck "to prevent our falling sick, by herding under deck," although many still fell ill during the voyage. The servants on that voyage seem to have received the same rations as the crew, but Moraley complained of the insufficient and bad food on shipboard, including "stinking butter," biscuits, an unsatisfactory daily "thimble full of bad brandy," and tough dried fish, occasionally supplemented by fresh fish caught by the crew.[8]

Servants were often in poor physical condition by the time they arrived after a long voyage, and Virginia strove to protect them through legislation in 1657 mandating that ships' captains had to provide "sufficient allowance of diet all the voyage" and "to take care that poor servants do not want cloathes and bedding in the voyage," warning that "if any shall offend they shall be liable to grievous censure here according to the merit of the offense."[9] There may have been some self-interest involved, as unsaleable sick servants would have been a burden to the colony. Once the ships arrived in the colonies, servants were sold from the ship's decks.[10] Richard Ligon described planters boarding ships in Barbados to purchase servants.[11] Elizabeth Ashbridge, travelling to indenture in the eighteenth century, wrote that she was sold on shipboard, two weeks after arriving in New York.[12]

Almost all indentured servants travelled to one of four colonies: Maryland, Virginia, Barbados, and Jamaica, with each colony receiving about a quarter of the migrants, though slightly more (52 per cent) went to the Chesapeake than to the Caribbean (45 per cent), with the remaining 3 per cent going to other continental colonies. More women and youths went to the continental colonies, while more men travelled to the Caribbean.[13] The colonies they arrived to were growing rapidly during the seventeenth century. By the end of that century, Maryland had a population of 32,000, including free and indentured whites, the enslaved, and Native Americans. In 1670, Governor Berkeley of Virginia estimated the colony's population at 40,000, including 2,000 enslaved people and 6,000 "Christian servants." Barbados, with approximately 30,000 slaves and 20,000 whites, was the most populous colony in 1670.[14]

PROVISIONS AND CLOTHING

Once servants disembarked, they often found the basic conditions of life to be very poor, especially in the earliest days of colonial settlement. There was considerable difference between colonies. Like enslaved people, indentured servants were generally treated best in the New England colonies and Pennsylvania, and worst in the Caribbean. Servants themselves seem to have been aware of these factors, and voluntary servants preferred mainland colonies to the Caribbean, even at the cost of longer terms of servitude.[15] The behaviour and attitudes of individual masters and mistresses also varied widely.

Life in servitude could be unrelentingly harsh and was particularly deadly in the early days of colonization. In the Virginia colony in the 1620s, Richard Frethorne described endemic disease, including scurvy and dysentery, and prevalent hunger. He described himself in the "most miserable and pittiful case" from "want of meat [i.e., food] and want of cloathes," and the lack of beer, liquor, sugar or spices.[16] Frethorne was fortunate in encountering his parents' acquaintances, Mr and Mrs Jackson, who had built him a cabin and provided him with fish and other food. Nonetheless, "I have eaten more in [a] day at home th[a]n I have allowed me here for a weeke." He begged to be freed, but realizing the unlikelihood of this, asked for more provisions to be sent to the colony. He emotionally described the hunger pervading the colony, and how his cloak had been stolen by another servant and traded for food.[17]

Barbados, a destination for many of the rebels, was the worst location to survive a term of servitude. In their 1659 petition to Parliament, Marcellus Rivers and Oxenbridge Foyle decried their poor food, diet of potatoes, and "sleeping in sties worse than hogs."[18] Father Biet was appalled at the treatment of servants, observing that "all are very badly treated" and fed poorly, receiving only potatoes for food.[19] Likewise, Monmouth rebel Henry Pitman complained of the poor conditions of life in 1660s Barbados, including the inadequate food, writing, "our diet was very mean. 5 pounds of Irish salt beef, or salt fish, a week, for each man, and Indian or Guinea corn … made into dumplings instead of bread," although the enslaved received worse.[20] Von Uchteritz, in Barbados in 1652, reported that white servants ate only sweet potatoes and cassava, but enslaved people received only cassava. While von Uchteritz was "poorly dressed," he wrote, "the Negroes and Indians … go about completely naked except for a cloth tied about their privities."[21]

Richard Ligon described how the servants' first task upon arrival to Barbados was to make a rudimentary "cabin" to sleep in, otherwise "they are to lye on the ground that night." The leaky cold cabins undermined servants' health and, "if they be not strong men," would "put them into a sickness," but "if they complain, they are beaten by the overseer." Beatings were common and vicious: "I have seen an overseer beat a servant with a cane about the head, till the blood has followed, for a fault that is not worth the speaking of."[22] Ligon maintained that some masters treated their servants better, however. For example, he enumerated the annual expenses for clothing for the servants on the plantation where he lived for two years, alongside the allocations for enslaved people. All servants received a "rug gown" for cold nights. Manservants were given six shirts, six pairs of drawers, twelve pairs of shoes, six pairs of stockings, three caps, two doublets, and six "holland [fine linen] bands." Men working in the fields received six shirts, six pairs of drawers, twelve pairs of shoes, and three caps. Servant women doing domestic labour in the house each received six smocks, three petticoats, three waistcoats, six coifs or caps, and twelve pairs of shoes, while women who worked in the fields received four smocks, three petticoats, four coifs, and twelve pairs of shoes. The total yearly expense for clothing thirty servants was £78. By contrast, for the hundred slaves on the plantation, who were left nearly naked, a total of £35 was spent to provide two petticoats for each woman and three pairs of drawers for each man.[23] Ligon deprecated former conditions in Barbados, but maintained that during his time conditions had improved, and "now, most of the servants lie in hamocks, and in warm rooms," could change into dry clothing if needed, and received meat "two or three times a week."[24] However, although Ligon provided a multi-dimensional, if simplistic, description of the lives of servants, he was notably less sympathetic to the enslaved, depicting them as "happy" without seeing or caring about the violence and degradation that they experienced in their lives.

Fictionalized accounts also corroborated these conditions, often more colourfully than prosaic autobiographies, but showing some real awareness of the deprivation servants experienced. In Virginia, *The Trappan'd Maiden* remained dressed in the "cloath that I brought in, / They are worn very thin" and described a lack of food, drinking only water (rather than beer), "which makes me pale and wan," and sleeping in a bed of straw infested by spiders.[25] James Revel decried his shabby apparel: once sold from the ship's deck, his clothing was taken, and he was left with no hat, shoes, or stockings, only "a canvas shirt and trowsers ... a hop-sack frock, in which I was a slave."[26]

Even the fictional accounts are valuable, because there is little evidence of conditions outside of personal narratives; court cases, the other main source on servants' lives, rarely mention daily life except when depositions note that a servant plaintiff was deprived of adequate food, shelter, or clothing. In December 1640, Virginia servant

William Huddleston complained that his master Mr Canhow had left him in "want of all manner of apparel." The court ordered Mr Canhow to provide "sufficient apparel of linen and woolen," and to make sure of his compliance, Huddleston's clothing was to be inspected by a court-appointed lawyer who would "have power to dispose of said servant" until Canhow complied.[27] Yet adequate clothing was not the same as satisfactory, as is evidenced by a court case on illegal marketing of cloth in Virginia in 1633, which mentioned in passing "course [coarse] wollen stuffs, servants shirts or course linnen to make shirts, or sheets for servants, or course wollen clothes fittinge for servants apparel."[28] Similarly, Lois Carr's work suggests that in the Chesapeake as a whole, both masters and servants consumed a greater amount of and more nutritive foods than in England, but often still inadequate and unpalatable.[29] Servants were also potentially faced with tight-fisted masters who restricted food.

Even as late as the 1730s, Elizabeth Ashbridge, serving her indenture in New York, described harsh conditions and lack of clothing, going barefoot even in winter, although by this time her hardships were due to the severity of her cruel master rather than the poverty of the colony.[30] Likewise, in 1756, Elizabeth Sprigs's letter from Maryland to her father described the violence and abuse she endured. She was provided little more than corn to eat, left shoeless and without adequate clothing – "almost naked" – and slept wrapped in a blanket on the ground. "Many Negroes are better used" than servants, she wrote, in a comparison made by many servants that underlined the ideal that whites should not do slaves' labour.[31]

PERSONAL RELATIONSHIPS IN SERVITUDE

By their very nature, most of the court cases discussed in this book emphasize the exploitation and abuse of servants by masters and mistresses. Yet there were some who behaved more moderately toward their servants. Such individuals left behind little evidence of their relationships because they didn't turn up in court complaints. The examples that exist are few. In Maryland in 1672, Randall Revell sued Thomas Poole to recover Mary Perymane, a servant whom the latter was detaining. Revell "did lend" the servant woman to Poole, but Poole refused to return her and "forceth the servant to stay in his house." Perymane herself was deposed and emphasized that she had been "much troubled" at leaving Mrs Revell, while Mrs Revell had been "grieved" but had reassured Perymane that she would soon be able to return. It's difficult to know if this testimony indicated genuine caring between the two women or merely Perymane's desire to get away from Poole, but the descriptive language suggests the former.[32] Occasionally, a master would voluntarily release a servant early from service.[33] For example, sixteen-year-old Anne Bowden, "having no indenture" contract, had served six years at the custom of the country and would have had five more years of service before her, but her master William Round had brought her before the Charles County Maryland Court to be released early.[34] In some cases, indentured servants received benefits in the wills of their former masters: for example, in the 1650s in Barbados, Demot O'Doyle was to receive six months off his time and his master's best suit of clothes and best hat; and Katherine Wilson, originally bound for seven years, was to be freed in five.[35] Some masters also appear to have been family members, a relationship that may have been more *in loco parentis* than a typical indenture contract. For instance, in 1673, after the death of his father, three-year-old Peter Macnemillion was bound to his godfather Peter Carr until the age of twenty-one. Peter Carr was probably also his uncle, as Macnemillion's mother's maiden name had been Carr.[36] Peter Carr was involved in a number of cases in which he acted at least partially in the interests of his servants. He paid the bastardy fine for his servant Margaret Evans in 1669, thereby saving her a whipping – although it is also possible that he was the child's father.[37] In 1671, he asked the Charles County Maryland Court to indenture the twelve-year-old Elizabeth Lylly to him. He had cared for her "ever since shee hath been borne," without receiving any recompense, and was now "feare full that shee may be enticed by some or other from him"; perhaps he now wished some recompense for her earlier boarding through her labour, but his deposition suggests that until that time he had not required any work from her.[38] Likely she was the illegitimate child of one of his servants – or perhaps his own. But some masters and mistresses did show consideration for servants, especially if they were children. Before Ricckett Mecane was sold, Mrs Speake, the new mistress of four of the eight boys kidnapped with him, sent food to Mecane and the other three boys still detained on the ship.[39] Likewise, the master of Peter Williamson raised him as a son and left him a large bequest in his will.

MEDICAL TREATMENT

Medical treatment of ill servants was seen as a requirement in both the colonies and England.[40] In 1645, the Virginia Assembly responded to what was apparently a trend among masters to not pay for medical care for sick servants. Although possibly a consequence of the impunity held by masters, the ruling implied that the neglect was caused by the high cost of medical care. Nonetheless, the language chastized the masters who had "hardened their hearts," thus risking their servants' lives. The assembly enacted a somewhat equivocal standard that mandated that doctors and surgeons could be arrested for excessive fees but also, if they neglected or refused to treat patients, "being thereunto required" to help "any person or persons in sicknes or extremity," that they could be punished in court.[41] These provisions were reiterated in 1660.[42] In Barbados, the governor issued an order that articulated both moral and economic concerns: since the masters of sick servants frequently released them from servitude rather than pay for their treatment, "whereby the said servants do miserably perish, or become a charge to the parish," any masters who did "not use all reasonable means for the recovery of their diseased servants," would be fined, the fees used to treat the servant, and the servant released.[43]

Many masters seem to have voluntarily had their ill servants cared for. In 1691, Mary Huett's master paid to have her "cured" of syphilis.[44] In 1678, Thomas Bland asked Robert Proctor to heal his ill servant Allice Spyer. Proctor was to take her into his house and care for her for a month to effect the cure, for which Bland promised a hogshead (400 pounds) of tobacco. Although there seems to have been a genuine desire on the part of Bland to care for Spyer, she still ended up valued as chattel: the case went to trial when Proctor claimed that his expenses ended up being much higher and claimed the servant woman herself as his fee, which was authorized by the court.[45] In 1670s Maryland, estate manager Peter Dennis first agreed, unusually, to pay one of his master's servants, Francis Story, a portion of the tobacco crop for his labour, and then hired a surgeon to heal a "venomous humour" involving "ulcerous sores" that afflicted Story, a cure that took a year.[46] The case came to court because Dennis's sympathy for Story did not extend to the surgeon, whom he attempted to avoid paying. But some masters refused to care for their ill servants: in Virginia, William Mansfield was subpoenaed for "takeing litle care" of his servant Mary Tabb, who had a lame leg. The court removed her to the home of a medical practitioner, with Mansfield responsible for charges for her accommodations and treatment.[47]

In a more complex and also telling case in Maryland in April 1667, John Corbett, an ill indentured servant "in a languishing condicon of body" complained to the court that his master, Joseph Tilly, was taking no action "for the cure of his distemper [chronic illness] that hangs upon hime." This case delineates the master's obligation to provide medical care for his ill servant. The court's judgment, which must have involved behind-the-scenes negotiations, strove to take the interest of several participants into account. It ordered Corbett's contract to be transferred to Dr John Stansby, who would attempt to cure Corbett. Stansby would pay Tilly 250 pounds of tobacco in exchange for Corbett's lost labour left in his contract.[48] Corbett would owe Stansby 2,000 pounds of tobacco or two years of additional servitude beyond the terms of his original contract in exchange for being cured. However, the case continued with a sequel. By December 1668, more than a year later, Dr Stansby had failed to cure Corbett, who was still "languishing." Corbett "did apply himselfe unto" Peter Sharpe, a prominent Quaker, "for help," and Sharpe took him into his home "out of charity." Stansby hired the lawyer William Morecroft to sue Sharpe for detaining Corbett. However, the court found in favour of Sharpe and Corbett, holding that Stansby had done little to cure Corbett's leg, that Sharpe was not liable for keeping Corbett since he had been unaware of the earlier court judgment, and further that the previous decistion had been conditional upon the curing of Corbett's leg, which had not occurred: Corbett was to be freed from servitude.[49] These two cases involving Corbett demonstrate the court's initial resolution to satisfy all parties with what it considered a fair settlement as well as its willingness to revisit the case to ensure adherence to its prior judgment. At the same time, it demonstrates that the rights and claims of the indentured servant might be equally considered in the dispensation of justice.

William Morecroft was a practicing physician as well as a lawyer, and he entered into an unusual agreement in 1669 to trade indentured servants with Thomas Dent, giving Dent an unnamed indentured servant of his and taking Dent's indentured servant John Richards. Morecroft's former servant still had five years to serve, but Richards, who must have been a desirable worker, had only two years and ten months left on his indenture. However, he had agreed to serve five additional years if Morecroft was successful in effecting "a firme and absolute cure" of his leg – otherwise he was only liable to serve the original length of his contract.[50] In a similar case in April 1667, Joseph Edloe, a boy of unspecified age with an "old ulcher in his legg," was appointed a guardian by the court. He was ordered to live with Thomas Powell until the age of twenty-one, presumably as an indentured servant, and Powell was also to provide a "speedy remedy" for his leg.[51]

In another case, servant Eliza Thompson was beaten and kicked by Thomas Hays, a neighbour, laming her leg and requiring medical care. Her master paid for a surgeon to treat her, but also brought a suit against Hays for the value of the cure and of Thompson's lost labour. However, he lost the case because, although Thompson herself as well as another witness testified to the beating, the surgeon attested that Thompson had previously told him that the disabling lesion had arisen spontaneously, "the sore bread of it selfe."[52] As in other cases, this incident hinged on the master's financial loss, and no one claimed that Thompson herself deserved any redress for the assault. The reality was that servants occupied an anonymous status, shifting between chattel and rights-bearing freeborn subjects. This meant that when a servant was ill or injured, the courts weighed not only the harm to the servant but also the potential loss or depreciation for their master or mistress.

SERVANTS' ECONOMIC AUTONOMY

Servants were typically not allowed to engage in business outside of the duties assigned by their masters.[53] The Virginia Assembly made clear its concern that independent trade encouraged servants, who possessed little, to "purloin and imbeazill the goods" of their masters.[54] Freemen who broke this rule also risked punishment. In 1640, Robert Newman was accused of trading with Captain Samuel Mathews's servants, bartering for 60 pounds of tobacco; as a penalty, he was fined four times the value, to be paid to Mathews.[55] In 1666, the Maryland Provincial Court awarded damages of 1,000 pounds of tobacco to one of its own justices, Colonel William Evans, with 1,000 pounds more payable to the court, to penalize a man who had engaged in a business transaction with one of Evan's indentured servants, "in breach" of the law.[56] The same Francis Gunby who had sued to recover his stolen contract attempted to take advantage of these rules by reneging on a business deal with Petronella Chivers, claiming that he was not obligated to pay the debt he owed her because "hee was then a servant upon indenture which hee is ready to averre." The court was not convinced by this argument and found for the plaintiff.[57] Gunby only had to pay his debt, but he had undertaken a significant risk incurring it in the first place. If convicted of a crime, servants potentially incurred harsh penalties because they were unable to pay fines. In 1665, the Virginia Assembly mandated that "in all cases where a freeman is punishable by fine, a servant shall receive corporall punishment" – "for every five hundred pounds of tobacco, twenty lashes" – unless another person paid the fine, contingent on the servant's agreeing to perform future service after his or her term of servitude was over.[58]

On the other hand, if a servant was acting under a master's orders, there was significantly more leeway. For example, a power of attorney could allow a trusted servant to engage in trade, as when Robert Simmons in Maryland in 1668 was allowed to buy and sell "wth all … liberties … belonging to any freeman" provided he continued to obey the orders of his master.[59] Even a servant committing a crime at the behest of a master or mistress might not be seen as culpable. When Elizabeth Greene ordered her servant Richard Jones to forge a receipt for goods in 1663, the Maryland Provincial Court punished Greene severely, with the loss of one ear, as well as the pillory, a fine of double the court costs, payment of damages, and one year's imprisonment, but Jones was not charged, perhaps because the court recognized that he was acting under constraint.[60] Indeed, he had stated in his deposition that "shee caused him to write it."[61] Likewise, in 1665, Raymond Staplefort made his servant boy Humphrey Jones aid him in a burglary in which Jones was lifted through a broken window and then opened the front door of the house. However, while Staplefort was indicted, Jones was not charged. Despite what appeared to be overwhelming evidence against him, Staplefort was ultimately found not guilty by the jury.[62]

Another incident in Somerset County Maryland in 1691 demonstrated the compulsion a master and mistress could bring to bear on their servants. Bridgett and Stephen Page and their servant Margarett Kenneday were charged with stealing and killing some of their neighbours' pigs. A rambling series of witness testimonials described the events, including Bridgett Page's outlandish claim to her children that the two pigs were "over grown possums." An onlooker described the

Pages' bribes and threats toward Elizabeth Larramore, another servant, including how Stephen Page offered Larramore "20: ay. 30: 40:
nay 50 pound" to lie for them, but the skeptical Larramore instead
poignantly replied, "ah Master yw promised to send me home for
England, but you did not." In her own testimony, Larramore described
how when she refused to help dress a hog, one of the Pages' slaves was
ordered to knock her unconscious. In the end, there was plenty of evidence of wrongdoing. The jury found all of the Pages, including their
children, as well as Kenneday guilty of slaughtering the pigs, but
imprisoned only Stephen, as head of the household, until financial
restitution could be made. Perhaps fortunately for Larramore, she had
been sold into the household of William Oswell shortly before the
case came to trial, removing her from possible reprisals for her testimony against the Pages.[63]

VIOLENCE AGAINST SERVANTS

The nature of servitude placed masters in a position of great power
over their servants, and many of them behaved as though they had
impunity to do anything they wanted. There were frequent instances
of violence against servants, usually revealed through court cases in
which servants complained of being excessively beaten, or when
courts established inquests and investigations when servants were
killed. It should be noted that some domestic violence was considered
normal in early modern society. It was acceptable for husbands to hit
or beat their wives, parents to beat their children, masters and mistresses to strike their apprentices and servants.[64] The latter individuals
were seen as subordinates within the household, and thus subject to
correction by their superiors. In early modern law and society, the
patriarchal father or husband in charge of a household had a special
role, akin to that of the monarch of the country. Murder of a husband
by a wife or of a master or mistress by a servant was termed petty or
"petit treason," a crime viewed with more gravity and incurring more
terrible punishments than ordinary murder.[65]

However, superiors did not have the legal right to scar, maim, inca-
pacitate, or sexually assault subordinates, although marital rape was
not a crime.[66] Servants who had offended in a significant way were
supposed to be brought before a town official to have punishment
administered rather than be whipped by their masters, and masters
could not whip "white Christian" servants naked.[67] The intent was to

both formalize the punishment and remove impunity for masters to beat their servants without restrictions. Masters who went beyond these guidelines could be punished, though in practice, the penalty was typically limited to court-mandated removal of the servants from their master's control. A more serious penalty was sometimes imposed for egregious cruelty. In 1640 Barbados, for example, John Thomas, a servant, appealed to the Barbados council that his master Francis Leavin and his brother-in-law Hodgs "did inhumanly and unchristianlike torture" him by hanging him by his hands and placing burning matches between his fingers. Their "cruelly dealing" had crippled Thomas, "whereby he has lost the use of the severall joynts and is in great danger to loose the use of his right hand." In response, the governor and council freed Thomas, imprisoned Leavin and Hodgs, ordered that they pay Thomas 5,000 pounds of cotton apiece within ten days, and decreed that Leavin have Thomas cured in "a speedy course" and pay for the treatment.[68]

In general, the expectation that masters would physically punish servants combined with the power balance between vested members of the community and lowly servants, and the difficulty of proving that excessive violence had occurred meant that, even when charged in court, many violent or even murderous masters escaped prosecution. "Misadventure," or accidental killing, was frequently invoked, even in England, when people murdered subordinates, such as masters who killed hired servants or husbands their wives, particularly when the deaths occurred while masters or husbands were striking as a form of chastisement.[69] Indentured servitude was even more inherently risky for servants, who were very distant from their home communities, and brutal masters appear more frequently in official records in the colonies than in England.[70]

Protections for Servants

Servants did gain some safeguards through legislation, such as a vague 1657 Virginia act that specifically stated that mistreated servants could complain in court about their master by informing one of the court commissioners if they experienced "harsh and bad usage, or else for want of diet or convenient necessaries." A commissioner finding "by just proofe" that the complaint was accurate could caution the master or mistress, who might also be punished in court.[71] The legislation seems well-intentioned, with a stated aim to insure "that no servant or servants be misused by their master or mistresse," but it neglected to specify penalties and was so full of loopholes, such as the repeated requirement for proof, that it must have been almost toothless. In contrast, two years later, an act established to ensure that "no servant lay violent hands on his master or overseer" mandated two extra years of service as a penalty with no requirement of proof.[72] In 1661, the Virginia Assembly tried again to protect servants, with slightly stronger language mandating that "every master shall provide for his servants component dyett, clothing and lodging, and that he shall not exceed the bounds of moderation in correcting them beyond the merit of their offences," while servants could complain against "harsh and bad usage," or if they were in "want of dyett or convenient necessaries." Again, if the court commissioner found "by just proofes" that the allegations were correct, the servant would "have remedy for his grievances."[73] Yet the court immediately followed this with an act "against unruly servants," punishing servants that laid "violent hands on his or her master, mistress or overseer," as well as another law limiting servants' autonomy by preventing them from engaging in business transactions, as Francis Gunby had tried to do with Petronella Chivers.[74]

The protection of the law, of the courts, and even of public opinion must have provided servants in the mainland colonies with some safeguard against violence, neglect, and other forms of exploitation. However, there were many cases in which masters and mistresses continued to act harmfully toward their servants. Sometimes murder trials hinged not on whether the killer had struck the blows but on whether the subordinate had initially offended and thereby deserved chastisement.[75] This dynamic could be overturned, so that occasionally juries considered servants who killed their masters or wives who killed their husbands to have acted in self-defence, and thus warranted mercy.[76] Yet these cases demonstrate that while it was difficult to prosecute murderous masters, and the bar for obtaining justice was high by modern standards, the law as well as societal expectations did possess some power to restrain masters' illegal actions and to provide some justice for servants. Similar inquiries did not occur in the case of enslaved people who suffered violence or murder. While servants existed in an ambiguous category between dependents and chattel, slaves definitively occupied the latter category.

Murder of Servants

Masters who murdered their servants could be punished for their crimes, but the burden of proof was high. A pair of criminal cases that illustrate this were tried before the Maryland Provincial Court in 1664. In a legal practice that would not be permissible today, the cases were tried in tandem before one jury, which delivered two verdicts at once. The cases, which had differing outcomes, were both against masters accused of killing their servants. One case involved the death of Jeffrey Haggman, servant of Joseph Fincher.[77] The other accused John Grammer of killing his servant Thomas Simmons.[78] In the Fincher case, an inquest jury at first determined that Haggman had been "a diseased person" who had "died of the scurvey."[79] Nonetheless, there was enough suspicion of murder that a jury trial was called, and Fincher was held in jail during the proceedings, which took several months. Several witnesses were called, who testified that they saw Fincher strike Haggman at various times, at least once with "a small sticke." One added, however, that he was "sure" that the blows were not severe – they "could doe him no hurt."[80] Much of the testimony centred around where the beatings had occurred – Haggman had died in the tobacco house, where tobacco was dried before being processed. Accordingly, the first two witnesses had clarified that the beatings that they had seen had not occurred in the tobacco house. Another testified to observing a more serious beating on the day of Haggman's death, inflicted by both Fincher and his wife who had repeatedly knocked down, beaten, and kicked Haggman, who apparently collapsed before stumbling into the tobacco house, where his master continued to beat him with a stick. The deponent had later heard a "great noise" in the tobacco house, then had heard Fincher crying out, "gett up, gett up," after which she had seen several people running back and forth from the tobacco house.[81] This testimony was corroborated by four others, who also added further details about Haggman's bleeding nose and apparent bruises.[82] The jury found that Fincher "an assault did make" and "feloniously and of malice forthought did kill and murder" Haggman. Fincher was sentenced to be hanged.[83]

The jury then heard the case of John Grammer, accused of killing Thomas Simmons. At the request of Grammer, who claimed that Simmons had been ailing for the past year, the jury viewed

Simmons's autopsied body and observed various evidence of "putrid ulcers," "putrifaccon," paleness, and "rotton" organs, by which it concluded that he was sickly and dying: "this person by course of nature could not have lived long."[84] While this suggested a death of natural causes, there were compelling reasons to try the case. Most crucially, there were several witnesses, the majority of them Grammer's own servants, who had observed Simmons receiving violent beatings. They testified that on the day of Simmons's death, Grammer had ordered another servant, Christopher Anderson, to whip Simmons, which he had obeyed with severity. One witness stated that Simmons received "neer uppon a hundred stripes wth a catt of ninetailes uppon his bare back and that those blowes were the occasion of his death." Other servants confirmed this, as well as an additional beating administered by Grammer. After Simmons collapsed in the field, Grammer had tried to revive him with a gourd of water, but Simmons was unable to walk. James Low, one of the witnesses, stated that he had confronted his master, saying "yow have kill'd this man, for he is a dead man," to which Grammer had replied, "hang him roage [rogue], hee is a dissembling roage." However, Anderson and John Eds, another servant, had had to drag Simmons into the house. Anderson was brought to the stand and testified that Simmons had tried to run away, and that his master had ordered him to beat Simmons. In a deviation from the others' testimony, who had described Grammer continuing the beating immediately after Anderson had whipped Simmons, Anderson asserted that between the two beatings Simmons had breakfasted and completed some work, presumably hoping to emphasize that it was Grammer's actions and not his own that were responsible for Simmons's death. Anderson was in a precarious position: potentially liable for the murder but, having been "commanded" (the word used in the depositions) to whip Simmons, not in a position to refuse his master's order. However, the other servants' testimony seemed to suggest that Anderson had gone beyond his duty in his abuse of Simmons. To bolster his claim of innocence, Anderson dubiously claimed that it was he who had said to Grammer that Simmons "was a dead man, and he told me noe, he was a dissembling roage." The week before the trial, Anderson had asked Susan Hunt, another fellow servant, to falsely testify that she had heard Grammer threaten to kill Simmons. Instead, she testified on the stand that Anderson had whipped Simmons, and when asked by their mistress if he "were not sorry for what he had done," Anderson had seemed to show no remorse, replying "noe, he could have given him tenn times more."[85]

Despite these depositions, the jury, asked to determine whether Grammer and Anderson "feloniously did kill" Simmons, responded with a verdict of "ignoramus," meaning that there was insufficient evidence. No one denied that Simmons had been beaten. However, the jury concluded that "noe evidence which appeared before us … did possitively sweare that any blowes given by John Grammer or his man could touch his life." They were in part swayed by the surgeon who performed the autopsy, who stated that "noe stripes given him had in the least toucht any principall part [vital organ]" and, consequently, "in his judgm[en]t according to the rules of physick, his life could not be toucht" – the blows could not have killed him.[86] In a telling aspect of the whole affair, a further viewing of the body led the jury to declare that "want of good dyett and lodging has been the cheife furtherance and cause of his death," apparently absolving Grammer of responsibility.[87] This statement neglected two facts: that Simmons's death immediately after he was beaten was inexplicable and that if his death had indeed been caused by malnutrition and exposure, Grammer should still have been culpable. After being held in prison for eight months, Grammer was released.[88] A further bleak consequence of this trial is that his servants who had testified against him would have had little protection against reprisals.

These two cases show that the courts regarded a servant's murder with some gravity. Considerations had been given to the facts of the crimes, and the deliberations of the jury were real. Yet the burden of proof was high, and the disparate verdicts illustrate the precariousness of servants' safety while in the power of their masters. The killing of Thomas Simmons illustrates that often masters could operate with considerable impunity: the testimony of the witnesses had essentially been disregarded in Grammer's favour. Furthermore, in neither case did the court question the right of masters to physically punish their servants.

There were many other similar trials; in some instances, those who murdered servants were punished, while in others they escaped charges. For example, in 1666, Walter Pake was hanged for murdering former servant William Price. Price was known to be a disreputable character and had had a restraining order taken out by his wife, while the murderer was Price's former attorney and a pillar of the community, although drunk at the time of the murder.[89] While by modern standards, this was a relatively clear-cut case, it again demonstrates that indentured servants (particularly after time of service, as in this case) were seen as vested members of the body politic. It should be noted that in seventeenth-century Maryland, at least, juries typically failed to convict on capital murder cases unless the evidence was overwhelming.[90] Even in Pake's case, the jury attempted to have the charge reduced to manslaughter because "Walter Pake was drunk and did not know what he did att the time of committing the fact," leaving it in the hands of the justices to determine if it was murder.[91]

The trial of Pope Alvey, a notorious troublemaker who was tried twice for capital crimes, showed a different outcome. In 1664, Alvey was found guilty of murder of his indentured servant, Alice Sanford, who had died half an hour after being beaten. Alvey was sentenced to be hanged but pleaded benefit of the clergy – he was then branded on the hand and released.[92] In the second case, in 1665, Alvey was again sentenced to be hanged for killing a neighbour's cow.[93] Benefit of the clergy was not allowed twice, but after "several persons" came "upon their knees humbly [to] beg" the court for lenience, Alvey was released by the court with a warning to "hence forward behave himself in his remaining course of life."[94] The original sentence was left to be reinstated "in full force" under the "pleasure of the governour" if he showed recidivism, but Alvey was given a full pardon nine years later by the Maryland Assembly.[95] One wonders whether he would have been treated so leniently if he had killed a freewoman rather than an indentured servant and a cow.[96]

Likewise, despite significant evidence of violence, Anne Nevell was found not guilty after being indicted for the beating death of her servant Margarett Redfearne. At the inquest, Redfearne's body was observed to be severely beaten. Witnesses had observed her being beaten several times and had heard her accusing Mrs Nevell. In the end, despite providing little defence, Mrs Nevell was found not guilty by the jury – the justification was not recorded.[97]

In another Maryland case, in 1664, a jury in the Provincial Court investigated whether servant Ann Beetle had been murdered or had committed suicide. Her mistress, Mrs Hunt, had shoved Ann Beetle after finding her in her husband's bed, which had resulted in Beetle falling and gashing her face. However, the wound – "a great cut" – was judged "not mortal" and the source of death was determined to be drowning. The jury thus determined that servant Ann Beetle had committed suicide, and she was "indited" for "willfully murthering her selfe."[98] While there does appear to have been a genuine attempt in this case to determine whether the servant herself had been physically harmed in the reported incident, the determination did not take into account a number of factors, including the difficulty for a servant woman to deny her lecherous master's wishes, the inevitable scandal and likely retaliation that would ensue from the servant's continuing to live in the household after the affair was discovered, or Beetle's possible resultant despair that led to her suicide. Elizabeth Ashbridge too had considered suicide after her master's advances and abuse.[99] Servants sometimes committed suicide due to the harsh conditions of their lives and the abuse that many suffered, but it was seen as an extreme action in a society where suicide was viewed as a sin. For example, a Virginia inquest jury in 1664 found that servant Edward Whittell, who hanged himself, "for want of grace was guilty of his owne death."[100]

A similar case in 1657 Maryland involved the prosecution and sentencing of John Dandy for killing his servant Henry Gouge, whose body was found in a creek near Dandy's house. The trial hinged on whether or not Gouge had drowned. Several witnesses described the pitiful condition of Gouge's body, and others described hearing or seeing Dandy beating Gouge. But perhaps the key evidence was that several of the witnesses described seeing an old axe wound on Gouge's face bleeding "afresh" when Dandy touched his body, giving credence to a popular belief that a victim's body would bleed in the presence of his killer.[101] It's difficult to know whether the body was actually emitting blood in an unusual fashion, but it's clear that the neighbours' belief that Gouge had been murdered was a powerful factor in the conviction of his master. This case demonstrates that while public opinion tolerated a significant amount of brutality toward servants, there was a limit to what could be condoned.

Servants held by brutal masters were in grave danger and help from the courts might come too late. In 1661, the Maryland Provincial Court heard a case about servant Thomas Watson, who was beaten to death by Mary Bradnox and her husband Captain Thomas Bradnox. The Bradnoxes had been violent toward Watson for some time, and witnesses, including other servants in the household, testified to multiple beatings. The final cause of death was a blow to Watson's head inflicted by Mrs Bradnox using a staff. Captain Bradnox died while the case was being tried, but the jury found Mrs Bradnox not guilty, despite ample evidence against her.[102] While the trial was ongoing, the Bradnoxes retaliated against Sarah Taylor, one of the servants who had testified against them. In response, Taylor separately complained in the Kent County Maryland Court that she had been beaten by Captain Bradnox, and Mrs Bradnox had abetted this by holding her down and guarding the door. Taylor showed numerous bruises, and Captain Bradnox admitted to the charge. As well, she was able to produce a witness to another beating, and the court possessed a record of her complaint of ill-treatment two years earlier when she had run away and been sheltered by a neighbour. She had also once been accused of theft by her master and mistress but had been found not guilty. Following these earlier incidents, the court had returned her to the violent Bradnox household. Ultimately, in the 1661 case, the court decided in Taylor's favour, ruling that there had been "no caus[e] at all" for one beating and that the punishment in the other instance was excessively harsh – "above measiour." Taylor was freed early, without having served her full term of servitude. The court did not punish her employers but did deliver an implicit reprimand in justifying Taylor's "discharge" from her indenture "in regard of the eminent danger likely to insew[ensue] by the invetterat mallice of hur master & mistres toward hure."[103] In light of the still-ongoing Thomas Watson case, this court decision may have saved Taylor's life.

Since servants were often the main witnesses against their masters in such cases, there was a significant risk of reprisal if the master was not convicted. In 1679, Mary Baines, servant of James Lewis, accused him of murder. She also asked to be removed from his household. Baines feared for her life because, although she had asked the court a year ago to punish Lewis for his violence toward her, he had avoided arrest and had become even more violent toward her and the other servants in the household. He had beaten servant Joseph Robinson to death. In addition, he had continued to abuse the other servants, beating them and treating them "cruelly," and Baines had been deprived of clothing, food, and a bed. If Lewis was left unchecked, it would lead to her "inevitable ruine." The court arrested Lewis and placed Baines, first, with the sheriff and then as a servant in another household. There is no record of a judgment against Lewis.[104]

Physical Abuse

Other forms of violence could also be claimed in the courts. On 27 April 1658, the Maryland Provincial Court heard a case brought by Margarett Roberts against her master, John Hambleton. Roberts complained that her master had kept her in servitude past the expiration of her time and had often struck her. Hambleton asked for the case to be respited until the next court session, when he would provide a defence. The court agreed and sent Roberts back to Hambleton's house, with the provision that he "use her well & not strike her." Although it made no determination about the outcome of the case, the court noted the provision that if Roberts was found to be free, Hambleton would also owe her payment for damages and her extra time in service.[105] The outcome of a further court encounter is not recorded, but Roberts had been returned by the court to a very vulnerable situation in which she was at risk of retaliation from a man who had already shown a propensity for violence.

In a very similar case, in 1652, Jane Latham complained to a Norfolk County Virginia court "of her ill usage by her master Mr Thomas Willoughby," which included physical abuse. The court ordered "that she return to her masters house there to doe her service ... until [th]e next Court" session. At that time the two parties were to come to court with witnesses, and Mr Willoughby was to bring "the ropes [that] struck [th]e s[ai]d Latham."[106] Although this statement seems to acknowledge the abuse, the court nevertheless left Latham in her master's house for at least a period of weeks, where she might expect reprisals for her testimony.

In June 1690, Thomas Everigon sued his former master Thomas Newbold. Newbold had consistently abused Everigon during his seven years of service, and now that he had completed the term, had denied him his freedom dues. Two days before Everigon was due to be released from indenture, Newbold had given him fifty lashes with a horsewhip, apparently out of anger that Everigon was being freed. The resulting injuries made Everigon "unfit for labour or travill at present," a serious concern for a man who had no likely means of support other than physical labour. Everigon brought in witnesses to both his past whippings and the most recent mistreatment at the hands of Newbold, and craved his freedom dues as well as monetary compensation. However, the court did not return a judgment on this case. Thomas Newbold was at that time a justice on the Somerset County Maryland Court.[107] Not only did his status seemingly give him immunity from Everigon's suit, but one wonders about his potential bias in other cases brought by maltreated servants.

Physical abuse was a common cause of complaint. It was probably some prior case of cruelty that led the Virginia quarter court to decide

in 1661 that Roger and Elizabeth Partridge would be prohibited from
keeping a maid servant for a three-year period, but there were many
examples where the nature of the violence was more clearly
described.[108] In 1664, Sarah Hall appeared before the Maryland
Provincial Court complaining of violence inflicted by her master and
mistress. Two witnesses were called, who verified that they had seen
Hall being hit, kicked, and threatened. The court did not punish her
employers, but it removed Hall from their household. As she had two
years of servitude remaining, she was to be resold to a new master.
Two appraisers were brought in, who valued her "att the most one
thowsand pounds of tobacco." The court ordered that she "be disposed off to some other p[e]rson," but mandated that her freedom
dues be remembered: "the buyer paying her att the expiracon of the
said servants servitude her corne and cloathes."[109] As with similar
cases, this case is filled with contradictions and disjunctions. The
court acknowledged that Hall had a right not to be beaten and moved
to remove her from the household. It also strove to protect her right
to receive freedom dues. The court also clung to the legality of the
contract, mandating that Hall continue to serve her two years. Yet it
relegated her to the status of chattel in having her appraised as though
she was any other form of property.

Likewise, in 1649 Virginia, when Charity Dollen was removed
from her mistress's custody due to severe physical abuse, the court
judgment indicating that her mistress had already had prior warning from the court to desist from beating her servant; in addition,
she had already lost custody of a "servant boy" who had run away,
but whom the court had found to have been maltreated. Dollen was
assigned to service under a new master appointed by the court.[110] In
a brief mention in the proceedings of the Kent County Court in
Maryland in 1657, a Mr Ward and his wife were fined for the "unlaw-
full correction" they had given their servant Alse Lutt, but she was
seemingly left in their custody.[111] In 1681, apparently responding to
a case of neglect and possibly abuse in which servant Jane Jones had
been taken in by a neighbour, the Maryland Provincial Court
ordered that "without delay" Elias Nuthall provide "sufficient apparel"
for his servant and also "give good security for his good usage of her"
before she would be returned to him.[112] Although in this case the
servant might have been a runaway, seen as serious misconduct, the
court acknowledged her reasons in admonishing her master. She
may have had a capable attorney, like Richard Boughton, who had

so effectively emphasized the brutality endured by Elizabeth Hasell
that he was able to win her freedom.[113] In a similar case, Ann Carter
complained to a York County Virginia justice that her master had
"severall times beat & abused her in a most barbarous manner"
and compelled her to work on Sundays. The justice, Henry Tyler,
ordered her to appear in court to pursue her complaint, but she
failed to appear. However, the court suspected that "she has been
prevented" by her master "with intent to obstruct the course of justice" and ordered the sheriff to take her into custody so that she
could prosecute her master.[114] Neighbours might step in to protect
a maltreated servant or apprentice. In 1712, William and Eliza
Young filed a petition on behalf of apprentice William Vernum
against Humphrey Nixon for maltreatment, including neglecting to
provide "wholesome diett" and whipping Vernum naked. Vernum
may have been sheltering with the Youngs at the time. They also
asked for 40 shillings in damages for Vernum. However, the court
decided that there was "no cause" of complaint and mandated that
Vernum return to his master.[115]

Although the servants in these cases succeeded in gaining the
attention of the court, not all of them gained significantly. Many
were left with their abusive masters and mistresses. Violent masters
mainly escaped punishment and so might conclude that they could
continue with impunity. Undoubtedly, many servants feared similar
treatment and never complained about ill-treatment, or were ignored
when they tried. Masters could also use the courts to retaliate against
their servants. In 1659, William Parrott sued his former servant, Alice
Brasse, for defamation. She had claimed to her new master, Captain
Waring, that Parrott had severely beaten her, breaking two of her ribs,
and imperilling her life. Parrott likely would have continued his violence against Brasse, but as she was in another household, his only
recourse was the courts. Two or three weeks after her sale to Waring,
Brasse still seemed "lame" and was observed to be covered with bruises.
However, the court dismissed both parties without action, thereby
leaving both parties responsible for their court fees.[116] A possible
interpretation of this non-judgment is that Brasse had demonstrated
the severity of the beating but not that it had threatened her life or
permanent health. This would have marginally voided the claim of
defamation, but not sufficiently to incline the court in her favour.
In addition, having been sold to Waring, the court no longer needed
to further protect her from Parrott. Sexual assault, an additional

form of violence that may have been implicit in some of these cases, is discussed in chapter 6.

DEFAMATION CASES

The burden of proof was high for servants, even when they were supposedly protected by the law. In May 1640, Patrick Hitchcock and Alexander Joyner, two servants in Barbados, alleged that their master, Captain Stanhope, "had vented some injurious and malicious speeches much tending to the dishonor and disgrace of" the Barbados governor. Stanhope confessed that while "in his drunkenesse" he had made "scurrilous speeches" against the governor. He was imprisoned to "remaine during the Governor's pleasure." However, the servants were also punished, ostensibly because they had "lewd and profane" lives and because there was some uncertainly about their statements: "they did varie much from their former depositions." They were imprisoned and whipped at the public whipping post, receiving twenty lashes each. One must speculate, however, that their punishment was a form of retaliation against servants who dared contradict their master.[117]

Defamation was a serious concern, but courts were relatively evenhanded when servants and masters clashed on this issue.[118] For example, in 1666, the Maryland Provincial Court heard a case for defamation against former indentured servant William Champ, who was being sued by his erstwhile master, William Morecroft, who had then just recently become an attorney. Champ had called his master "a cheating old knave," although it is unclear whether this occurred before or after he had finished his service. Champ himself admitted to the insult, even refused to retract it, but claimed that he had made it prior to Morecroft's assumption of position. The court's judgment was primarily concerned with this latter point, and it eventually determined that since the words had been uttered prior to Morecroft's swearing in, they were not actionable. The court thus decided in favour of the former servant against his master.[119] Champ flourished as a freeman shortly thereafter, marrying and working as a physician, although he died early in 1668.[120] In another case, a servant, James the Scot, was falsely accused of theft in seventeenth-century Virginia; the court awarded him 200 pounds of tobacco to compensate for the harm to his reputation.[121] On the other hand, in 1638 Virginia, servant Margaret Harrington sought revenge against her mistress, Sarah

Julian, for abuse, saying "now she would be even with her" and claiming Julian had engaged in "carnall capulation" with a man not her husband. Lack of evidence led to Harrington being punished for defamation with "100 stripes upon the bare shoulders" and also ordered to ask her mistress for forgiveness "heare now in court."[122] Richard Austin called his mistress a whore, for which the court sentenced him to "thirty lashes well laid on his bare backe."[123] These excessively harsh punishments could also be imposed on free individuals who alleged sexual impropriety without proof. Earlier in the same year, Debora Glascock alleged of Captain Sibsey that "his maide servant was with child by him" but then offered no proof; she was sentenced to "100 stripes on the bare shoulders and likewise [to] aske the s[ai]d Capt. Sibsey forgiveness heere now in court and the next sabath at the parish church."[124] Notably, the damage to the servant's reputation was not addressed.

DISPUTES ABOUT TERM OF SERVITUDE

Servants sought to employ the courts to protect their rights, sometimes suing for freedom, as did Ricckett Mecane and Hester Nicholls and her father, and other times suing their former masters or mistresses for delayed freedom dues or other obligations owed them by contract or custom. Many servants appeared in court protesting against unscrupulous masters who sought to keep them indentured past the legal termination of their contracts.

Richard Newman petitioned the Maryland Provincial Court for freedom in February 1679 after his appropriately named current master, Captain Slye, had refused to free him in November of the previous year. The court searched the papers from the estate of Newman's previous master, who had died three and a half years earlier, discovered a "certifficate" validating Newman's claim, and ordered that Captain Slye free Newman and pay his freedom dues.[125] Even servants without a paper contract could successfully sue for both their freedom and their freedom dues. Wiliam Knags sued his master Robert Kenly in the Maryland Provincial Court in 1660, arguing that despite "there being no indentures," he had served four years and ought to be freed. Kenly hoped to keep him in servitude for seven. However, the jury stated that "a servant comeing in at sixteene yeares of age w[i]thout indentures ought not to serve above fower yeares according to the custome of this province," and that not only was Knags free but also Kenly owed him freedom dues and was liable for the court costs.[126] In a comparable case, Joseph Inglesby, a servant brought from Virginia to Maryland, argued in the Maryland Provincial Court that his master was trying to keep him in indenture an extra year, based on the former colony's longer terms of indenture under the custom of the country. The court found in Inglesby's favour, ruling that Maryland was not bound by "that act in Vergenia concerning servants servitudes" and also mandated that Inglesby's master pay him his freedom dues according to Maryland custom.[127] In 1686 Virginia, Thomas Mountfort sold his servant woman Margery Crow to Alexander Mackdaniell for a three-year term. However, Crow was granted her freedom in court after two years. Mountfort was ordered to compensate Mackdaniell for the value of the lost year and pay the court fees.[128]

Elizabeth Cannee was the plaintiff in a more difficult dispute involving both her freedom and her freedom dues. She was obliged to go to the Maryland Provincial Court twice to obtain her rights. In February 1679, her master, Mark Cordea, had transferred her to his son-in-law, John Le Compt, who had agreed to let Cannee go free immediately if she would forego her freedom dues. However, Cordea had then arrested Cannee as a runaway and claimed extra time of servitude from her as a result. Cannee was able to produce her discharge document in court, but the court deemed it invalid and ordered her to serve the rest of her original time with Cordea, though it provided some protection against retaliation by mandating that Cordea "bee for ever debarred from takeing any advantage against the said Elizabeth for the time she absented her selfe." Yet on 12 May 1680, she was in court again because Cordea had refused to allow her freedom and freedom dues, owed on 6 May. The court found in her favour and ordered Cordea to free her and provide her corn and clothing.[129] The rapidity with which Cannee resorted to the court to obtain her rights suggests that she was an unusually proactive individual, and perhaps also that she had anticipated trouble with Cordea. The previous year, the court had made a similar decision in favour of another servant illegally detained past his time by the intractable Cordea.[130]

False contractual dealings were another reason that servants resorted to the courts. In 1670, the Maryland Provincial Court responded to the petition of John Griffith, a "poore" and "ignorant" indentured servant from Maryland who sued his erstwhile master Thomas Paine, claiming that he had been tricked out of the freedom dues owed him with a false document that the possibly illiterate Griffith had been "perswaded" to sign or mark ("putt his hand unto"). Griffith won, and the court ordered that Paine pay the "corne and clothes & other things accordinge to the custome of the country which is due to him."[131] In a similar case of fraud, Thomas Darner had signed a contract for a four-year indenture in England. But when in Maryland, Humphrey Warren, the factor for the shipper, had confiscated the document, erased Darner's name, and substituted the name of another servant. Darner was judged to be seventeen years old in 1668 and sold at the custom of the country for a seven-year period. In 1672, he sued for his freedom. The jury examined the indenture contract and awarded Darner his freedom. His master was made responsible for the cost of suit, perhaps under the assumption that he had colluded with Warren.[132] Similarly, when a Maryland master attempted to alter a contract made in 1739 by erasing a time of four years and replacing it with seven, and then selling his servant, the court found for the servant over his new master, who wanted to retain the servant's time based on the new sale contract.[133]

Altering a contract or neglecting its terms was cause for a lawsuit. Elizabeth Frame sued her master Thomas Davis in 1657 in the Maryland Provincial Court, alleging that she had been deprived of her freedom. The previous year, Davis had purchased her for three years from John Hawkins. The court ordered her to bring proof of her freedom to the next session. In the interim, she left Davis's service. Frame failed to bring in proof, and Davis sued her in 1658 for damages, including court costs and loss of her time, and asked for her to be returned to his service. He brought in a copy of a contract, which was transcribed in the court records, verifying that Frame had agreed to her purchase from her previous master, John Hawkins, for the period of three years beginning in 1656, which also added a half year to her original contract. However, Frame pointed out that the contract had also stated that Hawkins was to "give her a cow [and] calfe, as speedily as hee can," which he had not done.[134] Furthermore, in a facile argument that led the court recorder to dub her "Elizabeth the deft," she pointed out that she had been a servant when she had engaged in the contract, which was therefore invalid.[135] The court agreed that she had no "further obligation of service" and that she remained free. The irrepressible Frame then demanded freedom dues of clothing from Davis, which was granted by the court. Davis was left only with the advice of the court to sue Hawkins.[136]

Many servants sued their masters and mistresses for attempting to default on freedom dues, a more common occurrence if the master or mistress was not the original employer of a servant who had only served a short term with them. In 1693, Mary Cranshaw sued her former master Leonard Jones for not giving her freedom dues. She had been sold to Jones by William Gross and presented the court with a note signed by Gross in 1691 transferring the remaining three years and eight months of her service to Jones. The court ruled that Cranshaw was free and that Jones was to pay her clothing and corn, as well as court costs.[137] In 1710 Virginia, Abigail Obrian successfully sued her former master in court because, although she had been released from her service early "being greatly afflicted with sickness," she had not received her freedom dues.[138] A claim of poverty by the former master, or even his death, was insufficient cause for withholding the dues. This was verified in 1648 when Henry Spink petitioned the Maryland Provincial Court to recover his freedom dues from his deceased master Nicholas Hanvey's estate. The executor of the will claimed that he did not possess the requisite goods, "there being noe such assets to bee fownd in the estate," leading the court to assess the freedom dues' value in tobacco.[139] In Virginia in 1711, Robert Francis sued his master William Babb, who had inherited Francis after his former master John Babb died. The outcome is not recorded.[140] There were many more examples of servants suing for release from servitude, for withheld freedom dues, or for damages based on being held in servitude too long, indicating that the right to sue was widely known.[141]

The individual situations of indentured servants varied considerably, but always remained uncertain. Servants were at risk for many hazards, such as disease that threatened the entire settler community, as well as risks specific to indentured servitude. The latter included the dangerous passage across the ocean; poor living conditions involving bad or insufficient food, clothes and lodging; or excessively hard labour, as well as cruelty by vicious masters. Meanwhile, servants were limited in their ability to engage in economic transactions that might have bettered their situations. The servitude relationship gave masters and mistresses inordinate power to maltreat servants. While cultural norms in theory limited the amount of abuse, in actuality, masters had a great deal of impunity; often they were only punished in extreme cases, such as murder or severe physical abuse, while the burden of proof was high. There were some mitigating factors, including social norms that saw servants as "Englishmen" with certain rights, including medical care and fulfilling the provisions of their contracts. Further, many masters' and mistresses' behaviour remained within the bounds of appropriate social norms, and some even treated their servants with kindness. Nonetheless, these individual relationships could not completely alleviate the inherently exploitative nature of indentured servitude. Additionally, while the English state and colonial governments recognized servants as rights-bearing members of society and provided legal remedies against the worst forms of violence and abuse, in practice this generally depended on the awareness, ability, and resolve of individuals to utilize the courts, leaving many wrongs unredressed.

6

Women in Indentured Servitude

Approximately two-thirds of indentured servants were men, who were generally preferred by colonial masters. However, women were also in demand as domestic servants, and the colonies, beset by unequal gender ratios among English settlers (four males to each female), also hoped for marriageable women who would complete their servitude and marry colonial men.[1] Most shippers of indentured servants preferentially chose men, whose contracts were worth more at auction in the colonies, but there were increased ratios of women in servant cargos that included convicts, indigents, and kidnapped persons.

Early modern women who were indentured servants were in a precarious position. Often women's experiences in servitude paralleled those of men. However, women also experienced particular constraints and risks in servitude. In early modern England, women's rights were significantly limited in comparison with those of men and with modern conceptions of human rights. However, they included rights to life, subsistence, religious participation, some property, and inheritance, as well as various rights associated with social status and entitlements by birth.[2] In addition, women servants possessed a very significant right that equalled that of men: the right to petition for grievances in the courts. Indeed, in late seventeenth-century Maryland, women were considerably more likely than men to win suits for overextension of indenture and slightly more likely to win any suit.[3] Although they occupied an underprivileged social category, women and, as shown in the next chapter, children were still seen as rights-bearing members of society if they were of English, British, or Irish descent. Nonetheless, their overall rights remained limited in comparison with those of men.

Women additionally faced sexual double standards that restricted their autonomy and placed more stringent standards on their behaviour, although they sometimes found ways to subvert cultural norms to express agency. While all servants were at risk of abuse from their masters, women were more likely than men to be sexually harassed or assaulted by other males of the household, against which there was little recourse. Women's sexual lives were also subject to more coercive control than men's. Women were more likely than men to be punished for fornication, which was usually revealed through pregnancy. If they bore children while under contract, they were typically punished by a public whipping and the length of their contract could be lengthened to compensate for the labour lost during their pregnancy. As a consequence of the coverture laws, women servants who married slaves were sometimes enslaved themselves.

WOMEN'S ENTRY INTO SERVITUDE

Many female indentured servants agreed to enter servitude, like Mary Hillyard and her daughter. They likely travelled for the same reasons as men: to seek opportunity or escape destitution. When the *Conquer* was searched by British authorities, the two kidnapped women aboard were willing to continue with the voyage "if they had their clothes," while a dozen other rescued servants departed the ship, illustrating the fine line between the two alternatives.[4] Some women also saw indenture as a chance for independence and adventure, as shown in Elizabeth Ashbridge's autobiography. Later in her life, Elizabeth Ashbridge regretted disobeying her parents and entering indenture as a mistake of her headstrong youth. Yet she also wrote about her adolescent sense of being deprived opportunity as a woman: "I sometimes wept with sorrow that I was not a boy." Even after experiencing abuse by her master and reconciling with her parents, she rejected her father's offer to pay off her indenture, preferring to pay it off through her own needlework: "my proud heart would not consent to return in so mean a condition, and I therefore chose bondage rather."[5]

Women's experiences also significantly diverged from those of men. A larger percentage of indentured women than men were transported by force. Women in England earned lower wages than men and were eligible for fewer kinds of work. The large numbers of impoverished women and children roaming urban streets, with limited possibilities for earning a stable living, were viewed with consternation by the

authorities.[6] The indigence of so many early modern women, especially single women, meant that to survive many had to resort to crime,
especially theft, vagrancy, or prostitution. The narrow options women
faced must have made the expanded opportunities of indentured servitude seem more desirable. Yet to some extent, it was harder for women
to enter servitude than men. They were generally less desirable labourers and brought a lower price when sold in the colonies, making shippers hesitant to transport them.

EXPECTATIONS OF MARRIAGE

By the conventions and laws of early modern society, women were conceived of as inherently dependent.[7] Unlike men, who were expected to
become productive and independent members of society upon finishing their contracts, women were frequently sent overseas as future
wives, under the expectation that they would marry into colonial society – a form of productivity, but not one based upon autonomy or
independence. Coverture laws prevailed in the colonies as in England,
and a married woman, or *feme covert*, was theoretically a dependent of
her husband and lacked a legal persona. The latter precluded, for
example, her ability to engage in economic transactions or control
property, even an inheritance; to earn separate wages; to act as a witness in court; and, perhaps more beneficially, to bear responsibility for
crimes committed in the presence of her husband.[8] By way of illustra-
tion: in Sarah Taylor's case for abuse against her employers, the Bradnoxes, it is likely that the jury, though clearly sympathetic to Taylor, did
not find Mrs Bradnox guilty because her violence against Taylor had
been committed with the approval of her husband, whose early death
prevented his own prosecution.[9] To some degree, coverture expectations were moderated in the colonies, with both single and married
women taking on unexpected roles in legal cases and economic transactions through necessity.[10] For instance, in eighteenth-century Virginia, there were a number of instances of wives being granted power
of attorney in court.[11]

Single women, the most likely group to become servants, were allowed to take part in economic transactions, such as signing indenture
contracts, but were in a particularly difficult situation. "Masterless
women" were perceived as disorderly and liable to sinful behaviour. as
well as responsible for eliciting sinful behaviour in men. As a result,

The London Begger
Le Gueux de Londres
La pouera di Londra

Figure 6.1 Endemic poverty in London: a woman beggar and her children, from Marcellus Laroon, *The Cryes of the City of London Drawne after the Life* (1688).

many single women in England were forced into service with greater frequency than their male counterparts, with authorities setting their wages. A large percentage of young women spent some time in service even in Britain.[12] Servant women were held to be in a lower status category than married women or single women living in their relatives' household. In addition to being poor and dependent, they were viewed as lacking sexual morality, which justified strict restrictions on their sexuality. They were sometimes termed "wenches," a word that suggested a bondwoman, but also sexual immorality, filth, and disease; the label was even more commonly used to refer to young enslaved women.[13] For example, the term was casually used in Jone Nicculgutt's suit for freedom when one witness, a fellow servant, referred to her as "this wench."[14]

Most women came to the colonies as servants, but after their servitude, there was a significant expectation that they would marry men in colonial society. There were more enslaved African women in the colonies than free white women, but they were not usually considered marriage partners for white men; however, sex ratios were unequal among the enslaved as well, with men outnumbering women. In general, unmarried white women were believed to have excellent prospects for matrimony in the colonies, even if they had pasts that would have made marriage difficult in Britain.[15] Lois Carr's research suggests that poor women did have greater opportunities for marriage in the Chesapeake than in England.[16] John Hammond, the promoter of colonization, wrote that women could easily "advance themselves in marriage," yet at the same time, he cautioned against single women living alone: "I advise them to sojourn in a house of honest repute" because though even "loose" women "seldome live long unmarried," if they were to "match" with men who were "desolute," they would "never live handsomly or [be] ever respected."[17] Similarly, the more blunt George Alsop wrote: "the women that go over into this province as servants, have the best luck here as in any place of the world besides; for they are no sooner on shoar, but they are courted into a copulative matrimony."[18]

The possibility of marriage was used by recruiters to entice poor women in Britain into signing indenture contracts, some promising marriage within a few months.[19] The unequal gender ratio among English settlers also led to requests by colonial authorities to send women to marry into colonial society without the necessity of working in service, instigating transportation plans by the English government specifically targeting women.[20] From 1619, the first session of the Virginia Assembly, lawmakers discussed how to bring more English women into the colony. In 1620, Virginia requested one hundred "maids to made wives" as well as male servants. The women were not to be servants and not to be sold but, rather, allowed to choose a husband. The lack of a servitude requirement was intended to incentivize women to come to the colony, where they could gain the status of a wife and the safety of a household without committing to years of hard labour.[21] In 1660, James Ley Earl of Marlborough attempted to rectify the gender imbalance among English settlers in Jamaica by encouraging "poor maids," preferably not prisoners, to come to Jamaica "for planters' wives." Dowries were not necessary, he pointed out, because "the custom of the planter is to give, not to require anything with his wife," a point doubtlessly intended to reassure his English audience that such women would be acceptable partners for wealthy planters.[22] Indeed, while poor English women had traditionally provided their own wherewithal for a marriage, for higher levels of society, the frequent necessity of waiving dowries in the early colonial period may have contributed to the practice fading in the American colonies. Of course, servant women remained more likely to marry men from the same socio-economic level, like Abigail Shanks, whose future husband John Shanks, a well-to-do former servant, paid off her indenture and soon after married her.[23] However, the repeated attempts to bring in women suggest that, overall, the idea of an overseas marriage was not sufficiently enticing for many women.[24]

Potential marriage prospects aside, most transported women were sent to indentured labour, often by force. In 1653, a Bristol merchant applied to ship 250 Irish women to New England. This was turned down, but when he modified his request to a cargo of male and female "beggars and vagabonds" from Cork, it was granted.[25] Supplying marriageable women was likely a motivation behind Henry Cromwell's plans to send 1,000 Irish girls to Jamaica.[26] Most requests for women specified that only "respectable" poor women were to be sent over. However, in some cases, these schemes seem to have included women who would otherwise have been undesirable marriage partners, such as a 1656 proposal to send English prostitutes to Jamaica as potential wives. This scheme was eventually abandoned.[27] Even so, prostitutes could rise socio-economically by agreeing to travel to the colonies to marry colonial men, though in some cases, prostitutes appear to have seen the colonial milieu as an opportunity to continue practicing their trade rather than settle into a domestic arrangement.[28] For example, John Hammond wrote critically of the early days of the Virginia

Colony when, in order to supply servants for the colonies, there "were jayls emptied, youth seduced, infamous women drilled in."[29]

CONVICT WOMEN

Convict women represented a relatively small proportion of the servant women transported across the ocean, but because of their encounters with the courts, more records remain about them than about any other group. Their criminal records provide details not only about the reasons for their transportation but also about the stratagems that ordinary poor women developed to tackle the obstacles of survival in early modern London. Some women showed extraordinary initiative in forwarding their criminal careers, which usually revolved around subterfuge, deceit, and scams rather than the outright violence more common to male convicts.

A striking example can be found in the criminal career of Elizabeth Longman, a habitual lawbreaker, who was condemned to death in 1676 for repeated thievery and for returning early from transportation, the punishment for her prior offences. Longman had been gone overseas only fourteen months before her indenture contract was bought off through a "collection" of money by her criminal associates in England, referred to by the magistrate as "the brotherhood." However, by returning early, she was evading punishment. After returning to England, Longman resumed her career in theft, was caught and imprisoned in Newgate, and was then found to have coordinated the robbery of "a person of quality" while still imprisoned.[30] She was presented to the court as an audacious instigator who had reportedly incited her associates to theft, once seeing some unguarded silver in a wealthy household and opportunistically saying: "And will you only see it? ... then you deserve to starve indeed, when fortune puts booty, as it were, in your mouths, and you are such cowards, that you dare not take it."[31] Even when convicted of multiple crimes, Longman continued to fight for her life, claiming pregnancy, but to no avail.[32] The pregnancy defence or "pleading the belly" (discussed in greater detail below) conferred at least a temporary and usually a permanent reprieve from punishment – if the claimant was believed.[33] Longman represents a particularly interesting case. She appears to have been a leader in her criminal gang, which explains the collection in order to pay off her contract and return passage, and why she was essential to the later theft plans. It is difficult to determine how common it was for women to have risen to her position within the criminal hierarchy of directing the kind and number of men implied by the term "brotherhood." She was clearly a person of resourcefulness and proficiency in her trade, yet her allusion to starvation indicates a substantial incentive pushing poverty-stricken women into a life of crime. Longman's inability to escape her final sentence resulted from jury perceptions that she was a hardened criminal.

The life trajectory of Mall Floyd was one of dabbling in crime rather than participating in a criminal organization. In 1674, she was convicted of enticing an eight-year-old girl into an unfamiliar London neighbourhood, robbing her of her valuable clothing, and then abandoning her. Fortunately, the crying child was taken in by a kindly passerby, and her parents were eventually found. After being jailed, Floyd pleaded for transportation as a respite from a capital sentence, which was granted on 17 July 1674. She too appears to have been a habitual criminal, as the court clerk sarcastically wrote that she "was committed to Newgate (having been often a distressed lady before in that inchanted castle)."[34] She may have then been transported, or may have remained in England, resumed her crimes, and ultimately faced a worse punishment, because a year later, an unnamed woman described as "the woman that stripped the children of their cloaths" was sentenced to death at Newgate. Like Longman, this woman, who was perhaps Floyd, attempted to plead pregnancy but was turned down.[35]

A similar story was that of Mary Carleton, a notorious con artist convicted of fraud, polygamy, and theft. She was transported to Jamaica in 1671 but returned within two years. Carleton, who was known for her wit, wrote a popular memoir and acted in a play about her own life.[36] Even the *Newgate Calendar*, a collection of condemnatory stories about executed felons, half-admiringly described her as a "prodigious woman, who, had she been virtuously inclined, was capable of being the phoenix of her age." Nonetheless, she too died on the gallows after attempting a last-minute pregnancy plea.[37]

Like today, it was apparently difficult to leave a life of lawlessness because the desperation or incentives that had instigated criminal activities continued to exist. Another woman, Jane Voss, referred to as "a notorious theife," boldly stole the Lord Chancellor's symbolic mace as part of her extensive criminal history. Sentenced to death, she claimed she was pregnant, and her punishment was reduced to transportation. In Voss's case, the pregnancy claim was invalidated after "a long time continued in prison" proved it false, but her sentence of transportation still held. She returned to England at the end of her service, resumed her career of theft even after her husband was executed, and was herself eventually executed.[38] However, there must have been other women like Longman, Floyd, and Voss who managed to evade capture to continue their previous life paths, whether criminal or otherwise.

Pleading the Belly

One commonality in all of these cases was pleading the belly – the pregnancy defence. The available means of reprieve were different for men and women. Men could sometimes win reprieve for benefit of the clergy, but women did not legally receive benefit of the clergy until two statutes passed in 1623 and 1692.[39] For example, transcripts from the trial of a woman found guilty of bigamy in 1676 and condemned to die related that she was not eligible to be reprieved, "her sex not being capable of the benefit of the clergy."[40] Bigamy was a serious crime, especially for a woman, and probably limited the availability of recourse in this case. However, in other circumstances, convicted women could, and did, ask for reduced punishments. For women, these would normally consist of either branding on the hand or transportation. For instance, in December 1678, the sentences for a group of convicts condemned to capital sentences were reduced: "those to whom the benefit of clergy, as men, and the punishment of branding, as women, was allowed."[41] In capital cases, courts were more likely to be lenient toward those who were young, first-time offenders and those who seemed regretful.[42]

The existence of a pregnancy defence meant that both actual and claimed pregnancy could become a strategy for women to escape punishment when convicted of capital crimes. In theory, a woman was to be brought back before the court after delivering a baby to plead her case again; in practice, pregnancy reprieves usually turned into transportation or, more often, release through respite from the king.[43] One consideration was the financial cost of care for the infant if the mother was executed or transported. Parishes preferred for women to provide for their own children, even if the mother was considered to demonstrate depraved morals by bearing illegitimate children.[44] Contemporaries sometimes suspected that women might have deliberately incurred pregnancy in jail in order to be reprieved. For example, in

October 1685, Newgate's bishop berated the condemned criminals to repent, including three women who had successfully pled pregnancy. He expressed suspicion that their pregnancies had been incurred in jail, "a very sinful artifice to prevent a sudden execution, hoping thereby to get a transportation." He referred to "their respit from death" as a certain fact.[45] Early modern jails consisted of large open rooms in which criminals had opportunity to consort with each other as well as with guards, providing opportunities for both voluntary sexual activity and rape. Rape was not a concern for prison authorities, who seem to have assumed that pregnancies were deliberately incurred, consistent with the early modern perception that conception could only occur if a woman had consented to sex.[46] Thus, contemporaries often considered women who became pregnant in prison or single women who entered prison pregnant to be morally depraved. Indeed, pleading the belly normally only succeeded once. If women were recommitted for another crime, they could not use this defence again.[47] To some extent, this must have reduced the number of women claiming this defence.

Nonetheless, the pregnancy defence was often successful, despite medical and moral obstacles. In an age when medical knowledge was scant, pregnancy could only positively be established if women were "quick with child," meaning that there was perceptible motion from the fetus, usually at well past four months' gestation.[48] This could have been possible even for pregnancies that had begun during the time that a woman was imprisoned because offenders often waited weeks or months for a trial.

In order to verify pregnancy, courts looked to those with expertise. Rather than turning to medical practitioners, women's claims of pregnancy had to be attested to by a "jury of women" responsible for gauging whether a woman was pregnant. These women, also referred to as a "jury of matrons," were chosen for their respectability.[49] The term "jury" implies that they were expected to exercise juridical as well as medical expertise, as suggested in the statement, "the jury of women bringing in their verdict it was truth," yet officially they were appointed to make a medical determination.[50] Nonetheless, the unusually high percentage of positive "verdicts" as well as the statements of contemporaries indicates that these juries sometimes showed sympathy toward the accused. Between 1674 and 1750, out of 746 capital cases with a verdict of guilty at the Old Bailey, 200 women, or about 26.8 per cent, were able to successfully plead the belly.[51]

That means that more than a quarter of women found guilty of capital crimes were respited for pregnancy. This seems an extraordinarily high figure if those pregnancies were assumed to be real, especially if one considers that the proportion of women accused of capital crimes likely encompassed all ages of women and some who may have been too early in their term to be confirmed as pregnant. These figures are still more striking because some women convicts did not claim pregnancy or were excluded from the pregnancy defence because they had already employed it previously.[52] Legal commentators remarked on this trend, like seventeenth-century jurist Matthew Hale, who observed that "I have rarely found but the compassion of their sex is gentle to them in their verdict, if there be any colour to support a sparing verdict."[53]

One such case is that of a woman sentenced to be burnt at the stake for coining (counterfeiting). Coining was a felony, and a form of treason since 1555, punished by drawing and quartering of men and burning of women. However, most people regarded this as excessive punishment, and magistrates and jurors were often sympathetic to the accused.[54] In December 1677, the unnamed woman was sentenced to be burnt to death. Her situation was particularly egregious because after she had obtained her husband's acquittal by claiming that he was sleeping "in another room in bed" while she was melting down the stolen metal, he was asked in court if he regretted her conviction and had callously responded, "I am very willing the law should have its course: better one than both."[55] However, she claimed pregnancy, which was affirmed five days later by the jury of matrons. The execution was suspended by the court "that the innocent babe might not perish with the guilty mother."[56] What happened to her is not recorded, but women who were found pregnant were usually freed – in theory temporarily, but without efforts being made later to locate them.[57]

Hale's statement also implies the exercise of judicial judgment. A percentage of women claiming pregnancy were turned down by the jury of women, though accurate figures are difficult to come by. Court recorders usually did not record pleas, only final sentences or remission and reprieve of those sentences, although they sometimes included the reasons for the latter categories. Elizabeth Longman's case history, for example, demonstrated that she was a habitual criminal. If we assume that the juries of matrons were influenced by factors other than medical findings, we can also see them wielding negative judgments in cases involving incorrigibles and other unsympathetic individuals, who were indeed least likely to be found pregnant.

Coverture

A further defence available only to married women was through coverture, the legal precept that a married woman was not fully legally responsible for crimes committed with the awareness of her husband. In some cases, only the husband was prosecuted for crimes committed by a married couple.[58] Some women employed a kind of coverture defence in court, claiming that they had committed crimes while under their husband's authority, an argument that could potentially result in a complete dismissal of charges. For example, in December 1678, a woman was apprehended with a gang of horse thieves that included her two brothers and husband, but was freed after claiming "what she did, was done by coertion" even though she was caught riding one of the horses.[59] Another woman argued that one of her confederates in a theft was her husband; though she produced a marriage certificate, the jury decided it was counterfeit and found her guilty.[60] On the other hand, married women who were convicted of murdering their husbands – "petit treason" – were virtually always executed as hardened and incorrigible criminals. Women were far more likely to be executed for killing a spouse than men.[61]

Transportation

Like Mall Floyd, another way to stave off capital punishment was to angle for transportation as a lesser evil. This, of course, was also an option for men. However, it appears that women and men were not convicted at the same rates, with a higher percentage of women receiving the sentence of transportation than men. There were no legal guidelines advising more lenient sentencing for unmarried women, but the practice of the law was highly variable, and courts had significant discretion in both conviction and sentencing.[62]

In practice, disparities occurred for a number of reasons. It appears that some magistrates were more likely to reprieve women than men by transmuting women's sentences to transportation.[63] In other instances, it appears that courts were more likely to prosecute female rather than male offenders.[64] Likewise, juries often gave lesser penalties to both men and women in order to prevent death sentences, but also varied in their tendencies to be more or less favourable toward women. Often, lenience was based upon the character of the accused. However, this placed an additional onus on women to prove that they were dependents under coverture or mainly of good character.[65]

There were many individual cases in which sentencing was comparable for both sexes but also a significant number in which disparities existed, with women more likely to be acquitted, reprieved, or given reduced sentences, especially for capital crimes. This was particularly marked in cases where sentencing guidelines were dissimilar, as in capital offences with benefit of the clergy.[66] For example, in a case tried at the Old Bailey in October 1694, out of nine men and five women initially condemned to die, all of the women but none of the men had their sentences commuted to transportation.[67] Similarly, in 1718, out of twenty-two offenders convicted of capital offenses, seventeen were respited, including all seven of the women – five for transportation and two who successfully pled pregnancy presumably released.[68] These cases and others show women were less likely to be charged with transportable crimes (about 25 per cent of cases) but more likely to be sentenced to transportation than men (about 33 per cent).[69] The actual number may have been even higher because of the sparse reporting of sentences. In addition to the 200 out of 746 women respited for pregnancy mentioned earlier, another 38 women at the Old Bailey, or about 5 per cent, were respited for other reasons; the outcome is unknown for 491 or 65.8 per cent of the capital cases involving women.[70] One reason for passage of the 1718 Transportation Act was that courts were reluctant to give too many capital sentences for lesser crimes that could be respited to transportation, but shippers were disinclined to ship women. Making transportation a sentence instead of a respite allowed the government to ship away women who were accumulating in large numbers in prison.[71] While relieving women from execution, the tendency to punish women with transportation actually resulted in a higher frequency of punishment for women, some of whom would have been simply reprieved in the past.[72]

Convict women have left more records behind them than women from other populations, but most female indentured servants were not convicts. Rather, they were women who found themselves in extremely limiting circumstances, typically acute poverty. Indeed, the majority of indentured servants, men or women, were willing migrants who had contracted for their labour in London or Bristol. However, willing women servants also faced problems in becoming servants, especially in selling their labour, as they were often perceived as less valuable labourers than men.[73] On landing on the western shores of the Atlantic, captains sold servants' contracts to the highest bidders. From the captains' perspective, then, this meant that women were less lucrative cargos for shipping since they had a lower market value. Sometimes women were able to raise their labour value by agreeing to serve for longer contracts than men, up to seven years.[74] This was also true of child servants, who contracted (or were contracted) for the longest terms.

WOMEN'S WORK IN THE COLONIES

Once women arrived in the colonies, they mostly worked in typically female occupations such as domestic work in household, including cooking and child care; dairying; and working with poultry. However, many faced new labour arrangements, being required to take on male labour working in the fields.[75] Even though propagandist John Hammond had assured his readers that "the women are not (as is reported) put into the ground to worke, but occupie such domestique imployments and houswifery as in England, that is dressing victuals, righting up the house, milking, imployed about dayries, washing, sowing, &c. and both men and women have times of recreations, as much or more than in any part of the world besides," he had qualified his statement by adding that "som wenches that are nasty, beastly and not fit to be so imployed are put into the ground [i.e., employed at farm labour], for reason tells us, they must not at charge be transported and then mantained for nothing, but those that prove so aukward are rather burthensome then servants desirable or usefull."[76] Readers of his tract may well have been suspicious of his disclaimer of what "is reported" or the criterion that determined which "wenches" were "nasty" and "beastly" and destined to work in the fields. On the other hand, Revel described his first master owning six male servants who worked in the fields, "Besides four transport[ed] women in the house, / To wait upon his daughter and his spouse."[77]

Yet some indentured women were surprised and displeased to find that they were expected to do heavy farm labour that in England had been the purview of men. Often the tasks most associated with women's work were at least partially done by the mistress, while

women indentured servants were expected to take part in tilling, hoe-
ing, and other physically demanding work.[78] Part of the complaint of
The Trappan'd Maiden was that she was forced to do farm labour typically the role of men in England: "The axe and the hoe / have wrought
my overthrow," and "I have play'd my part, / Both at plow and at cart,"
while "Billats [billets, i.e., firewood] from the wood, / Upon my back
they load," in addition to duties at more typical female tasks such as
bringing water, grinding grain, and caring for a child.[79] In the satiric
Sot-weed Factor, on the other hand, an indentured woman was
described at domestic labour and "weeding corn or feeding swine,"
outdoor farm tasks but less heavy.[80] In colonies like Barbados, where
the work for servants consisted mainly of hard manual labour out-
doors, there were few women servants by the end of the seventeenth
century.[81] The reality, borne out by most of the court cases that mentioned women, seems to have been a mixture of a gendered division
of domestic labour and outside work.

WOMEN AND FREEDOM DUES

Women's indentures also differed from men's in the allotment of freedom dues: women's dues were usually less valuable than men's, which
is consistent with the lower rates of pay for women labourers in
Britain that were enshrined in tradition and contracts.[82] Men often
received land, tools, or money, but women frequently received dues of
clothing, a valuable form of moveable capital in some ways but not
necessarily as productive as the male dues. For example, in the 1654
scheme to entice Irish servants to the continent, men were to receive
money, while women would obtain clothing.[83] Clothing was particularly suitable for women who were expected to eventually marry into
a male-headed household, taking their goods with them.[84] During
their contracted period, women rarely received skilled vocational
training, except in domestic duties.

In the early days of settlement, when land was still relatively plentiful and cheap in the mainland colonies, there were some expectations of similar, though not always equal, freedom dues. A 1667
advertisement urging colonists to come to the Carolinas stated that
"every servant at the expiration of their service (which is four years)
are to have the same quantity of land for him or herself that their
master had for their bringing over ... also the master is bound to give

them two suits of apparel and a set of tools to work with when he is out of his time."[85]

Although the pronouns are not consistent, this seems to indicate an equal assurance for dues. Nonetheless, women servants were not counted equal to men. In the same document, masters were encouraged to bring male rather than female servants by being awarded headrights that bestowed more land per male servant: 100 acres for each family member and each male servant, and 50 acres for each female servant and each slave.[86] In 1669, the Lords Proprietors of Carolina issued similar provisions and announced that newly arrived free individuals over age sixteen would receive 150 acres, plus 150 acres for each man servant, but 100 acres for each woman servant or each male under sixteen. The servants themselves would receive equal amounts regardless of sex: 100 acres.[87] Two years later, the Lords Proprietors reduced the amount of land made available to women servants and ordained that subsequently arriving free persons and male servants would receive 100 acres, while women and males under sixteen would receive 70 acres "to his or her proper use when out of their time and to their heirs for ever."[88] This was reiterated in 1672, but the amount of land given in male servants' dues was reduced to 70 acres.[89] Thus in the Carolinas, as in other colonies, women were less valued as colonists and also received lower freedom dues than men. It is unclear whether the quality of land given to men and women varied, or whether women trained mainly as domestic servants could effectively cultivate their land.

As the availability of land decreased, the disparity between women's and men's dues persisted. By 1676, men's freedom dues for those serving at the custom of the country in Maryland consisted of clothing, corn, and tools, while women received only clothes and corn.[90] From 1715, both men and women were to receive clothing, but men obtained farm tools and a gun, while women got three barrels of corn. Thus, while men were given productive tools to enter independent life, women were given means of sustenance, presumably to provide for them until they married or entered new work arrangements.[91] It may also be that land was perceived as more appropriate dues for men since women's indentured servitude was encouraged by other means: from the 1680s, women's terms of indenture got shorter relative to men's, apparently to incentivize women to migrate into the colonies.[92]

VIOLENCE AGAINST SERVANT WOMEN

Like men, women servants were vulnerable to violence from their masters and mistresses, as several of the examples in this book show, such as the cases of Margarett Redfearne, Ann Beetle, Sarah Taylor, Mary Baines, Margarett Roberts, Charity Dollen, Sarah Hall, Alice Brasse, and others.[93] But women were more likely to be abused by their mistresses than men were. In addition, women's proximity to the house made them particularly vulnerable to hostile attentions from their masters and mistresses, and there appear to be more frequent cases of violent abuse of female than of male servants. For example, women were almost five times more likely than men to claim physical abuse in court cases in seventeenth-century Maryland.[94]

A poignant case comes from 1637 Virginia, in which Elizabeth Starkey complained in court of "diverse unjust and rigorous abuses done and offered unto her by Alexander Mountney." Starkey was in an exceptionally commodified position even for a servant, and her labour was shared between two men. Mountney possessed only a "halfe share in her" with the other half held by James Holloway, the two men having split the cost of her indenture. The Accomack County Virginia Court's decision was to transfer Starkey completely into Holloway's service, but left Holloway owing Mountney compensation for his initial payment.[95]

Beyond the more usual violence of beatings, women were more likely to be the targets of sexual violence. Women servants, whether indentured or not, were particularly vulnerable to unwelcome sexual advances and rape by their masters and other males within the household.[96] Likely these dangers were exacerbated in the more isolated, haphazard, and less-regulated life of the colonies. Although rape was illegal, it was difficult to prove and prosecute, particularly as women's statements were regarded as less trustworthy than those of men. In seventeenth-century Maryland, rape was usually presented as a charge in cases of illegitimate birth or repeated abuse by masters. While women might be removed from the household, the perpetrators were rarely punished. Rape was a felony, but as English jurist Matthew Hale argued in his seventeenth-century treatise on legal precedents, it was one of the crimes most difficult to prove (together with witchcraft) because although "many times persons are really guilty, yet such an evidence, as is satisfactory to prove it, can hardly be found."[97] It appears that in seventeenth-century Delaware, though rape was probably significantly under-reported, cases of rape and attempted rape were virtually always prosecuted with severity.[98] Nonetheless, women were often reluctant to report rape because of the difficulty of proof, the possibility of retaliation, and the potential damage to the victim's reputation, factors that still operate as deterrents today.

In her autobiography, Elizabeth Ashbridge alluded to a sexual assault by her master. She described how at first her indenture went "pretty well," but soon "the scale turned, occasioned by a difference that happened wherein I was innocent." After she had repulsed his advances or had attempted to, her formerly lenient master changed, having "set himself against me and was inhuman," giving her insufficient clothing and no shoes even in winter. Two years after "the difference" occurred, Ashbridge told another woman, who informed others, and "by her means he heard of it." Her "barbarous" master "sent for the town whipper to correct me" for spreading the rumour, even though "he knew it was true." She escaped the whipping because when ordered to strip, she begged her master to pity her "for my father's sake." After wrestling with himself during "a turn about the room," her master let her escape punishment – perhaps because, unlike most indentured servants, Ashbridge had a father who, as a surgeon, "had no great estates, yet he lived well" and she had some relatives in America. Yet her reputation had been damaged. She wrote: "but now I began to think my credit gone. For they said many things of me, which I thank God were not true. And here I suffered so much cruelty I could not bear it."[99]

In most cases, historical evidence of rape comes from the courts. In 1677, Judith Platts complained to the Suffolk County Massachusetts Court that her master was physically and sexually abusing her, engaging in "wanton and lascivious carriages towards her & cruell beating of her." Her master was fined, and Platt was freed from her indenture.[100]

In a sad case from 1659, Joseph Wicks sued Richard Owens in the Maryland Court of Chancery for deception in the sale of the contract of Ann Gould, a servant woman who had been severely infected with syphilis and who had died within a few months. She had been promised to be "in sownd & perfect health." Gould had described to witness Ann Hinson how she had been raped and beaten by Richard Owens, who "did make use of her body, after a very inhumane manner" and had infected her with "the pox." This case is notable for the way in which Gould, who remained an unnamed "servant woman" in most of the depositions, was treated as chattel by almost everyone concerned. The case revolved not around Owens's mistreatment of Gould but on his misrepresentation of her as sound merchandise and on the infection risk to the Wicks family, who had employed her to cook their food and wash their laundry before they realized the source of her condition. She was repeatedly described in the testimonies as "loathsome" and "stinking." The case records do describe Gould's plaintive cry that she had been "undone" by Owens and mention the "pitty" of some of the witnesses, who tried to provide palliatives to "ease or moderate the payne she endured" and "use their best skill & endeavor for her cure." Although the defendant's lawyer argued that Gould had appeared to be healthy when purchased and that Owens therefore had fulfilled the terms of the sale, Owens was ordered to provide the Wicks with another woman servant with a four-year contract and to pay the court fees. He does not appear to have incurred a penalty for rape, or for that matter, murder.[101]

The risk of making an accusation of rape is demonstrated by a 1657 Maryland case. Margreet Manning, servant to Thomas South, had charged her master with rape. After an interrogation by the court, she withdrew her complaint but was then prosecuted for slander and sentenced to ten lashes. She would also have had to continue serving in South's household, leaving her at risk of further assault and reprisals.[102] Likewise, when two servants of Captain Hilary Stringer accused their master of "occasioning the death" of his servant woman Ellinor Tanner in 1681, the Accomack County Virginia Court, after deliberating, decided that it was slander and ordered the servants extra time on their contracts.[103]

WOMEN SERVANTS AND SEXUAL REPUTATION

Even if women servants engaged in consensual sexual relations, the risks and penalties were potentially more severe for them than for men. Laura Gowing's work shows the importance of reputation for early modern women, a pitfall Elizabeth Ashbridge had experienced first-hand.[104] Early modern women who were indentured servants were in a precarious position according to societal norms, coming from a social class that was often assumed to be sexually promiscuous while often exposed to sexual harassment from males in the household, whether the master's family or fellow servants.[105] However, there was also potentially some legal protection against the most damaging claims.

In a case that illustrates the vulnerability of reputation for an indentured woman, in 1663, Henry Spinke accused Luke Barber of slander for calling Spinke's wife Elinor a whore. Barber had been the shipper who had brought the former Elinor Edwards to Maryland as an indentured servant. He acknowledged making the insult but defended his words by saying that "hee brought none but rogues & whoares out of England, some out of Bridewell, some out of Newgate, & some from the whipping post," and added further that he had previously observed her "divers[e] times" with "her coates up, & th[a]t rogue Thomas Hewes w[i]th his breeches downe."[106] Henry Spinke responded by asking for additional damages because of the harm to Elinor's reputation, asserting that she "has been almost five yeares in this country without the least blemish of immodesty," yet now, because of Barber's "slanderous speeches," she had been "wounded ... in her creditt, reputacon & honor," a harm that could only be remedied by "reparacon" awarded by the court. The jury awarded the Spinkes 30,000 pounds of tobacco, but unfortunately, on an appeal by Barber to the Maryland Assembly, inconsistencies between the deposition and the warrant led to a voiding of the case, with both parties responsible for their own court charges.[107] As in other cases where jury judgments were revisited by the Assembly, Barber's influence prevailed over the less-affluent Spinkes. While demonstrating the precariousness of servant women's reputations, this case also evidences that women servants could become respectable wives.

Although servant women's reputations were vulnerable, like male servants, they were members of the social body and thus theoretically protected from libelous accusations. In 1640s Virginia, Mary Jolly, an ailing servant woman, was accused by Francis Millicent of fornication, saying that she had been "in bed with" another man and also "if she were not with child, she was lately with child." However, Jolly's mistress, Elizabeth Neale, defended her and accused Millicent of "opprobrious speeches" against Jolly. After witnesses testified to both Millicent's slander and to Jolly's good behaviour, the court declared that Millicent had "unjustly and wrongfully scandalized and defamed Mary Jolly," ordered him to make a public apology in church, and sentenced him to thirty lashes.[108] It is not clear whether Jolly was an indentured servant or had been hired to work for wages, but this case illustrates the complex relationships of servitude. Her mistress, a *feme covert*, had sued Millicent on behalf of Jolly. Furthermore, Mrs Neale was caring for her own bedridden servant. However, this case seems to have hinged on the personal relationship between Mary Jolly and Elizabeth Neale; if Mrs Neale had not been so inclined, it is unlikely that anyone else would have defended Jolly's reputation.

In that regard, servant women rarely possessed advocates within the community, and especially so when first arriving in the colonies. In 1652, Judith Catchpole was accused before the Maryland Provincial Court of a number of offences that suggested witchcraft (though the term was not used in the charges). Her crimes supposedly occurred while Catchpole was shipboard crossing the ocean and included giving birth to and murdering a baby; cutting "a maids skinn off her throat and she never felt it and the said Judith Catchpole sowed the wound up againe"; grinding a knife with which she then "prickt a seaman in the back," apparently wounding or killing him, but then she "greased his back and he stood up again," after which she "was to kill three or four men more." The court was apparently skeptical of these charges, and the lack of victims and evidence, and ordered a jury of "able women" to examine Catchpole to ascertain whether she had borne a child. The jury of women returned their "verdict" that Catchpole had not recently done so. Based on this determination, and the opinion of the court that the main "party accusing was not in sound mind," Catchpole was acquitted.[109] This case demonstrates both the social disadvantages of servant women and the potential for even-handed protection by the law.

SERVANT WOMEN, "FORNICATION," AND "BASTARDY"

Although sex outside of marriage was a punishable offence for any-one, people were rarely punished unless they were caught in the act or the relationship produced a child. Women's sexuality was tightly controlled throughout early modern Europe as well as in the colonies. But because of the strict regulations governing indenture contracts, among the harshest penalties were imposed in the colonial context.[110] Typically, servant women were not allowed to marry or bear children while in servitude. Servant women who engaged in "fornication" were risking whipping, additional time in servitude, and the loss of their children.[111] Yet sex outside of marriage remained a relatively frequent charge in both Maryland and Virginia, and servants, who could not marry and were very vulnerable to coercion, were charged at a much higher rate than free women.[112]

From the earliest period, servant women and men required the permission of their master or mistress to marry while in servitude. For example, from 1619, Virginia laws stated that servants could not marry without penalties, which by 1643 meant an extra year in servitude for both spouses.[113] This was reiterated in a 1657 Virginia act mandating that if servants married without permission, they would be liable to serve an extra year of servitude.[114] In 1661, the law also added fines for ministers who presided over the marriages of servants without their masters' permission, and reiterated the additional time for those who married.[115]

Fornication outside of marriage was against the law, but was usually only prosecuted if a birth occurred, although a substantiated accusation could bring about a court case and penalties. In such cases, the penalty was usually less harsh, as when servants George Wakefield and Ursula Bayley were caught in the act in 1649 Virginia and made "to do penance" in the chapel "wearing a white sheet and a white rod in their hands."[116] In Virginia, couples were punished if a child was born too soon – six months or less – after the marriage.[117] Maryland apparently let these cases slide, as I have not seen any in the records. Early modern courts were somewhat haphazardly run by modern standards, providing leeway for avoiding punishment. Amy Markes, a spinster, was summoned to appear before the Maryland Provincial Court for fornication in 1670. She duly arrived at court, but fortunately for her, the informant did not appear, and she was acquitted.[118] Bastardy, however, was a serious accusation, one that tarnished not only the parents but also the child, as evinced by the case of James Lewis. The planter was sentenced to the harsh penalty of thirty-nine lashes for saying that the governor, the chancelor, and one of the Provincial Court justices were "all rouges" and that the justice was in addition a "bastard."[119]

The courts paid more attention when sexual encounters resulted in an infant who potentially required financial support from the parish in England or from the county in America, including the children of indentured servants. In England, men who were the fathers of illegitimate children were usually made to pay the parish for their maintenance, but the norms of English law were not always fully implemented in the colonies.[120] Courts did try to make fathers maintain the child, but if the father was a servant, the solution was usually to put the child into indenture until the father finished his term of service, at which time he was potentially liable for reimbursing the costs.[121] In practice, however, the children of indentured mothers were usually indentured themselves until age twenty-one. In Britain, a single woman with a bastard, if she was not a resident, could be forced from the parish without any provisions for subsistence. In the colonies, the same could happen to a single freewoman. For example, in 1693, Susanah Church, a single woman ("spinster") was charged with fornication and having a child out of wedlock. Because she stated that the child had been "[be]gott[en] and born" in Accomack County in Virginia, she was ordered to pay security and leave Somerset County in Maryland within two months.[122] However, servants who bore children were residents and not allowed to leave their servitude.

There was some contemporary understanding of the constraints under which women servants lived. A 1662 Virginia act expressed disapproval of "dissolute" masters who had "gotten their maides with child" while hoping to continue to have "benefitt of their service." However, the law continued with little sympathy. While it might seem that such a woman "should be freed from that service," such an approach was problematic because women would then make false claims about the parentage of their infants: "it might probably induce such loose persons to lay all their bastards to their masters." Thus, the law concluded, women who gave birth to their master's children would serve the rest of their indentures, and then be sold by the parish for a further two years.[123]

In theory, both parents of an illegitimate child were to receive punishment, but some women were unwilling, afraid, or unable to report the father, or their claim of paternity was not accepted by the court. Women were put under a lot of compulsion by the court to name their child's father.[124] Generally, if a father could be identified, the woman's penalty was often reduced, either because of her co-operativeness in naming in the father or because the father himself promised or was made to pay compensation to the county.[125] Most, but not all, women did in fact name the father of their child.[126] If the woman did not divulge the father's name, midwives were enjoined to try to force women to name the father of the child during labour.[127] Accusations of rape were rare in such cases, likely because of the belief that conception could only occur in consensual encounters.[128]

However, it was obviously difficult to prove the paternity of a reluctant man. A sizable minority of women, perhaps a third, do not seem to have named names, even though in both colonies, in addition to a penalty of extra servitude, women who bore illegitimate children could be whipped ten to forty lashes, "well laid on," "on the bare back," and until "the blood flows." This punishment was rarely inflicted on the fathers of illegitimate children, although fathers who were servants might suffer whippings or extra terms of labour.[129] Despite the wording of the 1662 Virginia law, there was little recognition of the compulsion a servant woman was under, either physical or psychological, to engage in sex with men in positions of power, especially their masters.[130] This is delineated by a 1661 Maryland bastardy case in which the paternity of Elesabeth Lockett's child was initially unclear because she had previously had sexual encounters with other men than the father of child, and her master had also sexually abused her. The women attending the birth had asked her "w[ha]t hur master dide to hure in the husks in the tobaco house" to which she replied that he "did butt tickell hur," which apparently referred to sexual contact short of intercourse, because she went on to say that "she never knew hur master but by his face and hands."[131]

Maryland laws, the first not passed until 1658, were somewhat more lenient toward women, focusing on the loss of income for the master, but also the costs of child care for the parish. If a pregnant woman could be made to testify to the identity of the father, he could be made responsible for any costs.[132] The laws stated that "bastard-bearing servant women not being able to prove the father shall satisfy damages by servitude, or otherwise," but if the father could be verified, "then the father, if a servant, shall pay half damages: if a freeman, he shall satisfy the whole damage by servitude, or otherwise, as the court shall think fit."[133] In a 1693 case, Elizabeth Lawrence became pregnant by her master, John Pope. She had previously complained of his "incessant, unwearied, pationate & violent alurements & temptations" to a witness, but ultimately succumbed. Although Pope tried to deny the charge, he was required to make bond for £50, pay for the support of the child, and maintain good behaviour. Lawrence was ordered twenty days of public work, which was paid off by another man, perhaps recognizing the compulsion she was under, and she was apparently transferred to another master.[134] When Walter Rowles and Joyce Cox, both of whom seem to have been free, had an illegitimate child, only the father, who was an influential man and a constable, was fined 1.000 pounds of tobacco, to be paid to the Lord Proprietary of Maryland.[135] This was double the typical fine of 500 pounds of tobacco per parent. A servant woman was in a more difficult situation, because at issue was the labour still owed the master, as well as the lost labour during the time of pregnancy and early child care. Furthermore, a servant did not possess the financial where-withal to make restitution through a fine. Thus, a servant typically would be whipped and sentenced to additional labour, although some were fined if they could find someone to pay security. For exam-ple, when Andrew Twotley fathered an illegitimate child with Eliza-beth Wharton, servant of Johnathan Kinemant, the penalties for the two parents were quite disparate. Twotley was ordered to pay Kine-mant 500 pounds of tobacco, while Wharton was sentenced to "thirty lashes well laid on her bare backe."[136] If the mother was free while the father was in servitude – an uncommon situation – his penalty might be the lesser because his master could still obtain work from him. In Norfolk County Virginia in 1637, Sarah Purslit, a widow, "being big with child and destitute of any place of abiding" complained to the court, who ordered that she be married to Thomas Hughs, a servant who was "the reported father of her child." The court also mandated that Hughs's master would provide a bushel of corn "for the mainte-nance" of Purslit and "give leave" to Hughs "to go to the said Sarah Purslit at convenient times, not hindering his master's business."[137] In this decision, the court seems to have aimed to facilitate the relation-ship of Sarah and Thomas so as to establish a self-sustaining Hughs household in future and avert the county's expense of supporting a destitute single mother. However, the case also strikingly illustrates the disparity of punishment between male and female servants who had illegitimate children.

In another example, while a servant to Anne Bishopp in Maryland, Rose Deaverley bore a child out of wedlock: she "hath most wickedly, sinfully and shamefully comitted fornication, and of her body born a basterd child" – a formulaic phrase used for other unwed mothers. In March 1691, she admitted her guilt in court and named the father, Alexander Mackswain, and then "prayed that a fine might be taken for her offence" rather than receiving a whipping. She "was ordered to pay twenty five dayes worke" in the parish. Security and her fine (pre-sumably the equivalent value of the work) were paid by Peter Bodkin and Peter Dent, who had paid security for other arrested people and were possibly hired by Mackswain.[138] By the winter of 1692, Deaver-ley had absconded, leaving her child in the care of her former mis-tress, Ann Bishopp, who was raising it.[139] Maryland laws stipulated that "bastard children of women servants shall be maintained by the master or owner of such servants, during the mother's servitude."[140] The extra expenses of the child's care would be paid for by additional servitude from the mother, which was obviously not an option in this case. Many people would have turned the baby over to the county to be indentured, but Bishopp continued to keep the infant, at least for the time being.

In 1663 Virginia, pregnant servant Anne Orthwood was removed from her master's house to the home of the midwife, Ellinor Gething, so she could force Orthwood to divulge the father's name during the birth; also, the court was worried that the master, Lt Col. William Walker, might be the baby's father.[141] Meanwhile, Walker accused Jacob Bishop, the man from whom he had purchased Orthwood, of selling him a pregnant servant. Bishop was fined. During the birth of twins, which resulted in Orthwood's death, the midwife succeeded in obtaining the name of John Kendall, son of Justice William Kendall, from Orthwood.[142] The court, seeking to protect "the said Kendalls future reputation," was at a quandary. On one hand, it insisted that Orthwood's claim of paternity was false because the possible timespan meant only a pregnancy of eight months (which is actually common for twins), but on the other hand, it felt itself bound by the fact that "the law peremptorily declareth that person, who shall at the delivery of such child or children be charged with gitting of the same, shall keep the child or children unavoidably."[143] Eventually, through four lawsuits, Kendall was made responsible, though not acknowledged as the father. Jasper, the one surviving infant, was indentured until age twenty-one; later, he successfully sued for his freedom when his master hoped to detain him for three more years.[144] A salient aspect of this case is the far greater concern for the reputation of the privileged defendant and for the financial obligation to care for the infants than for the death of a young woman.

The bastardy indictment of Owne Mackragh, an Irish woman from Somerset County Maryland in 1673, illustrates many of the typical features of these cases. Mackragh was no longer a servant, but her former status as a servant was entered into the record. The child's father, Francis Roberts, was still a servant. The court ordered that Mackragh either be whipped or provide security for twenty days work on the highways. The short summary implies that the latter course would be undertaken, with the work done by Francis Roberts, who would also be responsible for the child's upkeep.[145] Roberts may have been the same Francis Roberts who eighteen years later in the same county sired another bastard child, though by this time his profession was listed as "planter." That penalty accrued mainly to Roberts, who "hath most wickedly, sinfully & shamefully committed fornication, and upon the body of Mary Mackennie hath begot a basterd child." Mackennie was a "spinster," or single woman, rather than a servant. Her punishment of a whipping was remitted because she was prone to "fitts of sickness," and she was fined instead. Roberts was fined a steep penalty of £30 plus court costs and was required to provide for the upkeep of the child. In addition, he was to pay Mackennie 1,200 pounds of tobacco to maintain the child for the next twelve months.[146]

In contrast, the northern colonies appear to have been more egalitarian with respect to women's responsibility for fornication. In the Delaware Valley regions of Pennsylvania and Jersey, men were charged almost as frequently as women, and often incurred harsher penalties, such as in a seventeenth-century fornication case in which the man incurred twenty lashes to the woman's ten, and the couple were forced to marry.[147] In Barbados in 1652, the governor mandated that both the servant mother and the "reputed father," apparently whether free or not, of an illegitimate child serve three additional years each, or pay another to do the service.[148]

Most indentured women were without community support, in contrast to single freewomen, who still endured disapprobation but might be protected by their families. In Somerset County Maryland in 1791, Mary Hearne, a spinster, gave birth to an illegitimate child. The child's father, Lawrence Burfy, had fled, and Hearne "humbly requested that corporall punishment might be remitted and a fine taken, w[hi]ch was granted." William Hearne, her father, paid for both the fine and for the security for the care of the baby, who was his grandchild.[149] However, for an indentured woman, family members were less likely to be present in the area and to have the financial wherewithal to pay off fines.

SERVANT WOMEN AND MARRIAGE

A man who had promised marriage prior to sexual intercourse could be forced to carry it through, or pay compensation.[150] In Maryland, for example, if a servant woman was able to show proof of "a promise of marriage" and the father of her child was a freeman, "he shall be at his choice either to perform such promise, or recompence her abuse," according to a sum set by the court.[151] For example, pregnant servant Elesabeth Lockett was forced during childbirth to swear on the Bible to the paternity of Thomas Bright as the father of her child. She was originally sentenced to "twenty lashes on hur backe well layd on" but testified that Bright had broken a piece of money to be divided between the two in a betrothal promise, a fact confirmed by a witness. That led the court to give her indemnity, with Bright responsible for fines and court costs.[152] A promise of marriage could allow women servants caught in a bastardy case to attempt to use the law to gain restitution. Joane Langford, a servant woman, sued George Harris, "accusing the said George for begetting a bastard child on her body, and for nonperformance of his promise to marry her, or set her free thereupon." This represented a clever rearticulation of the situation, which implied that Harris was solely responsible. Harris was ordered by the court to provide a bond for 1,600 pounds of tobacco in case he failed to provide for maintaining the child and 250 pounds of tobacco to the woman who had cared for Langford during and after the birth; he apparently voluntarily agreed to pay 500 pounds of tobacco to prevent Langford from being whipped. The records do not mention whether she was freed or whether Harris agreed to marry her.[153]

If a servant woman bore a baby for which the father accepted responsibility and her master was willing to be reasonable, an accommodation could be reached. Servant Anne Carre was summoned to the Somerset County Maryland Court for bearing an illegitimate child in 1671. The father, Edward Hassards, acknowledged the child before the court. Carre was fined 500 pounds of tobacco, Hassards ordered to do work on the roads, and the couple were wed.[154] In 1693, Jone Needham and John Poore, who appears to have been a freeman, had an illegitimate baby. In this case, Needham's master was awarded an extra year of servitude, but agreed to pay her fine and to care for her. Poore was assessed twenty days of work, a bond of £30, and a promise to maintain the child; it appears the two were wed, because Jone later appears with the surname Poore.[155] In March 1671, Talbott County Maryland servants George Thirle and Mary Barnett had an illegitimate child and were sentenced by the court to receive twenty lashes each. However, their master, Henry Coursey, agreed to allow them to marry, and Thirle and Barnett settled with him that "for every child the[y] shall have in his sarvis," they would serve a court-determined additional period of time to compensate him "for loss of time, truble, & charge of bringing up each child."[156] This couple seems to have avoided the whippings and succeeded in constructing a household in which they could expect to remain together, to keep their child, and to receive sufficient wherewithal to raise it, as well as potential additional children, albeit at the cost of additional time of servitude. The agreement also prevented any children from being indentured. This arrangement was probably facilitated by the fact that the two worked for the same master.

Mistresses and masters of servants also sometimes married their servants, either before or after a pregnancy was incurred. Marriage did present a potential successful outcome for women servants. Women like Elinor Spinke could rise in status as a result. The reality, though, was that masters were not usually disposed to release women from indenture early and cobbled-together strategies might not come to fruition. In Maryland, servant Margarett Brent claimed the estate of the deceased Thomas White based on an informal agreement in which he had promised to give her his goods and hoped to marry her.[157] Brent was the servant of William Marshall, but White had hoped to "buy her off." The depositions suggest that the engagement went on for at least two years. By 1658, White seems to have known that he was dying, as he had made several statements mentioning both his proposal of marriage and his wish to pass his goods on to Brent, telling a witness "if it pleased God he the said White should dye, before he married William Marshalls maid Margarett, he would give her all he had."[158] Shortly before his death, he had been witnessed slaughtering a hog and saying that "hee was crasye & desyred to eate some fresh porke, saying I thinke I shall have noe great occasion to kill any more."[159] It's unclear what was wrong with White, who was perhaps ailing or elderly. However, from the beginning, the Maryland Provincial Court was skeptical, and when Brent attempted to claim the estate, the court recorded her to be "pretending her selfe exequutrix."[160] In the end, Brent's claim did not prevail, as "there could not bee proofe made of the will."[161]

INTERRACIAL RELATIONSHIPS

In a few cases, women servants or former servants married slaves or former slaves. There were harsh penalties for white women who had children with slaves or black men. Some colonial-era laws specified that freewomen, black or white, who married slaves automatically attained slave status, thus enslaving their future children. However, this was not true of women who had sexual relations with slaves outside of marriage; their children remained free. Thus, when marriages

occurred, they seem to have been voluntary affairs sanctified by ministers, rather than a stratagem by owners to increase their numbers of
slaves.[162] By comparison, women who married indentured Monmouth rebels in Barbados were to be fined and sentenced to a six-
month jail term.[163]

There were also significant penalties for white women who
engaged in sexual relations with black men. In Virginia in 1705, An
Act Concerning Servants and Slaves stated that servant women who
had illegitimate children by black or multiracial men, regardless of
the father's status as enslaved or free, were liable for an additional five
years of service or a fine. The child would be indentured until age
thirty-one.[164] The 1716 Maryland Act of Assembly stated that if "any
white woman whether free or a servant that shall suffer her-selfe to be
got with child by a negroe or other slave or free negroe ... if free, shall
become a servant for and dureing a terme of seven years, [and] if
[already] a servant, shall finish her time of servitude ... together with
the damage that shall accrue [i.e., serving extra time to make up for
her lost labour] ... and after such satisfaction made shall againe
become a servant for & during the terme of seven years." Not only
would the mother serve seven years in penalty, but if the "begetter" of
the child was a "free Negroe," he too would become a servant for seven
years, and any children resulting from "such unnaturall and inordinate copulations" were to be indentured until age thirty-one. In addition, "any white man that shall begett any Negroe woman with child,
whether freewoman or servant, shall undergoe the same penalties as
white women," a penalty that was notably not applied. Such child
servants could be sold or used by the county, and the proceeds of
their servitude would be "appropriated towards defraying the county
charge."[165] Since a child's status of servitude followed that of its mother,
the children of enslaved women automatically became the property of
their mother's master.[166]

In Kent County Maryland in 1733, several women were indicted for
bastardy during the same court session, but their differing penalties
are instructive about the ways that social standing shaped perceptions
of criminality. Single women were typically fined, while servants, who
had no property or funds, were sentenced to whippings and additional service. Whippings could be remitted, however, if the child's
father paid a fine. White women who engaged in fornication with
black men faced the steepest penalties, and their children were obligated to undergo ten more years of servitude than white children.

Servant Loveday Turner, whose child's white father was also a servant, was fined 311 pounds of tobacco and sentenced to receive fifteen lashes "on her bare back tell the blood appear."[167] Mary Spearman, a spinster, had a bastard child with an unnamed "certain Negro person" and was sentenced to seven years of indenture and a fine.[168] Phebe Gilbert, a spinster, had a child with a white man, and was fined 30 shillings and 221 pounds tobacco.[169] The father, Thomas Morsell, was also fined, but his fine, and probably Gilbert's also, was remitted when he agreed to raise the child.[170] Spinster Jane Flanagan was likewise fined 30 shillings and 267 pounds of tobacco.[171] Lawrence Neale, the father of Flanagan's child, was fined 30 shillings and 449 pounds of tobacco, apparently remitting the fines of Flanagan.[172] Mary Graves, "a free Mullatto and [a] servant" [in other words, she was not enslaved, but was indentured] who had an illegitimate child was fined, ordered to serve her master for an additional year, and then serve an additional seven years to the county. "Two Mullatto children," probably the children of Mary Graves and Mary Spearman, were to serve Mary Graves's master until the age of thirty-one.[173]

Early modern women were expected to be humble, deferential, and compliant. Servant women suffered from poverty and were particularly vulnerable to unwelcome sexual advances and everyday violence. Nonetheless, women also resisted the demands of authority, for example, by contributing to or leading complicated heists and scams, returning early from a sentence of transportation, running away from their masters, and in some cases refusing to name names of their criminal associates or the fathers of their infants, even when the alternative was physical punishment, transportation, or death.[174] In addition, women's involvement in the criminal underworld expanded options, though it is always questionable to what degree participation in crime was a choice or a necessity of survival. Servant women tried to better their prospects and, in the colonies, sometimes appear in the records trying to obtain a just portion of freedom dues or accusing their masters and mistresses of mistreatment – evidence of both their vulnerable position and their willingness to fight for what they saw as their rights.

This chapter has been able to detail only a few of the ways in which women servants, despite being restricted by their circumstances, endeavoured to shape their own lives and act as autonomous agents. Nonetheless, a considerable number of servant women were able to partially circumvent the constraints imposed upon them and find the most advantageous way to chart their own course in life. Many of the women described in this chapter defied convention, despite coming from the poorest and least-influential levels of their society. They negotiated, signed, and broke indenture contracts; travelled to the colonies; sued for their rights; and evaded criminal penalties. They also broke the law and engaged in theft and disorderly conduct, sometimes persistently, and in one case led a criminal organization. Women who participated in the juries of matrons exercised judicial judgment and endorsed their own visions of justice. Even indentured women servants, frequently thought of as the lowest of the low, were often able to navigate a course through the many obstacles before them, some thereby perhaps bettering their prospects. Although many of the sources available to present-day historians reflect the unlucky women who failed or were caught in their endeavours, these probably represent only a few of the working and servant women who strove to insure a better future for themselves. Additionally, the presence of colonial women, including servant women, in the courtroom highlighted disjunctions in early modern gender norms, and established that colonial women possessed certain rights of subjecthood, albeit within a clearly patriarchal framework.

Indentured Children

Most indentured servants entered servitude in their late teens or early twenties, but the most vulnerable servants sent to the colonies were children in their early teens or younger. Most of these were older than ten, but some even younger children were transported. Child servants also included the indentured children of indentured mothers. Transported children presented particular difficulties in the servant market because they were inherently less desirable to overseas masters. Colonial interest in child servants was never high and diminished over the seventeenth century, with children more sought-after in the mainland colonies rather than in the Caribbean, where plantation labour prevailed. Nonetheless, the government continued to ship children as it weighed the utility of removing certain populations at home against actual labour needs overseas. In addition, children were shipped by spirits because they were relatively easy to seize. Even so, the servitude of white children remained an emotionally resonant issue throughout the seventeenth century because of changing ideas about the need to nurture children, and also because such children were expected to grow into contributing members of colonial society, and like other British and Irish servants, possessed inherent rights as citizens.

TRANSPORTING POOR CHILDREN

Poor children were often targeted for transportation by the government, under the belief that they were destined to become beggars and vagrants. In addition to removing them from Britain or Ireland, they were seen as nascent colonists once they had finished their terms of indentured servitude. Such children were sometimes orphans or merely destitute. Shipments of children were generally planned on a larger scale than those of adult voluntary servants, often one hundred or more, although there were exceptions. The government displayed considerably more ambiguity about its motives for transporting children than it showed in the case of adults, and the implementation of such policies was virtually always justified on the grounds that transportation was morally and economically beneficial to the youths. There was also a small percentage of children who were indentured with the permission of their parents, usually because of family poverty but also because of incorrigible behaviour, the death of one parent, or adverse family dynamics such as coveting a child's inheritance.[1]

The government in London periodically swept indigent children off the streets and sent them to the colonies. They did this without much concern for the welfare of the children, with hundreds dying during and after transportation in ships such as the notorious *Seaflower*, which accidentally blew up in 1623.[2] The incentive for these roundups was unease about widespread poverty and vagabondage in both Britain and Ireland; indenture removed itinerant street children from both the public view and the public expense, and it was widely believed that domestic service would be morally redeeming for them.[3] In addition, as with adults, professional kidnappers tricked or coerced children into indenture. As mentioned at the beginning of chapter 2, the very word "kidnap" comes from the practice of nabbing kids off the street to send them to colonial plantations.[4] Children were easy targets, though of low value at sale for servants. Once in the colonies, children worked for longer terms than adults, usually until age twenty-one. Nonetheless, there was considerable controversy regarding the indenture of children since public opinion opposed child stealing, parents complained of lost children, and colonial planters petitioned for able-bodied adult labourers. Although there were feeble official attempts to halt child kidnapping, official half-heartedness, conflicting social attitudes, and government weakness and corruption mainly resulted in inaction. However, the practice was inherently limited by economics as well as, to some degree, ambiguities about how to view children and childhood.

EARLY MODERN CHILDHOOD

There is a considerable scholarship on children and childhood in early modern Europe. Historians from the mid-twentieth century argued that early modern child rearing was characterized by both neglect and strictness, and that the era did not possess a defined concept of childhood.[5] However, more recent historiography has detailed relationships shaped by love and concern, though also coloured by early modern ideas about patriarchy, deferential behaviour, and social norms.[6] In the early modern era, children of modest means were expected to work in the household or in the profession of their parents. It was considered perfectly acceptable to make children work, and work hard.[7] Although very young children were not considered productive, children from the age of seven years or so were expected to contribute to the household economy.[8]

Working, for able-bodied children, meant that they were supporting themselves through their labour, rather than relying on society through the parish, and that they were behaving in socially and morally acceptable ways. Yet there was also recognition of children's developing physical and cognitive abilities, and of the need for guardians to provide moral guidance and education, despite little acknowledgement by governing officials of the emotional or psychological needs of children. On a more informal and implicit level, parents do seem to have had an appreciation of children's psychological needs to some degree. When children were indentured, courts and magistrates envisioned the labour arrangement as paying for the child's keep, but also saw the masters and mistresses of children as *in loco parentis*. Children, removed from the supposedly malign influence of their parents, were placed in a proper patriarchal household, and perhaps trained in a skill so that they could become competent and moral adults.

Children were among the earliest groups sent into indentured servitude. The Elizabethan poor laws provided the guidelines for the practice of child indenture, with rules about apprenticeships that were not too fussy about training poor children in a trade.[9] As early as 1618, the Virginia Company, which had been requesting transports of vagrant adults to labour in the fields, changed its request to children. A plan was set up for "a hundred young boys and girls who lay starving in the streets" to be shipped from London to Virginia.[10] Before the City of London agreed, there were a series of tense negotiations between the city and the Virginia Company over the value of the freedom dues that the children would receive upon completing their indentures.[11] Yet further obstacles appeared. Even children could protest against forcible transportation overseas. Most of the "ill-disposed children, who under severe masters in Virginia may be brought to goodness, and of whom the City is especially desirous to be disburdened" were reluctant to go, making a Privy Council order necessary to transport the children "against their will." In 1620, the City of London was able to hand over these children "from their superfluous multitude" to be sent to Virginia as servants.[12] Perhaps included was Richard Frethorne, who left for Virginia in the early 1620s. This incident is particularly instructive because it illustrates a number of contested moral, legal, and economic positions that would continue to reverberate in later initiatives to transport indentured servants, particularly children: the City of London's attempt to provide for the children in its care by negotiating a more fair settlement of freedom dues for them and its inability to transport them against their will conflicted with its desire to "disburden" itself of a population deemed "ill-disposed" and "superfluous." The transportation of children continued throughout the seventeenth century and typically occurred in an extremely coercive fashion. It was also extremely dangerous: approximately 8,500 poor children were sent from London to Virginia from 1619 to 1625, but fewer than 1,250 were alive two years after transportation. The rest had died from Indian attacks, disease, and starvation.[13] Yet unlike typical pauper apprenticeships served in England, arrangements with the Virginia Company included relatively generous freedom dues that would provide each child with 50 acres of land, a house, a cow, tools, clothing, and corn.[14]

Perhaps as a result of the 1618 fiasco, in 1623, it was proposed by the Council of New England that laws binding poor children as apprentices be adapted to indenturing children to send to the colonies, thus explicitly employing the Elizabethan Statute of Artificers to justify this newer punitive system.[15] On 31 January 1643, New Englanders petitioned Parliament for a collection for the next two fast days to pay for "poor fatherless children" either "driven out of Ireland" or "of this kingdom [England]" that "are out of employment" to be "transplanted to New England." The first shipment of these children arrived the same year.[16] A significant number of "voluntary" migrant children were orphans without other means of supporting themselves.[17]

CRITICISMS OF CHILD INDENTURE

Fundamentally, shipments of children failed to meet the Caribbean demand for labour. While children were apparently somewhat desirable in the mainland colonies, presumably because they were bound

for much longer terms than adults and were employable as household
workers, they were less sought-after on farms and plantations where
hard labour was the main work for servants. In 1661, for example, the
Barbados masters and servants act stipulated that children under the
age of fourteen not be brought in as servants.[18] In 1697, the Barbados
Assembly specified that they were willing to take people "fit for labo-
rious service," even convicts, "but no women, children nor other
infirm persons."[19] Jamaican merchants also complained in 1697 about
the overabundance of women and children.[20]

   In addition, public opinion mitigated against the forcible indenture
of children. The coerced apprenticing of pauper children had always
been controversial, and even more so when the children were being
sent to the colonies.[21] The practice of child stealing was generally
regarded as especially atrocious and saw earlier preventative legislation
than against the kidnapping of adults. In 1645, Parliament ordered that
stealing children would result in "severe and exemplary punishment"
and mandated that all ships at dock in London be immediately
searched.[22] During the colonial period, the last time that the government deliberately attempted to transplant English children seems to
have been 1643.[23] This cessation was likely a combination of increased
public concern over forced indenture practices, especially in the case of
children, and an increase in appeals from colonial planters to transport
only adult servants. Vagrant or available children continued to be
transported by spirits and unscrupulous government contractors, however, and Irish children, perhaps seen as more expendable, continued
to be sent overseas as well. In 1653, the Council of State agreed to grant
a licence to a New England merchant to take 400 Irish children to
plantations in New England and Virginia.[24] Soon after, an act was
drafted supporting the transportation of poor Irish children to England and the western plantations.[25] The topic of shipping children,
including those from Ireland, was debated in government circles from
the early 1660s, although without much resolution.[26] The government
did mandate in 1660 that registration of servants be implemented so
that it could be clear that "all servants and children" who were to be
transported to Virginia or Barbados would first "declare their willingness to go."[27]

KIDNAPPING

Kidnapping children was illegal, though not a felony, perhaps the reason it continued to occur.[28] Like Ricckett Mecane, some autobiographers revealed how they had been kidnapped as children – including Charles Bayly, who was "cunningly" tricked onto a ship at age thirteen in the 1640s and. "being once aboard, could never get on shore until I came to America."[29] Peter Williamson was only eight when he was kidnapped from Aberdeen, along with several other boys, in the 1730s.[30] There was significant public and governmental disapprobation of the practice of making away with children. In 1660, the Privy Council referred to the kidnapping of children as "a thing so barbarous and inhumane that Nature itself, much more Christians, cannot but abhorre," but without agreeing on further legislation.[31] In 1682, a broadside that purported to be the text of a letter written from Jamaica to London about child kidnapping grieved that "the great abuses in the spiriting away of children, makes a very sad story" and was "a lamentable grief to their parents that have lost them."[32] Narcissus Luttrell mentioned that the increasing prevalence of child kidnapping led the authorities to aim more strenuously at "putting a stop to so prodigious a villany" by stepping up the number of prosecutions, and promulgating a royal proclamation against child stealing in 1682, as well as an Order of Council against kidnapping in general in 1686.[33]

The kidnapping of children reflected the fear of every parent of harm coming to their children. Servitude itself was not safe for children. While all indentured servants were at risk of violence, children were particularly vulnerable. Even if indentured children survived their period of indenture, even if they were not abused by their masters, they were likely to lose contact with their parents forever. Random indenture of children was also a denial of the rights of fathers to determine what happened to their family members – hence the usual disclaimer in the official government sweeps of indigent children that the children were orphans. For example, the c.1650 broadsheet printed by the Admiralty aimed to disavow the "most false aspersion" that "there were diverse little children taken up and shipped ... to be transported for the plantations." The "begger boyes" in the ship described in the text were carefully documented to be both "willing" and orphans.[34]

Parents who strove to recover kidnapped children were supported
by the authorities on an individual basis. In 1682, Narcissus Luttrell
described an order to arrest merchant John Wilmore for "haveing kidnapped a boy of 13 years of age to Jamaica."[35] Wilmore seems to have
been a prominent shipper, but also a known spirit, while Richard
Siviter, the kidnapped thirteen-year-old, appears to have come from a
middling-level family.[36] The authorities took the case seriously. It
came to trial before the King's Bench after the parents of Richard
Siviter had appeared before the mayor of Gravesend to claim their
lost son, and the mayor had summoned Wilmore. Wilmore attempted
to justify taking the boy by producing a copy of the boy's contract,
claiming that the boy "was very willing to goe with him" and that he
had done the boy "a very good act of charity, haveing bound him to a
carpenter there, and so provided for him better then his parents
could." He also attempted to force the parents to compensate him for
the boy's passage across the ocean and back and his clothing before
he would agree to return him.[37] Wilmore lost the case, and the other
parties involved in the kidnapping were also prosecuted, including
the mayor of Gravesend, who had defended Wilmore after the fact
and who was fined "for his countenancing such a practice." The ship's
captain also was arrested. He had been brought in as a witness on
Wilmore's behalf, but his dubious testimony in which he "supposed
to have witnessed what he knew not" had been full of "several contradictions and unlikelyhoods."[38] After the decision of the court, in
"hopes to mitigate his fine," Wilmore urgently "sent an expresse to
Jamaica" to recover the boy "as soon as possible."[39] The fine would
have been a steep one; Luttrell records the typical penalty for kidnapping children as £500, sometimes with time in the pillory
added.[40] The judgment was delivered by a jury, but during the trial
the Lord Chief Justice made leading remarks "against the horrid prac-
tise of kidnapping children."[41] He afterwards congratulated the jury
for giving "a good verdict."[42] The multiple prosecutions as well as the
unanimity of the jury and the justice testify to a societal distaste for
the kidnapping of children. Yet this was not followed through by
legislation, which meant child stealing remained a misdemeanour
rather than a felony.[43]

Richard Siviter's story ended well – he was rapidly "brought over"
the ocean on Wilmore's express ship and restored to his parents.
Although Siviter's parents recovered their son, most parents of kidnapped children probably did not. Indeed, the merchant Wilmore

had been a known shipper of children in the past.[44] The public embarrassment of this case led Wilmore to publish a sixteen-page tract that claimed the boy had entered indenture willingly.[45] The likelihood of rescuing a child must have been much higher if the parents were able to trace their child prior to shipping, which did sometimes occur.[46] In November 1653, the father of Bart Broome, an eleven-year-old boy, traced his son to a ship berthed at London. The ship's master was served a warrant for stealing the boy and forced to return the boy to his father. Like Wilmore, the captain of the ship at first refused to comply until the father returned with a magistrate, who warned the captain that he would resist the warrant "at his peril."[47] In April 1668, the "lost child John Brookes" was rescued "after much trouble and charge" from a docked ship, but the three other ships still held several children "enticed from their parents." The ships masters required payment from the parents to recover their children, or each child would have required individual government warrants if they were to be released.[48] When the spirits Edward Harrison and Captain Azariah Daniel were apprehended, 150 children were rescued. They had been confined for three weeks in the holds of ships that had been waiting to sail. Two boys were found "bound in a garrett."[49] In none of these incidents were merchants or ships' masters prosecuted.

In some instances, kidnapping was arranged by acquaintances or even family members. In a partially recorded case from Maryland in 1677, James Disborow petitioned the Provincial Court that his father had agreed for him to become the assistant to a Maryland merchant, paying his passage across the ocean. However, when he arrived, he was "disposed of" as a servant. The court ordered the ship's master to appear and testify, and the ship to remain in port until this was done. There is no record of how the case was resolved.[50] A more unusual case was that of John Baker, orphaned at the age of twelve, who through his adult sister's "cruell contrivance" was sent as an indentured servant to Virginia and forced by threats to sign his inheritance over to her. In 1660, having reached adulthood at twenty-one, he returned to petition Parliament for redress, but the outcome is not recorded.[51]

AGE DETERMINATION FOR INDENTURED CHILDREN

Once in the colonies, unlike voluntarily indentured adults, most children did not possess a paper contract and were expected to serve at the custom of the country. This usually meant seven years for adults

without contracts, but children were indentured until age twenty-
one, legal adulthood, because of their reduced earning potential and
the belief that they needed to be contained within a patriarchal
household.[52] For a child indentured at a young age, this could mean
many years of servitude, perhaps ten or more. Because the length of
indenture depended on the determination of a child's age, which
could potentially be contested later by either a master or a servant,
colonial legislatures mandated that within one to three months after
purchasing a child, the master or mistress had to bring them before
the court to determine their age, providing a public record of the term
to serve.[53] Older youths could be expected to serve past the age of
twenty-one to give them adult-length terms of servitude, like Mary
Taylor, judged seventeen and indentured for seven years, and Margaret
Ohderoh, judged twenty and ordered to serve six years in seventeenth-
century Maryland.[54] Often the servant's age was not recorded, only
the future term of servitude. For example, John Couch, who must
have been adjudged about eight years old, was ordered to serve thirteen years, while Roger Allen, who was merely described as "very
young," received only six years.[55] There was some arbitrariness to these
terms, probably in part because of the impreciseness of age determination, and neither the servant nor the master appears to have had
much control over the length of servitude. A few lucky youths might
have a contract in hand; on the second Tuesday of April 1669, the
Charles County Court began proceedings by judging the ages of
twenty-two servants, including two pairs of siblings. While the
Hoskins brothers were indentured to the same master, the Bawlding
siblings received separate masters and also separate fates. Robert
Bawlding was judged to be twenty-one, and would have been
required to serve five years, but his sister's new master was probably
disappointed to see Mary's proof "she had an indenture," which likely
limited her term to four years regardless of her age.[56]

Each colony established its own rules for managing the custom of
the country. Although they were broadly similar, terms did vary
between colonies and changed over time. In Virginia, in 1642, servants from thirteen to nineteen of age were to serve five years, while
those twelve and under served seven, as compared to adults, who
served four.[57] In 1657, this was amended, with those sixteen and over
serving four years, and children under sixteen typically till age twenty-
one.[58] In 1661, this was raised to five years for those over sixteen
and until age twenty-four for those under sixteen.[59] Masters were

legally obligated to bring young servants into court within four months of receiving them for judgment of their ages, or their term of indenture could be no longer than what was assessed for those aged sixteen or above.[60] In 1638, the Maryland Assembly assessed a term of four years for those over eighteen but until age twenty-four for younger boys, though girls were to serve seven years if under twelve or four years if older, perhaps under the assumption that they would soon marry.[61] In 1661, the Maryland Assembly mandated that servants aged twenty-two and over without contracts were to serve four years; if aged eighteen to twenty-two, then five years; if fifteen to eighteen, then six years; and if under fifteen, till age twenty-one. Masters and mistresses were to bring new youths into their local county court for age determination within three months, or risk losing one year of the servant's service.[62] From 1666, this was amended so that Maryland masters were legally obligated to bring young servants into court within six months of receiving them for judgment of their ages, unless they planned to ask for only a five-year contract.[63] In the meantime, in 1664, the Maryland Assembly again attempted to regularize the status of incoming child servants without contracts, ruling that those who were under fifteen were to serve until age twenty-two, those between fifteen and eighteen to serve six years, and those between eighteen and twenty-two to serve five years.[64]

The existence of trade between Maryland and Virginia, in servants as well as slaves, led to the colonies honouring prior arrangements. The 1676 Act Relateing to Servants and Slaves enacted in Maryland mandated that servants transported from Virginia "shall compleat their time of servitude here which they ought to have served in Virginia & noe more." In addition, Maryland masters bringing or buying a servant from Virginia were to bring them into the court for age determination within six months. After reiterating the term limits for young servants without contracts, the law also stated that no servant could be compelled to serve longer than his initial indenture had specified."[65] A 1715 compilation of Maryland laws added the provision that servitude began upon arrival to the colony, regardless of whether the master or mistress delayed in asking for age determination: "the time of servitude of all servants imported, shall commence from the first anchoring of the vessel within this province."[66]

These laws typically clarified that both master and servant could challenge the determination of age in court, though in reality that would have been difficult or impossible for a child or youth arriving alone to an unfamiliar territory. Yet the courts did take the question of age determination seriously, recording youthful servant's ages so that the register could be referred to in instances of dispute. Maryland courts also aimed to enforce regulations protecting servants, such as requiring a minimum number of jurors for age determinations. For example, in 1662, the Talbot County Maryland Court refused to judge a servant's age on a day when a full quorum was not in session.[67] In 1676, the Somerset County Maryland Court refused to determine the age of an apprentice whose master was attempting to resell him as a servant.[68] In 1665, when Lott Richards sold his eleven-year-old servant boy William Freeman, who had no indenture contract, in Surry County Virginia, the transaction was recorded in the register of deeds, specifying that the boy was to serve eight years "from the arrival of the ship he came in," and after that, he was "to be absolutly free" and to receive his freedom dues.[69]

There are many records of masters and mistresses bringing in children, usually youths in their mid-teens.[70] For example, there are 181 records of servants having their ages determined in the nine-year period from 1666 to 1674 in the Charles County Maryland Court.[71] In Maryland, age determinations before the central Provincial Court began to occur with such frequency that from 1688 on, the Provincial Court refused to take further cases, stating that such determinations were the purview of the lower county courts.[72] Nonetheless, evidence suggests that many masters neglected to obtain age determinations – there are simply too few of them recorded in court records. Presumably there are multiple reasons – some masters simply didn't bother or didn't live in the vicinity of a court; others might have had a more malevolent intention to hold children in service longer than their legal terms, especially in an era when few people knew their exact ages or the calendar date of their arrival into the colony.

In 1661, when Ricckett Mecane took his master to court, the crux of the trial hinged on age determination. Mecane argued that after serving six and a half years, he was now twenty-one and should be released from servitude. His master Thomas Gerrard contended that Mecane still had eight and a half more years to serve, implausibly implying that Mecane at that point in time in 1661 was about twelve years old. Mecane had been one of eight Irish boys kidnapped in 1654 and sold, four to Thomas Gerrard and four to Colonel Speake. Gerrard had not brought Mecane in for age determination when he was first indentured. The jury decided that Mecane was nineteen and had to serve two more years. A crucial facet of the case was the testimony of witnesses about the initial arrival and sale of the eight boys just over six years earlier, which revealed the disapproval of community members regarding the indenturing of young children. The witnesses took an ambiguous role, acknowledging the boys' young age at the time of their arrival, which would have suggested the boys had a longer term left to serve, but simultaneously expressing their disapprobation. Witness Nicholas Lansdowne declared that the "the eldest of those boyes in my judgement then was not above tenn yeares of age and many of them not neere soe much." Judith Love, apparently a servant of Gerrard's in 1654, testified that she had seen Captain Hinfeild, who had brought the boys across the ocean, threaten to beat them with his cane while telling them that they were to serve fifteen years. James Salstceme, a servant of Colonel Speake, who had taken the other four boys, stated that Mrs Speake had been shocked by their youthfulness when her husband first brought the boys home, asking sarcastically, "why had not yo[u]r master brought some cradles to have rocked them in?" She was likely anticipating the additional work that caring for four young boys would create for her. However, her response also indicated sympathy for the children; the next morning, she was concerned enough to dispatch Salstceme with bread and cheese for the remaining four boys still on Hinfeild's ship.[73]

The case provides evidence for the kidnapping of boys, in this case from Ireland in the 1650s, but also shows that the indenture of very young children was not a normal practice in Maryland at the time. Mrs Speake's parcel of food for the remaining boys on the ship also indicates a sense that children deserved special consideration and care. Thomas Gerrard seems to have taken the case to heart since soon after he presented his new Irish servant Dearmid Dormer before the court to have his age determined. Dormer was a youth, but not as young as the previous boys – the court determined that he was fifteen years old.[74]

The instances of contestation of the age of indentured children demonstrates the unscrupulousness of certain masters. In Somerset County Maryland in June 1694, servant Robert Atkins argued that he was due to be freed because the court had determined him to be thirteen in June 1686, after having arrived in the fall of 1685, and had ordered that he should serve nine years. His master maintained that he had not yet served the full term, but the court ordered that Atkins be freed and receive his freedom dues.[75] This case provides a good example of the protectiveness of age determinations for young servants and also demonstrates why some masters might attempt to avoid them.

EXPLOITATION OF CHILD SERVANTS

In addition to potential exploitation of the length of contracts, masters and mistresses had inordinate power over child servants, who were even more vulnerable to maltreatment than adults and were less able to defend themselves in court. Charles Bayly, though he eventually prospered as an adult, described in his autobiography how he was kidnapped by a spirit in the 1640s at age thirteen and sent to the Chesapeake region. While a child servant, he suffered "hunger, cold and nakednesse, beatings, whippings, and the like," while kept at "soare and grievous labour."[76] A master's impunity might even extend to murder. In March 1665, planter Francis Carpenter was tried in the Maryland Provincial Court for murdering an indentured servant boy, Samuel Youngman. A post-mortem examination of the boy found severe head injuries and a fractured skull. Witnesses described the wounded boy left exposed in a "cold and bleake" cabin in February, lying on the ground "w[i]th out any clothes to cover" him. The jury, which included Carpenter's neighbours, delivered a verdict of manslaughter. To avoid the death penalty, Carpenter pleaded benefit of the clergy, possible because the verdict had not been murder. He was burnt on the hand and ordered to pay court costs of 3,000 pounds of tobacco.[77] It is difficult to know whether the lenience of Carpenter's sentencing was due to the reluctance of peers to prosecute for the death of a servant, because his victim had been a child, or because it was not considered proven that Carpenter had intended to kill the boy.

In another example, in Virginia in 1640, Anne Belson sued her master Theodore Moyses after having completed seven years of an eight-year contract. Indentured at a young age, her contract had promised that Moyses would "use her more like his child than his servant and that he would teach her to read and instruct her in the rudiments of religion and have a paternal care over her." Instead, she was grinding grain for the household. The court took Belson's side, "taking into consideration the grievous and tyrannical usage of the said Moyses to the said Belson." It mandated that she be immediately freed from her service; that Moyses owed her freedom dues of a cow and calf, and an additional amount of clothing and corn; and that Moyses was obligated to pay all court fees.[78]

If living parents were present in the community, they might attempt to protect their indentured children by interfering with the indenture arrangement. The case of Hester Nicholls, mentioned earlier, is worth revisiting here. Her initial indenture in 1659 had been for seven years when she was about ten or eleven years old. When Hester's father, John Nicholls, objected in 1662 that Thomas Cornwallis had breached the contract, the basis of his claim was that Cornwallis had supposedly agreed to treat Hester like his own child, and to teach her to read and sew, conditions that had been nullified by Hester's sale.[79] Cornwallis, meanwhile, tried to configure Hester as an adult, arguing that Mr Nicholl's case was instigated because his main witness wanted to marry the then thirteen- or fourteen-year-old Hester.[80] The case did demonstrate the potential obligations impinging on the master of an indentured child. The case is possibly also indicative of genuine concern for Hester Nicholls's welfare by her father, although an impending marriage for his daughter might signal another motive.

There was an even greater obligation incumbent on the master of an apprentice. Apprenticeship was different from servitude in that it presupposed that the apprenticed child or youth was to be taught a skill preparing them for a trade, rather than working at any task the master required. They were normally apprenticed by their parents or perhaps the local parish if their parents were deceased or indigent. The master of an apprentice usually accepted a payment to defer costs of training, housing, and feeding the apprentice. Apprenticeship implied that the master would care for his apprentice more like his own child than as a labourer with a monetary value.[81] For example, in 1632 Virginia, Jane Winlee sued James Knott for "the misse usage" of her son Pharaoh, Knott's apprentice. The court's judgment was for Knott to "remedie what had beene formerly amisse," pay court fees, and if he were again "justly complained of," to release Pharaoh from his apprenticeship.[82] Pharaoh here received some protection from the proximity of his mother in the community. There were a number of court cases in the mainland colonies in which apprentices or their parents sued because the apprentice was being forced to work at general labour rather than being trained in the trade they had been apprenticed to.[83]

However, apprenticeship had been the basis from which indentured servitude practices were developed, and apprentices were, like

servants, contracted to serve and obey their master for a term of usually seven years. The similarity of apprenticeship to the practice of
indenture could lead to abuses. In February 1676, the Somerset Maryland County Court was presented with a case in which Francis
Roberts asked the court to determine the age of Tristram Davis, having bought him from Thomas Davis (apparently no relation), ship's
master of the *Endeavor* from Barbados. The court demurred, finding
evidence that Tristram was in fact apprenticed to Thomas to learn "the
art of navigation," and thus could not be sold.[84] However, despite con-
demning the fraud, the court apparently left the boy in Thomas
Davis's care. Thomas Davis was unwavering in his duplicitousness
since later that month he was sued by Edward Gibbs for the same
cause. This time, Thomas had succeeded in selling Tristram to Gibbs
for 1,200 pounds of tobacco; Gibbs wanted compensation when he
realized that he "cannot enjoy th[e] s[ai]d Tristram as his serv[an]t,"
and was awarded 1,800 pounds of tobacco.[85] Tristram had by this time
been away from Thomas Davis's service, but the record does not relate
what became of him; the court had already demonstrated its inability
or unwillingness to truly protect his interests.

The death of a parent, very common in the early modern era, was
often what precipitated children into indenture, especially if it was
the male head of a family who died. A poor widow was often left
without the wherewithal to care for her children.[86] On the American
mainland, orphans were usually placed in "apprenticeships," much
like the orphaned poor children in England. These orphan apprenticeships, however, were more like indenture than the craft apprenticeships of England.[87] It is possible that Pharaoh Winlee's case was
more like this than a typical craft apprenticeship. Sometimes, even if
the mother survived, the child was considered an orphan, a group
lumped with illegitimate and abandoned children.[88] That said, in seventeenth-century Maryland, most single mothers raised their own
children, even if illegitimate.[89] In 1638 Virginia, after widow Mary
Bibby died, the disposition of her children includes much contradictory language. The executors of the estate, "out of charity to her children," took them "to be sould" but not on the open market, instead
finding homes to place them in through "the advice of some of the
most judiciall neighbors adjacent" for "the best behoofe of the said
children."[90] Unlike in England, such arrangements were made by the
courts rather than by the parish authorities, but the children's situation was more like indenture – they served till twenty-one, working

for their master. However, because of court oversight, it was easier for them to complain to the courts about ill-treatment and, if necessary, ask for a new master.[91] Also, in such cases the children did not always seem to expect freedom dues, but often expected training in skills, including reading, especially for boys.[92] For example, in Somerset County Maryland in 1692, Valentine and Mary Trubshaw, the daughters of the deceased John Trubshaw, were "apprenticed" to two masters. The girls were to be taught to sew and read and to receive a ewe and a heifer respectively when they turned twelve, while their six-year-old brother John, also apprenticed, was to be taught to read.[93] The five children of Arthur Turner, who had died at the end of 1667 in Charles County Maryland, were parcelled off to their father's acquaintances, or as apprentices, including a baby girl just one month old whose mother may have died at her birth. The baby was put under the care of "George Taylors wife Susannah Taylor," who was to receive an allowance of 1,600 pounds of tobacco per year, which was to be reduced if the baby died before a half year was up.[94] The court appears to have continued in its oversight of the Turner orphans because a half year later, it abruptly moved Anne Turner, one of the older children, into an apprenticeship with a new master; no reason was provided.[95] Very young orphaned babies were invariably sent to a woman to care for them during their early years. Thus Dorothie Jones was awarded a maintenance of several bushels and barrels of corn, 300 pounds of tobacco, and the milk of one cow for maintaining James Ravis's child, who was probably illegitimate.[96] However, if they were able, parents appear to have tried to make provisions, through wills or arrangements with relatives or friends, to prevent this happening to their children.[97]

INDENTURED INFANTS

Women who bore children while under indenture were usually seen as unfit parents because they had engaged in fornication, and additionally, caring for the children would have interfered with their duties. The child was usually indentured by the courts, from weaning at two or three years of age until twenty-one, unless someone made provision for its care.[98] In some cases, single freewomen appear to have voluntarily given up their children to indenture. Infants' contracts did not usually provide much special considerations for child servants, but both written contracts and the custom of the country

stipulated that servants were to have adequate food, clothing, and
shelter; receive freedom dues; and particularly specified that very
young children were to receive some education and religious training.
Such was the case of Thomas Ducaloon, one year and eight months
old, who was to be indentured from age two to twenty-two by his
mother, Dorothy Stoddard. In an unusual arrangement, Ducaloon
was to be treated more like an apprentice, trained to work as an artisan and taught to read and write; additionally, he was to have some
contact with his mother in his early years, as she was responsible for
clothing him during the first five years.[99] More typically, in 1693, the
Somerset Maryland County Court separately indentured two boys
with this provision. The very young (four years old) Edward Camplin,
indentured for 1,000 pounds of tobacco by his father, was to be taught
to read and given a heifer. More equivocally, John Chancelor, probably also quite little, was to be taught to read, provided his master "can
have it done in his own house."[100]

Sometimes adults in the community, usually women, stepped in to
care for indigent children, but they usually expected some compensation.[101] For example, Anne Bishopp, mentioned in chapter 6, cared for
the illegitimate child left behind by her runaway servant Rose Deaverley.[102] Bishopp's care may have been grudging – she complained that
the baby's upkeep was a "real detrement" and had caused her "damage
and trouble." She sought reimbursement in court for expenses
incurred in rearing the child, which she had undertaken for more than
one year at that point, as well as penalties from Deaverley. Yet Bishopp
never suggested abandoning the infant or asked for it to be removed
from her household to be raised by the county, as she could have done.
The record hints at some real concern for the baby's welfare, with
Bishopp referring to how she had "nourished, kept, and mentained"
the infant. Ultimately, her case against the absent Deaverley was dismissed, while it is unrecorded whether she received any funds from
the county.[103] In a similar case, a bleak existence probably awaited
seven-month-old William Shuttlesworth, whose mother was dead and
whose father "is [a] runaway." He was indentured in June 1675 to
Roger Woollford, who had cared for him since his birth and who had
probably been his mother's master. Woollford was to provide
"cloth[ing], meat, drinke, washing, and lodging, provided it [the baby]
may be ordered to serve him from the time it is able to worke till
it come to the age of one and twenty yeares."[104] In 1672, Sarah Bass, an
eight-year-old "mallatto" girl whose parents were "a negro man servant

and an English woman servant" living in the household of John White, was indentured as White's servant until age twenty-one, with the expectation of freedom dues of a cow and calf. This appears to be a formalization of a relationship that already existed, perhaps because Sarah had reached an age where she could do some light work. Her parents must have had long terms if they had already been in White's service for eight years, or perhaps they were hired servants who worked for wages. Bass's mother might also have served additional time for bearing a child. It is also possible that her father was enslaved. Assuming that her parents continued to remain in White's household, this arrangement allowed young Sarah to remain with her parents and assured her some assets and her freedom when she reached adulthood. In some, probably rare, cases, an indentured child may have been treated more like a son or daughter, as with Peter Williamson. His master, "having no children of his own, and commiserating my condition, he took care of me, indulged me in going to school," and left Williamson a large bequest in his will.[105] Williamson's case was unusual, however, and the relationships of most indentured children with their masters were probably more adversarial.

In a very different arrangement, Elizabeth Copper, the wife of John Copper, gave up all rights to her three-year-old daughter Mary Curtis to Anthony Hodgkins. Hodgkins was to keep little Mary "as his own natural child" and to care for her "as becometh a natural parent."[106] Mary was probably an illegitimate child born before Elizabeth Copper's marriage, with Hodgkins likely the girl's father. The baby had been kept by her mother until weaned, and could enter the new household. As a freewoman, Copper had not had to risk the indenture of her child. In Dartmouth Massachusetts in 1716, Abigail Bryant indentured her son James, "an Indian lad," for a seven-year term. She received 20 shillings and "a good fat sheep" in a transaction that was akin to an exchange.[107]

An indentured woman had little recourse to prevent her child from being indentured, especially if it was illegitimate, but some parents were determined to attempt it. For example, Bethea Cunningham had arrived in Somerset County Maryland in 1690 as "a free woman," but had then contracted herself to serve Lawrence Crawford for a year. Before the year was over, she "committed a fault, that hath offended the law of God and man," which was apparently a sexual encounter resulting in the birth of a child. Her master then tried to deceive her in order to keep her labouring for a longer period: he "pretended he had a great kindness for your peti[ti]oner, and did pretend he would keep your petitioner harmless from the law, provided your petitioner would indent with him for four years." Cunningham, unaware of the law, agreed, provided that her child would continue to live with her for the four years and "to have mentannce according as a child ought to have," and when Cunningham's term of labour was completed, "your petitioners child to be free" along with Cunningham. The case showed up in court because Cunningham's child died eight days after birth, and she was seeking to have her indenture agreement cancelled.[108] Cunningham had done her best to both keep her child and prevent it from entering indenture.

These cases also demonstrate that there must have been a significant minority of unmarried women in seventeenth-century Maryland living with their illegitimate children, even under indenture. Another example is revealed in a 1660 case, in which John Dabb sued Mathew Reede for detaining his unnamed maidservant and her child. The child in this case was likely an infant or toddler still breast-feeding, who had apparently continued to reside with its mother within Dabb's household.[109] Even Lawrence Crawford, for all his unscrupulousness about the contract, had been willing to allow the unmarried Bethea Cunningham to keep her illegitimate child with her in his household.

In 1674, Elizabeth Goodale arrived in Maryland with her five-year-old son Gilbert. Although she had contracted for her son to remain with her and to be free at the end of her five-year contract, John Quigley, the ship's captain, had sold them both to the same master, but the boy at the custom of the country for nineteen years. She complained to the Provincial Court, which drew up a new indenture clearly stating her conditions and also ordering Quigley to pay 2,000 pounds of tobacco to compensate their master for the future loss of the boy's labour.[110] Very few women entered into indenture together with their children unless they had borne the child while under indenture. Another exception can be found in the example of Mary Hillyard and her daughter Mary Hillyard, who may have been an adult, whose contracts were discussed in chapter 4.[111]

If a child was indentured until age twenty-one, the long period of indenture coupled with the scanty levels of knowledge about one's age meant that masters could try to take advantage and keep former child servants in indenture past their times. In August 1690 in Somerset County Maryland, Hannah Holland petitioned the county "supposing her selfe ... to be of age" and thus "free." She had asked her master Walter Lane "to goe and search the records" to determine whether she was of age, but he had refused. Holland, who was illegitimate, had been indentured in court while a child by her unmarried mother, a servant woman.[112] In her complaint, she was not asking for compensation, but for the court to order "that the records may be searched."[113] The persistent Holland had to return to court in November, because although the court had done as she asked and Holland had been "informed she is a free woman," she was still being "deteined and kept a servant."[114] Holland presumably won her freedom, but appeared in court again in 1692 complaining that she had contracted to serve Edmund Beauchamp for a year, but he had not provided her dues of 600 pounds of tobacco and two shifts.[115] She won this case as well, but in a sad coda to her tale, that same year she gave birth to a bastard child – repeating the conditions of her own birth – for which she received "one & twenty lashes on her bare back well laid on" as well as a fine.[116] The father of the child was her master Edmund Beauchamp. He was probably fairly young because it was Thomas Beauchamp, perhaps his father, who undertook his portion of the fine. At first, Beauchamp denied paternity, and the Beauchamps appear to have had little interest in their descendent, baby John, who took the surname of his mother.[117] Two years later, John Holland was indentured, to start at age three until twenty-one to John Kirk, with a heifer and one year of schooling as freedom dues.[118] John Kirk had been Hannah Holland's original master when she had been a child.[119] This case illustrates the difficulty of breaking the cycle of poverty, illegitimate birth, and child indenture, even for an individual as willing to use the courts to fight for her rights as Hannah Holland.

Occasionally, legal cases unveil the pain of parents at losing their children. In 1693, Mary Windsley petitioned the Somerset Maryland County Court to return her two children who had been "detained" by the suitably named Devorax Dregers. The court judged the children to be twelve and fourteen years of age, apparently without consulting Windsley about their ages. Clearly considering her an unfit parent, either because she was a poor widow or because she was a single mother, the court awarded the children to Dregers, with the proviso that he give Windsley's son one year of schooling and a heifer to each child. Dregers was to keep them "in custody" until the boy, the younger of the children, was of age, presumably thus able to take his older sister into his care.[120] Parents did not often succeed in recovering their children from indenture. Hester Nicholls's father's suit is a case in point. In 1692, Anne Walker petitioned the court to release her two sons whom she had indentured after her husband died, because she "craves to have her children again," but the outcome was not recorded.[121] Alexander Gold, with "great grief & sorrow of heart" sought to end the indenture of his fourteen-year-old daughter Elizabeth, who had already served many years. The original 1684 document of indenture, produced in court, proved almost unintelligible, calling into question whether it referred to Elizabeth's age of nine at her initial indenture, or a term of nine years, with the court ultimately ruling against the Golds and selecting the latter option.[122] Elizabeth Shelbourne was arrested in Virginia in 1693 because she was sheltering her son, a runaway apprentice.[123]

Early modern people generally regarded orphaned and poor children as a troublesome population to be slotted into preconceived legal and political categories: vagrants, occasionally criminals, and labourers. The state and community also strove to limit financial costs for their care. While a small part of the indentured servant trade, child labour saved government funds while providing low-priced labour to masters. Yet this practice came into increasing conflict with evolving early modern perceptions of children and childhood, which had already begun to see children as a special category of people requiring nurture and care. The complex reactions to the indenture of children illustrate the changing attitudes to the nature of childhood in the early modern period. Perhaps even more than the servitude of adults, the servitude of children also laid bare the ambiguities, contradictions, and weaknesses of the early modern state.

Resistance to Servitude

Indentured servants possessed few effective ways of resisting servitude. Still, for some, any form of escape appeared worthwhile. One legitimate avenue of resistance was in using the courts to contest ill-treatment by masters and mistresses, whether physical or sexual abuse; detaining a servant past the end of their terms; stealing freedom dues; or other forms of harm. As has been seen throughout this book, many servants used this recourse effectively. Yet other servants, whether they were poorly informed about their rights, had their petitions to the court rejected, or lacked means to get to court, did not utilize this approach. Instead, they resorted to other methods of resistance, of small and large magnitude. These could range from minor acts such as theft to more overt opposition such as refusing to work, running away, using violence against masters and mistresses, uttering threats and insults, and the most confrontational resistance: engaging in open rebellion. Of course, all of these forms of revolt involved risk, but for some servants, it may have been safer than remaining in an exploitative or dangerous situation of servitude. At the heart of all of these modes of resistance was the conviction that servants were humans who deserved dignity and autonomy.

REBELLION

Although open rebellion was a last resort, it did occur. The most famous is Bacon's Rebellion in 1676 Virginia, which was not exclusively a servant rebellion, but did involve significant participation by servants.[1] There were also several other attempted rebellions.[2] In

Virginia, this included the Gloucester County Conspiracy in 1663, a planned servant rebellion in which servants, termed by the authorities "false traytors" who were "seduced by the instigation of the devil," planned an insurrection that was betrayed by John Berkenhead, one of their fellows, who was rewarded with his freedom and 5,000 pounds of tobacco, as "an encouragement to others."[3] In the Middlesex County Conspiracy of 1687, also discovered before it began, a few "ill disposed servants" and enslaved people planned to run away and use stolen weapons to defend themselves against the authorities.[4]

There were a number of smaller rebellions by servants in Barbados, some in collusion with the enslaved, who were perhaps seen as compatriots in oppression.[5] Ligon described a servant rebellion shortly before he arrived: "their sufferings being grown to a great height" by "the intolerable burdens they labor'd under ... at the last, some among them, whose spirits were not able to endure such slavery, resolved to break through it or dye in the act." Although the "discontented party ... were the greatest numbers of servants in the island," the servants lost their nerve, the plot failed, and eighteen leaders were executed.[6] Yet most servants did not engage in open revolt; the promise of eventual freedom must have limited the instances of this to some extent.

VIOLENCE AND CRIME

Servants who killed their masters, the ultimate act of resistance, were guilty not of murder, but of petit treason, a much more serious charge.[7] A case of petit treason was heard by a Maryland grand jury in 1671, in which three servants, James Sail, Robert Warry, and Robert Spear, as well as two men recorded as servants who may actually have been enslaved, John the Negro and Tony the Negro, were convicted of "traytorously" killing their master, John Hawkins. The three servants and John the Negro were put to death. Tony the Negro, who "could speake no English," was acquitted, but was made to serve as executioner at the hanging of the other four men.[8]

On a lower scale, servants engaged in disorderly behaviour and violence. In 1669 Maryland, Robert Pennywell, an indentured servant, was sentenced to twenty lashes for smashing the glass windows of a chapel, an action that may have had a religious motivation.[9] In 1659, Owen Morgan not only ran away from his Maryland master but also cursed and beat him.[10] In 1679, the "barbarous and villanous" servant

Thomas Jones attempted to rape his mistress and cut her severely about the face and hands with a rapier and knife when she resisted. In response to his "horrid offense," the Accomack County Virginia Court sentenced Jones to thirty-nine lashes, three additional years of servitude, and an iron collar.[11] In 1715 Virginia, John Watson was made to serve an additional year for "lifting up his hand in opposition" and "assaulting" his master.[12]

Theft could be another means of resistance. In the mainland colonies, it was usually a misdemeanour, in contrast to the felony charge it incurred in England. In 1684, the Accomack County Virginia Court heard the cases of several servants who had been accused of theft by their master. The thefts, some in collusion with an enslaved man, were of food, that was subsequently eaten; livestock: three turkeys, a lamb, two sheep, a sow, six piglets; and a sack of potatoes. The record also includes one of the servants' sardonic statement that if he was caught, he would send his master "a very loveing letter" commending how "very fat" his livestock was. The judgment is not recorded, but the stolen food as well as the sarcasm about fat livestock indicate the hunger experienced by the servants.[13] In 1670, Maryland servant Nicholas Bradley was sentenced to receive six lashes for rebelliousness and theft.[14] In 1638 Virginia, servant Anthony Delamons was punished with "30 stripes on the bare shoulders" because he "hath conveyed and made away the goods of his said master, and bartered and bargained contrary to the lawes and customes of the country."[15] In 1650 Virginia, Magrat, a servant, was caught after she had "broken up the doors of the house and stolen certain goods" from a neighbour.[16] In 1674 Massachusetts, Hanna Steward was imprisoned on suspicion of stealing from her master. However, as the theft "could not bee fully proved ag[ains]t her," she was "admonished" by the suspicious court, ordered to pay court and prison fees, and dismissed.[17] However, in 1679, another Massachusetts servant, Sarah Phillips, not only stole from her master but also bore an illegitimate child and perhaps had run away, "rideing away in mans apparell." She was sentenced to two weeks' imprisonment, to receive fifteen lashes twice, and to pay her master's court fees. If her master refused to pay off her prison fees, she would be sold, with the surplus going to her master.[18]

Close knowledge of the household facilitated James Southward and Anthony D'Mondidier's plot to forge the will of D'Mondidier's master Jeremiah Hasling. Hasling had been "totally deprived of his reason and sences" for some time, and the two men had kept others in the

household out of the bedchamber during Hasling's death.[19] The new
will, written by D'Mondidier, made Southward the heir to Hasling's
substantial estate, including a plantation, and disinherited Hasling's
two adult married daughters, the beneficiaries of his previous will.
D'Mondidier's incentive was made obvious in his boast immediately
after the death that "now there is a cow, calfe & a sow for Anthony
Mondidier" in a bequest from the false will.[20] Although Hasling's relatives (the suit was brought by his sons-in-law) regained his assets,
Southward and D'Mondidier do not seem to have been prosecuted
for their fraud.

STRIKES

Work stoppages were also a means of defiance. Six servants went on
strike on the Patuxent Maryland plantation of Richard Preston.
They announced they would "peremptorily & positively refuse to
goe & doe their ordinary labour" because of excessive hard work
and a diet of only beans and bread without meat. Both Preston and
four of the "obstinate rebellious" servants sent petitions to the
Maryland Provincial Court. The court did not view this rebellion
lightly – the four petitioning servants were sentenced to thirty lashes each, and with a stroke of cruelty, the court mandated that the
whipping be administered by the two "mildest" and "not soe refractory" servants. The four ringleaders escaped punishment by "kneel-
ing on their knees, asking & craving forgiveness" and "promising all
compliance & obedience hereafter," causing the court to suspend
their punishment as long as they remained of "good behavior
towards their s[ai]d Master ever hereafter."[21] This peaceful resolution might have occurred because Preston indicated that he would
not seek punishment as long as the servants returned to work. This
case illustrates the harsh lives of the servants, the impunity of the
master, and the favouring of the master by the court, but also the
social expectation of benevolence and patronage.

In Norfolk County Virginia in 1638, several servants of Captain
John Sibsey engaged in what the court called "a mutiny," but which
seems actually to have been some kind of work stoppage against the
overseer during a time of Sibsey's absence. The punishment was
harsh: the servants were to receive "100 strippes apiece" on their "bare
shoulders."[22] A similar kind of strike was implemented by an
unnamed Maryland servant in 1643, when she refused to work for

anyone who was not her master. After she had become "lame" on arrival to Kent County, her master had apparently handed her over to another man who brought her back to St Mary's County. He had expected her to also do work for him, but she stated that "shee was noe servant of his." Although brought to court, the lack of proof meant she was not punished.[23]

Servants also deployed their intimate knowledge of their masters' households to devise ways to better their situations. In another case, a servant inveigled her mistress to sell her. The matter emerged during litigation in the Maryland Provincial Court in 1664 over a large debt when one of the deponents mentioned in passing that John Hawkins, the plaintiff, had also encouraged a maidservant, Debory Webb, to "speake to your dame [mistress] and give her high words that will be the way to make her sell yow[you]." Webb had responded enthusiastically, saying, "I will give her all the bad language I cann to gett cleare of her." The plan seems to have worked, with Webb soon after being sold to Hawkins.[24] Although this stratagem was imputed to Hawkins, it's clear that Webb put it into action to further her own interests.

Returning early to Britain from a criminal sentence of indenture was also a potential means of resistance. The records are scanty about this, but a subset of criminal cases prosecuted at the Old Bailey in London included allegations of returning early from servitude.[25] One such was the trial of Elizabeth Longman, the leader of a theft ring that had bought off her indenture before she served the full term.[26] Returning early was evading punishment and thus a felony, because the convict had been reprieved from a death penalty conditional to serving the indenture.[27] Margaret Riggs, another repeat offender, "a year or two ago transported for stealing silks; but returning before her time, was now again convicted of stealing, and call'd to her former judgement" of capital punishment.[28] However, there must have been some number of convicted felons who left their indentures early and managed to avoid being recaptured.

RUNAWAYS

The most common way of attempting to evade a master's dominion was running away.[29] A relatively high proportion of servants ran away during the eighteenth century; scholars have estimated between 5 and 10 per cent of servants, which probably tallies with rates

for the seventeenth century.[30] It's difficult to know how many runaways were apprehended. On one hand, the authorities had limited
ability to trace runaways. On the other hand, it might have been
difficult for runaways to get assistance. Since the act was regarded as
a serious crime, and the population of the colonies was relatively
small in the seventeenth century, there was a persistent risk that a
fleeing person would be recognized. Nonetheless, running away
must have presented an obvious temptation to servants who had
been abused or who had entered servitude unwillingly. One case
that suggests that it was difficult to catch servants who had left the
area was brought by Thomas Bennett, who had been sent to
Delaware Bay in 1666 as a bounty hunter to recover a Maryland runaway servant. Bennett had been promised payment of a cow and calf
for his search and provided an affidavit of his journey, but the case
went to court when the servant's master, not recovering the servant,
refused to pay Bennett.[31] That said, many servants who tried to
escape were caught and punished.

Most legislation regarding servants dealt with the problem of runaways. The usual penalty in both Maryland and Virgina was additional
time added to the indenture, and often whipping.[32] For example, the
1676 Act Relateing to Servants and Slaves enacted in Maryland primarily focused on this issue. The law tried to disincentivize running
away and to make it more difficult. It mandated that no servants,
whether indentured or conventionally hired for wages, were to travel
more than 10 miles from their master or mistress without a notice. It
also established that for every day servants were unlawfully absent
from their master's or mistress's service, they would serve an additional ten days, while anyone helping absconding servants would be
fined 500 pounds of tobacco for every day of the servant's absence.[33]
For example, in 1666 William Loveridge, who was gone three months
and eight days, was sentenced to serve his original term plus ten days
for each day he had been absent – adding almost three years to his
term of servitude.[34] In 1680 Virginia, Adam Ballentine "voluntaryly"
agreed in court to serve his master for two and half years after his term
was over.[35] In another case, that had a more obscure resolution,
Robert Jones took his servant Robert Davies to court for running
away. Davies claimed, however, that his absence was due to being sold
by Jones to another master. The court, clearly unsure of its ground,
ordered Davies to serve extra time, but with the caveat that if he was
able to prove his contention, then Jones had to compensate him: "if

he makes appeare that he was sold by vertue of the said Robert Jones his power as aforesaid ... then the said Robert Jones shall make the said Robert Davies sattis faccon for all the time he shall serve the said Jones from this prsent day."[36] Popular culture recognized the risks of running away, and James Revel described how "if we offer once to run away, / for every hour we must serve a day, / For every day a week, they're so severe, / Every week a month, and every month a year."[37]

The courts heard many cases involving runaway servants. In Maryland, runaways were seen as a serious enough issue that they were usually dealt with by the Provincial Court rather than the local county court. Absconding from servitude was seen as a denial of proper societal relations that could disincline a court in a person's favour. On the same day in 1673, the Maryland Provincial Court heard two back-to-back cases of servants suing for their freedom dues from the same master. Elizabeth Thompson was freed and the court ordered that her master "pay her freedome corne & clothes." But because Walter Jefferys had previously run away, the court, after "making examinacon into the matter," decided that he had to serve an additional seven months.[38]

Although courts saw running away as malingering, it is not unlikely that most runaways were fleeing cruelty and maltreatment. A telling case is that of Ursula Bayley, who was brought to court in Virginia in 1650 for both running away and theft. Bayley was sentenced to "30 lashes on the bare backe," but the record also implies that she had absconded because of maltreatment, a factor the court seemed to recognize in mandating that her master George Heighham "shall provide meals, drinks, & clothing for her & further cure of her legge that hereafter no more complaints bee made by her" nor by "none of his sarvants." Heigham was also made responsible for court costs and other charges.[39]

Whipping of runaways was customary, but in 1668, the Virginia General Court felt the need to codify that while runaway indentured servants were liable to extra time of servitude by law, masters and magistrates could still inflict "moderate corporall punishment" in order, somewhat paradoxically, "to reclayme them from persisting in that idle course."[40] Apprehended runaways were to be whipped by the constable of each precinct "severely" as they were handed from district to district on their return to their master's home.[41] Recidivists suffered even worse punishment: Virginia imposed whipping and branding with an R after the second offence, as well as additional time.[42] When

Hugh George's three servants were apprehended in Maryland in 1640, he planned to cut his losses and sell them where they were. But the Virginia General Court ordered them to be brought back to Virginia, to be given "such exemplary and condign punishment as the nature of their offense shall justly deserve."[43]

Collusion

Enslaved people who conspired with servants to run away could not be punished with additional time, and additional violence was likely to be imposed on their persons; the same applied to Africans who were still free. In July 1640, Hugo Gwyn traced his three runaway servants to Maryland. The Virginia court ordered that they receive thirty lashes each, but then devised disparate punishments for the white and black servants. The two white servants, of Dutch and Scottish origins, were ordered to serve their master an additional year, and then the colony for three more years. The black servant, John Punch, suffered a much more severe punishment, being ordered to serve his master or his heirs "for the time of his natural life" – essentially becoming a slave.[44] Through such severity, punishments sought to deter runaways and also complicity between whites and blacks. If runaway slaves, of both African and Native American descent, were injured or killed, the owner was to receive compensation.[45] Injuring servants, on the other hand, was seen as a wrong done to the servant. The prospect of servants collaborating with the enslaved remained a significant fear, and there were attempts to divide the interests of the two groups. In 1660, Virginia aimed to disincentivize servants escaping with enslaved people, mandating that any "English servants who shall run away in company with any Negroes" would have to serve additional time to make up for the absence of the latter, who were "incapable of makeing satisfaction by addition of time." In fact, if enslaved people, as property, were "lost or killed," the captured servant would be liable for additional fines or service. [46]

In addition, the authorities were concerned about the collusion of servants who ran away together. In 1640, six of Captain William Pierce's servants, several of whom were Dutch, and Emanuel, slave of a Mr Reginald, stole a boat, food, and arms to escape to the Dutch "plantation" (the Dutch colonies of New Netherland and New Amsterdam). The court regarded this as "a dangerous precedent" and punished them harshly. The two ringleaders were punished with thirty lashes, branded on the cheek with the letter *R*, given added servitude to the colony of seven and three years respectively after they had finished their indentures, and forced to wear irons at the discretion of their master. The enslaved Emanuel suffered the same punishment, without the added time, which was superfluous. The other four men received lesser punishments, variously an additional seven years of servitude to the colony, an additional two and a half years, thirty lashes, and for one relatively lucky servant, "to remain upon his good behavior," although he too apparently served an additional unspecified term because the entry ends with: "all those who are condemned" were to "serve the colony after their time are expired with their masters."[47]

These severe punishments were in part imposed because the courts saw the attempt of several servants to escape together as a conspiracy that risked inciting a more general seditiousness among servants and perceived the collusion of servants with enslaved people as increasing the danger of general insurrection among the subordinate peoples, who were the majority of the colony's residents. In addition, it appears that there was concern that servants would continue to try to escape to the Dutch plantation. The Dutch practised both indentured servitude and slavery but mitigated by legislation and cultural expectations that allowed some freedoms and protections, as well as paths for the enslaved to rise out of slavery.[48] Fleeing to Dutch territory offered a zone out of reach of English law enforcement. In 1663, the Virginia Assembly mandated that if runaway servants managed to "escape to any of the Dutch plantations," then "it is enacted that letters be written" by Virginia magistrates "to the respective governours of those plantations to make seizure of all such fugitive servants, and to retorne them."[49] Within a few years, this ceased to be an escape option: in 1664 New Amsterdam and in 1674 New Netherland became British territories.

Another group escape attempt in 1640 was described as "a dangerous conspiracy" because the two leaders, William Wooton and John Bradye, had been "inticing divers others" to join them. They had been joined by six other men and a woman, Margaret Brandan. Wooton and Bradye, as the instigators, were to be whipped from the gallows to the courthouse, and then branded, Wooton on the shoulder and Bradye on the forehead, and then to work for the colony seven years after they had finished their terms. Two freemen who had joined them were to be whipped and serve two years; wthe other five, who were servants, would be whipped and their masters would pay fines for them, but would be recompensed by an additional year of labour each. They were to be kept in irons until released by the court's order.[50]

In some cases, if the runaway servant's master was amenable, a compromise was possible. In 1693, Nicholas Cornewell petitioned the Somerset County Maryland Court to assess additional time to the indenture of his servant Edward Hogg, who had run away for 101 days. The court granted the petition, and Hogg admitted that he had absconded. However, Cornewell also stated that if Hogg gave good service, he would reduce the additional time by half.[51] In the rare cases in which a servant could be shown to be justified in running away, the courts might impose no penalty. Japhet Griphin had been indentured for seven years, but his master claimed that he had the right to hold him in bondage for ten. When Griphin had finally run away, his master had recovered him through a public search. However, Griphin maintained that his master had no right to hold him, saying, "I did not run away but went away," and demanded his freedom and freedom dues. The court agreed, and Griphin was freed.[52] Likewise, David Ralston claimed his freedom from his master, who argued that because Ralston had been a runaway, he deserved extra time of servitude. However, Ralston argued, and the court agreed, that he had already served additional time before he had run away, and so he should be freed.[53]

Pursuit of Runaways

During the seventeenth century, runaways were announced by a "hue and cry" or announcement in pursuit of a felon, which might include placards advising passersby to be on the alert for a runaway.[54] William Moraley described "printed and written advertisements" to apprehend runaways that were "set up against the trees and publick places in the town," as well as notices in the newspapers in 1730s Pennsylvania.[55] There is only one such broadsheet extant from the seventeenth century, meant to recover Matthew Jones, a runaway servant of Hannah Bosworth in Hull, Massachusetts, in 1683. According to the announcement, Jones was a tailor, relatively well dressed, and a large reward of 40 shillings was offered for his capture.[56] However, most early runaway advertisements come from eighteenth-century newspaper advertisements, which still provide some insights into the conditions of earlier runaways.[57] The earliest such ads I have seen

date from the 1720s and 1730s, when American newspapers first
began to be published. They can provide some insights into runaways from previous decades. The *Virginia Gazette* started publishing
in 1736 and with its fifth issue began to solicit ads from "All persons
who have occasion to buy or sell houses, land, goods, or cattle; or
have servants or slaves runaway; or have lost horses or cattle &c., or
who want to give any publick notice."[58] Even earlier, the 1729 *Maryland Gazette* (which printed its first issue in 1727) announced the
disappearance of twenty-three-year-old Samuel Davis, "of middle
stature, very swarthy, down-look'd with a turn'd up nose," dressed
fairly well, in "a sinnamon colour'd jacket, with large brass buttons,
strip'd flannel breeches, and a speckled shirt, a pair of light colour'd
old worsted stockings, a pair of indifferent good shoes, and a felt hat,
with a brown wig." It included another ad for the less well-dressed
Eleanor Barry, an Irish woman, "pock-mark'd and of a swarthy com-
plexion." She had been wearing "a white-stuff gown and petticoat"
and had also taken a blue gown with her.[59] In the next issue, along
with a repeat of the ad for Davis, there was one for John Jones, a nine-
teen-year-old native of Maryland "of middling stature, short light
brown hair," dressed more modestly with "a cropt hat ... a white cotton jacket, and an oznabrig [coarse cloth] shirt and breeches." He
had also stolen a hoe.[60] Even before it began soliciting runaway ads,
the *Virginia Gazette* already included ads for runaways as of its third
issue in September 1736: readers were asked to help apprehend
Thomas Rennolds, a "convict servant-man" who was a shoemaker
and took with him several shoemaking tools, as well as clothing and
a horse and tack.[61] Its fourth issue included an ad for runaway Anne
Harmon, age twenty, "of a middle stature, well featur'd, and has black
hair and eyes" wearing "a cotton gown and petticoat, strip'd with red
and blue, and an English straw hat, lined with white callico." Harmon was notable for the quantity of additional goods that she took
with her: 11 yards of "fine Scotch plaid," 4 dozen Scotch handkerchiefs, several Holland [fine linen] shifts and aprons, three pairs of
fine worsted stockings, and several caps. She was also suspected of
stealing some other goods that had disappeared from storage about
ten days before she left: 11 dozen Scotch handkerchiefs, a piece of
fine plaid, some thread, 4 dozen cravats, and a felt hat. Her master
must have been a textile or clothing dealer.[62] On 15 October 1736,
the *Virginia Gazette* recorded three runaways who fled together: John
Connor, an Irish man (who had come from Bristol) who "talks upon

the brogue," was red haired, freckled, and pock marked; Ralph Taylor, an Englishman; and Sarah Miers, a Dutch woman who "talks
broken English." The three had also taken extra clothing, other goods
"in particular a red rug" and a "long-boat, with one mast and a square
sail."[63] The same issue included an ad to apprehend Robert Croson,
a tailor, who ran away wearing "a pair of brown breeches with green
puffs, a pair of brown yarn stockings, a blue and white stript waste-
coat, and a white shirt." Croson had been previously captured in
Charles County, but "he swore that he was no servant, and so was
whipt and discharged."[64]

These ads show servants putting into effect carefully devised plans
of escape, rather than fleeing without forethought. They took valuable clothing and gear with them, and Anne Harmon had planned
ahead to provision herself, taking lightweight but valuable goods
that were associated with women's property and easier for a woman
to sell.[65] The three servants who had fled together must have
planned ahead to take the boat as a means of escape and to depart
with valuable goods; Thomas Rennolds likewise took a horse to
facilitate his escape. In addition to providing transportation, the
boat and the horse and tack had value in themselves and could later
be sold. Robert Croson, when caught, was prepared with a lie, and
although he suffered a whipping as an idle vagrant, had been able to
continue with his escape.

Sympathy for Runaways

In some instances, runaways were aided by members of the community. Those who sheltered runaways, like the Quaker Peter Sharpe who
harboured the ill servant John Corbett, mentioned in chapter 5, were
liable to penalties from the courts. Sharpe escaped penalty only
because the court concluded that Corbett had not been cured by his
master as agreed upon and was therefore no longer a servant, and so
Sharpe had committed no crime in taking him into his home.[66] Many
who sheltered a runaway servant were not so fortunate: for example,
in 1667, Henry and Dorothy Robinson were sued successfully by
James Humes for sheltering his indentured servant Catherine How,
and Thomas Sprigg, a Maryland justice, was sued by Edmund Lindsey
for sheltering his indentured servant Robert Leeds. The latter two
took the case to arbitration, and Sprigg was ordered to pay Lindsey
5,000 pounds of tobacco, receiving "a generall release" from the

charge. This may also have meant that the servant's time was bought out.[67] Another influential man harbouring a fugitive was Augustine Herman, a wealthy landowner, who took in Francis Hill's runaway servant, George Taylor, in 1670, and refused to give him up to his master without a payment of 1,400 pounds of tobacco. As it often did with influential individuals, the court seems to have given Herman some benefit of the doubt, mandating that he receive 400 pounds of tobacco from Hill for a servant that Herman was unlawfully detaining, but that he return Taylor to Hill.[68] This case may have begun with Taylor fleeing to Herman for shelter but then devolved into a monetary exchange in which Taylor's interests were trivialized. In 1665, the Maryland Provincial Court fined Thomas Sprigg, then the sheriff, who apparently had deliberately let a servant escape rather than incur a severe punishment. (The sympathetic Sprigg is apparently the same man who two years later would be sued for sheltering Robert Leeds.) The servant in the 1665 case, Richard Newell, was one of three men charged in the Calvert County Court with stealing and killing hogs. The two freemen involved in the theft were each fined 2,000 pounds of tobacco, but Newell, "being incapable to satisfy in tob[acco] or goods because [he was] a servant," was sentenced to the pillory and twenty lashes at three separate court meetings. Sprigg may have found the punishment excessive, or perhaps was persuaded by the claim of the accused men that they had mistaken the earmarks of the hogs. In any event, he had "willfully" allowed Newell to escape. He was ordered to bring in Newell or, barring that (the court apparently recognizing that Sprigg might be recalcitrant or unable to do so), to pay the fine of 2,000 pounds of tobacco.[69]

The many cases of sympathetic bystanders helping runaway servants indicates that some felt the penalties were disproportionate or were sympathetic to the plight of abused servants, and potentially also accepted servants as rights-bearing members of society. Virginia laws reiterated that those who "entertained" runaways were fined for each day the runaway was at their place.[70] Apparently this was not a sufficient deterrent, though, because the issue of abetting runaways was revisted a number of times. In 1657, because "huy [hue] and cries after runnaway servants hath been much neglected," the Virginia Assembly mandated that the notice of a runaway be passed from household to household or a fine would be incurred.[71] The implication is that people in the community were not always very zealous in their supposed duty of tracking runaway servants. The following year, perhaps in desperation, the assembly mandated that a returned runaways' hair be cut "close above their ears" so that they could be "with more ease discovered and apprehended."[72] This provision was repeated in 1669.[73] The assumption behind this appears to have been that most runaways would try to abscond again and so, perhaps implicitly, to prevent members of the public from claiming that they could not be responsible for turning in runaways because they were too difficult to identify. Possibly, there was also a shaming aspect. However, hair clipping was considerably milder than the branding, mutilation, amputations, or outright murder typically suffered by recaptured enslaved runaways.[74] Nonetheless, in 1660, further legislation was passed in Virginia because "the pursuit and takeing of runawaies is hindred chiefly by the neglect of constables in making search according to their warrants." Officers were now enjoined to "make diligent search" and further encouraged by a reward of 200 pounds of tobacco, to be supplied by the servant's master, or fined 350 pounds of tobacco if they neglected to search.[75] In 1663, admitting that "the ordinary way of makeing pursuites after runawaye servants by hues and cryes is by experience found ineffectual," the Virginia Assembly established that the master of a runaway was "required" to make a strenuous effort for the servant's recovery, which would involve public agents, and had to repay the costs of recapturing the servant, though they would gain extra time served.[76] Nonetheless, it appears that many remained sympathetic to runaways, continuing to abet their escapes. With increasing desperation, bemoaning the "divers good laws" to deter and recapture runaway servants that had been "proved ineffectual, chiefly through the wickednesse of servants … and partly by the remisnes of some planters" who not only had not captured servants but also had "given them assistance and directions how to escape," the Virginia Assembly enacted a law in 1669 to reward anyone who apprehended a runaway with 1,000 pounds of tobacco from public funds, to be repaid by the servant's labour to the county upon finishing his or her original contract.[77] A few days later, the Assembly sheepishly reduced the reward to 200 pounds of tobacco, the previous amount being "too burthensome to the publique." Perhaps to bolster their claim to severity, however, the Assembly reiterated that servants would be given an extended term of servitude, that masters should cut the hair of previous runaways short, that any constable who took custody of fugitives should "whip them severely," that constables be fined if fugitives escaped, and that masters pay authorities for recovery costs.[78] The reward of 200 pounds of tobacco still appears to have offered some incentive to capture fleeing servants since the following year the legislature passed a law to limit the reward for each runaway to one person only; apparently it had become common for "sundry persons" to simultaneously claim the reward.[79] In 1676, in the aftermath of Bacon's Rebellion, the Virginia legislature reiterated that anyone sheltering someone who remotely appeared to be a servant, such as "any person not well knowne" in the locality, including newly hired servants, was potentially guilty of harbouring a runaway unless they immediately turned the person over to the authorities. No penalty was mentioned, perhaps because the events of "those late rebellious tymes" were assumed to have given an added seriousness to the mandate.[80]

"Detaining" Runaways

The problem of the public abetting runaways also existed in Maryland. Individuals could be prosecuted for "entertaining" or "detaining" the servants of others and would be ordered by the courts through a writ of replevin to "deliver" the absconded servants in question.[81] Perhaps because the courts treated the cases as a question of property, the nuances of the disputes, such as whether the accused individuals were sheltering runaways, stealing the labour of someone else's employee, or actually kidnapping servants, were not recorded. Some of these cases do suggest some form of kidnapping. For example, in a 1672 Maryland Court of Chancery case, widow Verlinda Stone complained with a public "clamour" about Edmund Lindsey who "took" and was "unjustly detaining" her servant Henry Dorman.[82] No mention was made of punishment to the servant, which suggests some form of abduction. Other cases employing similar language, including the "clamor" of the aggrieved master or mistress, the "taking" and "unjust" detaining of the servants, and lack of mention of punishments incurred by the servants occurred with some regularity: in 1673, John Wahob complained of Abell James's detention of Wahob's servant George Mills; in 1676, a servant named Johnathan Tosse was reclaimed from Johnathan Athey; in 1677, servant Johnathan Tassell was to be restored to Thomas Bowdie by Charles Boteler; in 1678, Thomas Waghob complained that Jacob Lotun had taken his servant William Simpson and Humphrey Davenport sued Thomas Hothud for the return of a servant woman named Sheely

Donnoughway; Thomas Harris sued Thomas Pattison to recover servant Rowland Morgan; and Johnathan Blomfield sued Garrett Van-
sweringen to get back a servant named James Wilkin.[83] In one
extreme case in 1677, George Parker sued Joseph Tilly not only for the
retrieval of two servants, Thomas Norris and Elizabeth Moore, but
also for the theft of his horses, cattle, hogs, and a quantity of goods
including tools, kitchen implements, clothing, and furniture. Charles
Boteler, himself once accused of "detaining" a servant, represented
Parker in court.[84] This last case clearly suggests that along with the
theft of the livestock and goods, the servants had been held against
their will. It's impossible to say with certainty how Tilly could have
taken what seems to be a large quantity, maybe most, of Parker's
goods and employees – perhaps it occurred when Parker was away
from the region for an extended period. The outcomes of these cases
are not recorded, but the courts would have called witness to confirm
the contentions of the plaintiffs and the accused. The mention of
writs of replevin suggests that rather than moving the cases to trial,
the courts were immediately ordering the return of the servants to
their original master or mistress.

In a similar case in late 1692 in Somerset Maryland County Court,
Thomas Davis sued John Carter for taking Davis's servant Mary
Armitage into his service, claiming 50,000 pounds of tobacco in damages. Armitage had been Carter's servant until August 1689 but then
had been recontracted to serve Davis, an arrangement to which all
parties had agreed. However, Carter had then enticed Armitage back
through unspecified means. Through his attorney, Carter admitted
fault and was assessed a penalty of 340 pounds of tobacco in damages
to Davis. It's not clear whether he also received Armitage back into his
service, since the two years and six months specified in her contract
were already over – perhaps the reason for the lower assessment of
damages by the court.[85]

A more complex case was that of Mary Maxwell, whose former master John Strawbridge sued Edward Jones in 1691 because Jones did
"detein and fraudulently and unjustly keep" the servant woman. Jones
claimed he had made a "swap," by supplying Strawbridge with another
servant woman, Margaret Williams, but Strawbridge contended that
Williams "was a poore indigent sickly creature" who was "not able to
do any manner of service," and within two weeks, "took her bed …
and died." However, the court ruled the transaction had been legitimate.[86] In a later hearing, Strawbridge was fined for "taking up his

wench, Mary Maxwell, which was runn away."[87] Despite the ambiguous language, the penalty was assessed to Strawbridge, which suggests that Maxwell was not actually perceived to be a runaway. Yet perhaps there had been some element of volition in the case; one year later, Mary Maxwell was brought to court by Jones for running away and stealing tobacco, for which she was ordered to serve an additional five months.[88] Maxwell also was willing to advocate for herself, as evidenced by her appearance in court in 1693, stating that "she has completed her service" and petitioning for her freedom dues from Jones, which were granted.[89] Searches and prosecutions of runaway servants provide evidence of the cruelty and exploitation of some masters, whose abusiveness caused their servants to flee, and of the sometimes unsympathetic courts. Yet, conversely, these narratives also show increasing recognition by those in the middling and even upper echelons of society, including magistrates and parish officials, of the shared citizenship of white servants.

Indentured servants who resented servitude or who were faced with cruel, exploitative, or neglectful masters had no really safe path before them. Yet many servants were willing to risk their safety and health, and even their lives, in order to resist. They rebelled through many means, including through the courts; engaging in crime, including theft, violence, and murder; levelling insults; manipulating their masters; refusing to work; running away; and outright rebellion. While most of these forms of resistance were viewed with severity, the many instances of individuals aiding runaway servants show widespread acceptance that servants and masters shared some essential rights. The records of these various forms of revolt are sadly fragmentary. However, they do illustrate ambivalent attitudes about white servitude within the larger colonial society and provide insights into the resilience and resourcefulness of servants as they attempted to attain dignity and agency.

9

After Indenture

From the beginnings of indentured servitude, servants received some rudimentary protections from English law. However, the articulation of the rights of indentured servants differed by geographic location and, especially, were expressed in the attention paid the legal grievances and court cases brought by indentured servants.

Indentured servants were the most protected in the continental colonies. Laws in Britain did protect individual rights, but the government retained the right to forcibly indenture large groups, a right that colonial authorities were unable to impose. Servants' protections, whether stated in indenture contracts made in Britain or protected by law under the custom of the country, provided inalienable rights to indentured servants that could be defended in court. These rights were so ingrained that the legal system mandated a remission of court fees and the provision of court-appointed lawyers to ensure protections to servants who were inherently *in pauperis*. By doing so, the colonial governments demonstrated that indentured servants, although in a temporary state of unequal dependence, were part of the body politic. The new definition of rights would prove critical to the growth of an American sense of citizenship in the state. Indeed, these rights were particularly far-reaching, extending not only to men but also to some extent to women, underage youths, and children.

The Caribbean colonies, while still recognizing some servant rights and personhood, generally provided the least recognition of rights and recourse to legal relief. It was in the mainland colonies where the servant class – during the seventeenth century, a group encompassing a significant proportion of the population – experienced official recognition of themselves as subjects with rights. The experience with inden-

tured servitude was not the only factor in the new conceptions of
nationalism and citizenship that arose in the American colonies in the
late eighteenth century. But it was a crucial component of the mainland
colonists' understanding of themselves as independent actors and pos-
sessors of individual rights that required legislative acknowledgement.

As servants completed their indentures, they entered the political
and social body of the British Atlantic colonies. A number of outcomes were possible for servants after they had completed their
indentures. While the period of servitude presented dangers, perhaps
most acutely the risk of dying from disease, once servitude was completed, colonial society presented opportunities that were not available in crowded and land-scarce Britain and Ireland. In the early days
of indentured servitude on the mainland, landownership through relatively generous freedom dues was a significant benefit. In other
cases, freedom dues also included some training in a trade, serving
partly as a kind of apprenticeship that left servants with serviceable
skills. Women were largely excluded from these opportunities but
had a reasonable chance of socio-economic gain through marriage,
like the former servant Abigail Shanks, whose status rose after she
married John Shanks, a former servant himself, who had become a
moderately prosperous planter and minor office-holder.[1] Many servants – some mentioned in this book – flourished. One such was
Thomas Doughty, or Dowty, a Scottish royalist soldier captured in
1650 at the Battle of Dunbar. He was sent to Massachusetts as an
indentured servant. After finishing his term of servitude, Doughty
seems to have prospered. He moved around New England, married,
had children, owned two mills, and acquired land, finally ending up
in Salem.[2] Charles Bayly, kidnapped as a child in the 1640s, eventually
became governor of the Hudson's Bay Company.[3] A number of the
eighteenth-century autobiographers discussed in this book made
good lives for themselves, including Peter Williamson, William Moraley, Elizabeth Ashbridge, and John Harrower. Cuthbert Fenwick, who
had tried to cheat Jone Nicculgutt during her indenture in the 1660s,
was a justice in Calvert County and referred to as a gentleman, yet he
was also the son of an indentured servant of the same name.[4] Russell
Menard's study of 275 Maryland servant men in the 1640s suggests
that "opportunity was abundant" if servants survived their term of
servitude. More than 40 per cent of the servants he followed eventually disappeared from the records, probably deceased during the period
of servitude or some dying after. But of the rest, about 80 became

landowners, mostly small planters, and about a dozen became substantial planters. Seventy-five served as jurors or public officials, with
some attaining prominent roles such as justices of the peace, and two
becoming part of Maryland's governing council.

Outcomes varied: some servants went on to economic and social
success; others remained at the lowest levels of free society, or even
reindentured themselves for lack of employment opportunities. After
the mid-seventeenth century, when freedom dues no longer included
substantial allotments of land, the basis for prosperity became more
precarious, dooming many former servants to poverty and dependence.[5] In Maryland, the province did acknowledge some responsibility toward them. For example, in 1676, the Maryland Provincial
Court ordered that Anne Williams, a former servant in a "miserable
and distressed condition," be assessed a yearly amount of tobacco "for
her maintinance and releife."[6] Former servant Alexander Howell
asked for "clemency" from the Charles County Court in 1666 after he
was disabled by palsy; he was awarded 1,400 pounds of tobacco yearly
as well as food, laundry, and lodging paid for by the county. A year
later, the county paid for his transportation back to England.[7] In
Barbados, most freed servants joined a labouring underclass, but
some prospered.[8]

Over time, while freedom dues diminished, there was increasing
regularization of the practices that served to protect servants from the
worst vagaries of the servant trade and abusive masters. Yet there continued to be considerable variation among servants' experiences. One
group who initially suffered particularly harsh terms of servitude
were eighteenth-century "redemptioners" from Germany and other
parts of Central Europe.[9] Unlike previous servants, this group often
included families with children, who were separated upon arrival.
Meanwhile, distinctions were increasingly made between servants
and enslaved people that established norms of citizenship for white
servants and other "freeborn Englishmen," as well as white women,
Scots, and the Irish, while specifying enslavement as a condition
appropriate only for those descended from Africans. Defining indentured servitude became central to delineating the nature of both citizenship and racial inequity.

After the American Revolution, the British state began transporting
convicts to Australia, while the practice of white indentured servitude
disappeared in British territories. After Britain's loss of the American
mainland colonies, it was still potentially possible for British inden-

tured servants to be sent to the Caribbean, but there was increasing distaste for the idea of whites labouring alongside African slaves. Australia offered a zone that was more clearly a penal colony.[10] In addition, as the Enlightenment approached, politicians and intellectuals began to express doubts about excessively harsh punishments for petty crimes, sometimes singling out transportation and forced servitude as examples of unjust forms of punishment.[11]

During the nineteenth century, redemptioners continued to arrive in Pennsylvania, while in British Caribbean territories, a form of indentured servitude was restored after the abolition of slavery. Hundreds of thousands of Indian and Chinese indentured servants began arriving after the abolition of slavery in 1833. These Asian servants, not protected by British subjecthood, were often shipped forcibly, with the collaboration of the local authorities in their homelands (in the case of India, under British control). They typically served many years of hard labour while accruing debts for food and upkeep, forcing many to repeatedly reindenture themselves after finishing a term, unlike previous generations of European servants.[12] Additionally, coercive laws were devised to maintain restrictions on the descendants of enslaved people in the British Caribbean.[13]

By that time, indentured servitude had helped shape many aspects of British and Irish economics, politics, and societal norms. The practice of indentured servitude was a crucial factor in shaping ideals of citizenship on both sides of the Atlantic. By situating indentured servants in an amorphous category between free English people and the enslaved, the need to define the status of indentured servants forced English and colonial societies to grapple with understanding the relationship of the subject to the state. The conclusion that servants possessed English rights helped codify an understanding of what those rights actually meant, and how they were expressed for an individual. These rights encompassed not only English servants but also the Scots and the Irish, even though the last group was often viewed with extreme bias. Paradoxically, the inhering of rights in people of British and Irish descent was part of the same process by which enslaved Africans and their descendants were defined as inferior.

Indentured servitude was a key element of many aspects of British and colonial life and society, and significantly shaped discourses about labour, citizenship, race, and gender. It simultaneously institutionalized inequality and helped establish a class system in the colonies while undermining it by engendering cultural norms expecting opportunity and social mobility. While initially placing whites in positions of servitude similar to those of Africans, the practice of indentured servitude ultimately contributed to the hardening of perceptions about racial disparities: both servants themselves and the British authorities demonstrated increasing disquiet about the employment of whites in bondage. It was also an important influence on the development of the Atlantic and British economies, shifting populations away from Europe, contributing to the commercialization of criminal justice, helping to pave the way for the accrual of vast fortunes for early capitalists, and laying the ground for slavery as well as transatlantic trade more generally. The existence of the practice of indentured servitude also forced a confrontation with and conceptualization of the nature of citizenship in England as well as in its growing empire in both Ireland and the colonies across the Atlantic.

Notes

ABBREVIATIONS

BNA Barbados National Archives
CSPC *Calendar of State Papers, Colonial Series*
FSL Folger Shakespeare Library
LMA London Metropolitan Archives
MAO Archives of Maryland Online (with shortened book titles)
MHS Massachusetts Historical Society
OBP *Old Bailey Proceedings Online*
OED *Oxford English Dictionary*
TNA The National Archives (London)

CHAPTER ONE

1 *Provincial Court*, MAO, v. 41, 476–8; on this case, see also Daniels, "Liberty to Complaine," 244.
2 *General Assembly*, MAO, v. 1, 403.
3 *Provincial Court*, MAO, v. 41, 476–8.
4 Ibid., 478.
5 *Provincial Court*, MAO, v. 49, 114, 122–3, 136, 138. Mecane was also spelled Micall.
6 *Provincial Court*, MAO, v. 41, 515–16; *General Assembly*, MAO, v. 1, 463–4; and editor's comments, *Provincial Court*, MAO, v. 49, xi.
7 Norton, "'Either Married," 36.
8 *Provincial Court*, MAO, v. 41, 515–16; *Provincial Court*, MAO, v. 49, xiii, 122, 137; *General Assembly*, MAO, v. 1, 463–4.

9 *Provincial Court*, MAO, v. 41, 515.

10 *General Assembly*, MAO, v. 1, 463.

11 Ibid., 463–6, 481. See also *Provincial Court*, MAO, v. 49, 137.

12 *General Assembly*, MAO, v. 1, 463–4.

13 Ibid., 464.

14 Wood, *Origins*, 17.

15 Rugemar, "Development of Mastery and Race," 443–7; Tomlins, *Freedom Bound*, 263–72; P. Morgan, "Virginia Slavery"; Halliday, "Brase's Case."

16 Examples of this pseudohistorical trend include Sean O'Callaghan, *To Hell or Barbados* (Dingle: Brandon, 2001); Michael Hoffman, *They Were White and They Were Slaves* (Dresden, NY: Wiswell Ruffin House, 1993); Lawrence Kelleher, *To Shed a Tear* (Lincoln, NE: Writers Club Press, 2001). A more accurate though still exaggerated and distorted discussion occurs in Don Jordan and Michael Walsh, *White Cargo* (New York: New York University Press, 2008), 137–54.

17 Handler and Reilly, "Contesting 'White Slavery'"; Rogers, *Ireland*, 45–6; Wareing, *Indentured Migration*, 41–3.

18 Handler and Reilly, "Contesting 'White Slavery," 48–9.

19 Tomlins, "Early British America," 122; Hay, "England," 78.

20 Many works adress the implications of slavery. A few include Wood, *Origins*; E. Morgan, *American Slavery*; K. Morgan, *Slavery*; Walvin, *Black Ivory*; Eltis, *Rise of African Slavery*; Dunn, *Sugar and Slaves*; Menard, *Sweet Negotiations*; Davis, *Inhuman Bondage*.

21 Daniels, "Liberty to Complaine"; see also Menard, "Servant to Freeholder," 48.

22 Handler, "Custom and Law," 13–14; Beckles, *History of Barbados*, 86–8.

23 Handler and Reilly, "Contesting 'White Slavery," 39.

24 Baxter, *Trelawny Papers*, v. 3, 166–7. Bickford does appear to have been indentured – see p. 291.

25 Carr, "Emigration," 272–4.

26 Elliott, *Empires*, 56; Wareing, *Indentured Migration*, 67; E. Morgan, *American Slavery*, 405; Tomlins, *Freedom Bound*, 583–5.

27 Billings, *Old Dominion*, 133.

28 Tomlins, *Freedom Bound*, 297.

29 Ibid., 583–7.

30 Newman, *New World*, 92.

31 Burnard, "European Migration," 775–80.

32 Eric Foner, *Give Me Liberty*, 100; Cooper, *Liberty*, 9; E. Morgan, *American Slavery*, 270; Rice, *Bacon's Rebellion*, especially 14–16, 90, 119, 195–6, 220–1; Tomlins, *Freedom Bound*, 276.

33 On Bacon's Rebellion in general, see E. Morgan, *American Slavery*, 250–70; Rice, *Bacon's Rebellion*; Nash, *Red, White & Black*, 110–5.

34 Tomlins, *Freedom Bound*, 40–2.

35 Handler, "Custom and Law," 5–8, 10, and throughout.

36 Coke, *Institutes*, v. 1, 117.

37 CSPC *1661–1668*, 229. See Wareing on the dating of this document, *Indentured Migration*, 41–2.

38 See Handler, "Custom and Law," 1, 12, and following.

39 Ibid., throughout.

40 *General Assembly*, MAO, v. 30, 291; Hening, *Statutes*, v. 1, 226.

41 Handler, "Early Edict."

42 *General Assembly*, MAO, v. 1, 80.

43 Ibid., 409.

44 *General Assembly*, MAO, v. 2, 528.

45 An Act for the Better Ordering and Governing of Negroes, 1661. The code is discussed in Handler, "Custom and Law," 14–15 and in Rugemar, "Development of Mastery and Race."

46 CSPC, *1675–1676*, 394, cited in Rugemar, "Development of Mastery and Race," 445.

47 For example, in 1631, 1632, 1645, Hening, *Statutes*, v. 1, 157, 182, 312. For New England, see Tomlins, *Freedom Bound*, 255.

48 Hening, *Statutes*, v. 2, 260.

49 Franklin, *Runaway Slaves*, 16, 45–6.

50 Hening, *Statutes*, v. 2, 270.

51 "An Act Concerning Servants and Slaves," (1705), in Hening, *Statutes*, v. 3, 447–63.

52 *General Assembly*, MAO, v. 30, 288–9.

53 The summation of Bryan's life appears on the first page, but he is discussed throughout the book, as is Pegg. Bryan, a "laborer," likely arrived as an indentured servant, but was free when he made his threats because he was ordered to leave Barbados. Instead, he remained and prospered over the next thirty years. Shaw, *Everyday Life*.

54 Shaw, 96. See also Handler, "Father Antoine Biet," 67; Hilary Beckles also mentions other Irish servants in Barbados who threatened the English: Beckles, "Riotous and Unruly," 513–14.

55 E. Morgan, *American Slavery*, 295–315; Eltis, "Rise and Fall."

56 Hening, *Statutes*, v. 2, 283; see also 252, 298, 447–62, 490–3; McIlwaine, *Journals*, 174. See also "An Act Concerning Servants and Slaves," (1705), in Hening, *Statutes*, v. 3, 447–63. On indenture and enslavement of Native Americans, see Rountree, *Pocahontas's People*, 86, 87, 94–9, 101–3,

109, 121, 130–45, 168–9; Reséndez, *The Other Slavery*; Fisher, "Shall Wee Have Peace"; Ethridge and Shuck-Hall, *Mississippian Shatter Zone*; Gallay, *Indian Slavery*; Gallay, *Indian Slave Trade*; E. Morgan, *American Slavery*, 99–100, 34, 163–4, 328–30; Nash, *Red, White & Black*, 109, 119–27.

57 Cited in Wareing, *Indentured Migration*, 4.

58 Galenson, "Rise and Fall; Beckles and Downes, "Economics of Transition"; Beckles and Downes, "Economic Formalization; Newman, *New World of Labor*; E. Morgan, *American Slavery*, 39–3; Menard, *Migrants, Servants, and Slaves*; Menard, "Popular Slave Society"; K. Morgan, *Slavery and Servitude*, 26–43.

59 See the OED, definition 2a.

60 Thomas, *Dictionarium Linguae Latinae*.

61 E. Morgan, *Inventing the People*, 28, 34, 46–7, 66, 71; Kettner, *Development*, especially chapter 1; Muller, *Subjects and Sovereign*, especially 1–7, 47–65, 217; Riesenberg, *Citizenship*, especially 203–51; *Hulsebosch*, "Ancient Constitution"; Dummett and Nicol, *Subjects, Citizens*.

62 Foxley, *The Levellers*; Donoghue, "Out of the Land of Bondage"; Pestana, *The English Atlantic*, especially 162–70.

63 Discussions of the growing sense of citizenship in British territories, and its antecedents, can be found in Tomlins, *Freedom Bound*, especially 140, 214, 245, 260, 276, 383, 409; Somers, "Rights, Relationality and Membership"; Somers, "Citizenship"; Goldie, "Unacknowledged Republic"; Pagden, "Human Rights"; E. Morgan, *Inventing the People*, especially 24, 38, 46–7, 66, 71, and chapter 4; Kettner, *Development*, especially 7–10, 15–18, 34, 52, 58–69, 78–90, 106–14, 127; Wells, *Law and Citizenship*; Gelderen and Skinner, "Introduction"; Skinner, "Classical Liberty"; Worder, "Republicanism, Regicide, and Republic"; Riesenberg, *Citizenship*, especially 231–51; Peltonen, "Citizenship and Republicanism"; Peltonen, *Classical Humanism and Republicanism*; Withington, *Politics of Commonwealth*; Hulsebosch, "Ancient Constitution"; Haskell, "Part of that Commonwealth"; Fitzmaurice, "Company-commonwealth."

64 Patterson, *Slavery and Social Death*, viii–ix; E. Morgan, *American Slavery*, 363–87; E. Morgan, "Slavery and Freedom"; Jordan, *White over Black*.

65 For example, Barbados's enslaved population had just surpassed the white population by the implementation of the 1661 slave code. Rugemar, "Development of Mastery and Race," 444; Menard, *Sweet Negotiations*, 25.

CHAPTER TWO

1 See the OED on "spirit" as a verb: "To carry off or away, to make away with or remove in a mysterious or dexterous manner" and "to kidnap, in order to transport to the plantations in America."

2 According to the OED: "kidnap" meant "originally, to steal or carry off (children or others) in order to provide servants or labourers for the American plantations; hence, in general use, to steal (a child), to carry off (a person) by illegal force."

3 "Trapan" probably arose from the word "trap," as in "entrap." See the OED, "trapan."

4 Wareing, *Indentured Migration*, 2, 23–4, 39, 51, 56, 91; Games, "Migration," 36–46; Smith, *Colonists in Bondage*, 336; Tomlins, *Freedom Bound*, 30, 35, 64–5, 573–82; Galenson, *White Servitude*, 18–33, 81–96; Fogelman, "Migrations." There was also substantial internal migration within the British Isles and to continental Europe.

5 The fifty-year-old was Thomas Middleton, sailing in 1682. LMA, CLC/521/MS006679

6 On spiriting and resistance to it, see Wareing, *Indentured Migration*, especially 141–9; Griffiths, *Lost Londons*, 288–9; Beckles, *White Servitude*, 50–2.

7 Wareing, Indentured Migration, 184–249.

8 On banishment as a form of punishment, see G. Morgan and Rushton, *Banishment*.

9 Palmer, *Virginia Calendar*, 185–6.

10 Wareing, *Indentured Migration*, 46–8; see also Galenson, *White Servitude*, 13–15.

11 See Wareing, *Indentured Migration*, chapter 4, and throughout the narrative.

12 On the Statute of Artificiers, see Hay, "England," 59–104; Tomlins, "Early British America, 1585–1830," 126–9, 135–6.

13 On hired servitude in England, see Kussmaul, *Servants in Husbandry* and Ben-Amos, *Adolescence and Youth*.

14 Ben-Amos, *Adolescence and Youth*, 39–40.

15 Ibid., 39.

16 Kussmaul, Servants in Husbandry, 4.

17 Ibid., 4, 70; Meldrum, *Domestic Service*, table 2.2.

18 Kussmaul, *Servants in Husbandry*, 8; Ben-Amos, *Adolescence and Youth*, 7; Amussen, *Ordered Society*. Steve Hindle addresses attempts by govern-

ment and parishes to "reconstitute" suitable households for poor children through apprenticeships. Hindle, *On the Parish*, 193–5.

19 Kussmaul, Servants in Husbandry, 5–6.

20 Ben-Amos, Adolescence and Youth, 43–5, 92–3; Kussmaul, Servants in Husbandry, 4.

21 Ben-Amos, Adolescence and Youth, 90–3.

22 King James Version, Deut. 15:12.

23 Kussmaul, Servants in Husbandry, 4.

24 Ibid., 4; Ben-Amos, *Adolescence and Youth*, 98–100.

25 Kussmaul, Servants in Husbandry, 24.

26 Hajnal, "European Marriage Patterns"; Hajnal, "Preindustrial Household Formation"; Laslett, "Size and Structure"; Ben-Amos, *Adolescence and Youth*, 5, 32.

27 Hay, "England," 62–3.

28 Ibid., 59–104; Tomlins, "Early British America," 135–6; Ewen, "Poore Soules," 141–2.

29 See Slack, *English Poor Law*, 17–25 and following; Hay, "England," 64–6.

30 Gwynn, "Cromwell's Policy," 617; Hindle, *On the Parish?* 191–219; Hay and Craven, *Masters, Servants, and Magistrates*.

31 G. Morgan and Rushton, *Banishment*, 11.

32 Ibid., 10–11.

33 Ibid., 15–16.

34 It seems likely that Gardenier's daughter was also an indentured servant. LMA, MJ/SP/1691/02/021.

35 King James Version, Deut. 15:13–4.

36 On consenting to sale, see Pagan, *Anne Orthwood's Bastard*, 23. Tomlins, however, argues that indentured servitude was more similar than not to hired servitude, *Freedom Bound*, 275–6.

37 Brown, *Good Wives*, 86–7.

38 Wareing, *Indentured Migration*, 50; G. Morgan and Rushton, *Criminal Transportation*, 4; Games, "Migration," 42–3.

39 On early modern poverty and public responses, see Beier, *Masterless Men*; Fumerton, *Unsettled*; Pound, *Poverty and Vagrancy*; Sharpe, *Crime*; Linda Woodbridge, *Vagrancy*; Slack, *Poverty and Policy*; Slack, *From Reformation to Improvement*; Boulton, "The Poor"; Griffiths, "Masterless Young People." On the dramatic growth of population, see Wrigley and Schofield, *Population History*; Slack, *Impact of Plague*; Thirsk, *Agrarian History*, v. 4. On the prevalence of child vagrancy in early modern Europe, see Cunningham, *Children and Childhood*, chapter 5.

40 On the patriarchal household, see Brown, *Good Wives*, chapter 1, and Fleetwood's sermons, *Relative Duties*, 339–418.

41 Hindle, "'Waste' Children," 17.

42 Blenerhasset, Plantation in Ulster.

43 Edwin Sandys, quoted in Rabb, *Jacobean Gentleman*, 240.

44 Carr, "Emigration," 282–6; Menard, "From Servant to Freeholder"; E. Morgan, *American Slavery*, 158–79; Salinger, *To Serve Well*, 32–46.

45 Wareing argues for the complexity of choice, *Indentured Migration*, 254–6; David Galenson argues for indentures as negotiated bargaining between contending parties, *White Servitude*, 99; while Smith describes passive human flotsam caught by an overwhelming tide, *Colonists in Bondage*, 39.

46 A discussion of early modern hierarchical ordering of society can be found in Amussen, "Social Hierarchies." Examples of sixteenth- and seventeenth-century treatises on master/servant relations include Fit John, *A Diamonde most precious*; Fosset, *The Servants Dutie*; Cleaver, *A godly forme*; Gouge, *Domesticall Duties*; Gother, *Instructions for Masters*.

47 Mather, A good master.

48 Ibid., 5.

49 Ibid., 34.

50 Ibid., 10.

51 Ibid., 10–19.

52 Ibid., 15.

53 Ibid., 23.

54 Ibid., 53–4. Although Mather expressed some compassion toward slaves, he rejected abolition.

55 William Fleetwood, *Relative Duties*, 339–418.

56 Ibid., 339–45. See also 386–8.

57 Ibid., 352.

58 Ibid., 408.

59 Ibid., 408–10.

60 Ibid., 353. See also 396–9.

61 Ibid., 354, 399. See also 400.

62 Ibid., 354.

63 Ibid., 393–6.

64 Ibid., 404–5.

65 Ibid., 397–8.

66 Ibid., 411.

67 Ibid., 345–8.

68 Mather, 51–2.

69 Fleetwood, 385.

70 Ibid., 409.

71 Ibid., 356–7, 359.

72 Fleetwood's book came out again in 1716, 1722, 1732, and 1753. Similar works include Gother, *Instructions for Masters*; Parkyns, *A Method Proposed*; Dutton, *Law of Masters and Servants in Ireland*; and legal treatises, such as *Jus Imperij & Servitutis*.

73 Hakluyt, *Discourse*, 37.

74 Ibid., 36.

75 Ibid., 107. See also Wareing, *Indentured Migration*, 17–19; Tomlins, *Freedom Bound*, 195–7.

76 Donne, *Major Works*, 321. For some other examples, including metaphors of biological purity, see Ewen, "Poore Soules," 146.

77 Hammond, *Leah and Rachel*, n.p.

78 Ibid.

79 Ibid.

80 Alsop, *A Character*, 491–516.

81 Ibid., 443–4.

82 Ibid., 447–51, 454–5.

83 Ibid., 457.

84 Ibid., 454–5.

85 Ibid., 460–3.

86 Ibid., 463–7.

87 Frethorne, "Letters," 41–2, 58–62, and mentioned in passing 161, 186, 239. On Frethorne, see Dahlberg, "'Do Not Forget Me,'" which provides some useful information on the context of Frethorne's indenture.

88 Frethorne, 59–60.

89 Bayly, *True and Faithful Warning*, 7–9; Carroll, "Bond Slave to Governor," 20–1.

90 von Uchteritz, "German Indentured Servant," 93–5.

91 Stock, *Proceedings*, 249 and Burton, "25 March 1658–9," *Diary*, 254–73.

92 Stock, *Proceedings*, 248–53, 263.

93 Ibid., 249 and Burton, "25 March 1658–9," *Diary*, 254–73.

94 Pitman, *A Relation*, 443–4.

95 Coad, *Memorandum*, 32, 34–5, 38–9.

96 Ibid., 94.

97 Ibid., 129–32; Appendix, 5–11. See also von Uchteritz, "German Indentured Servant," 98n5.

98 Richard Ligon, *History of Barbados*.

99 Ibid., 44; see also Handler and Reilly "Contesting 'White Slavery,'" 37.

100 Ligon, *History of Barbados*, 44–5. Implicit in the first comment is that cruelties to non-Christians, i.e., enslaved Africans, were more permissible.

101 Handler, "Father Biet," 65–7.

102 Cooke, *Sot-weed Factor*, 1. This work, while satirical, is generally regarded by historians as referring to an actual voyage taken by the author. See Coers, "New Light," 604–6; Beyers, "Ebenezer Cooke's Satire."

103 Moraley, *Infortunate*, 14, 23–7, 58–60.

104 Williamson, *French and Indian Cruelty*, 216–17. On kidnapping of children from Aberdeen in the mid-eighteenth century, see Coldham, *Emigrants in Chains*, 89–97. Williamson wrote that £200 in colonial currency was equivalent to about £120 sterling; it would be worth approximately £20,000 in Britain in 2020, "Purchasing Power."

105 Williamson, "French and Indian Cruelty," 216–17.

106 Harrower, "Diary."

107 Ibid., 91.

108 Ashbridge, *Quaker Grey*, 11, 13–14, 21–6.

109 Sprigs, "Letter," 151–2.

110 G. Morgan and Rushton, *Criminal Transportation*, 85–95, as well as G. Morgan and Rushton, "Print Culture."

111 See Wareing, *Indentured Migration*, 72, 137–8, 163–5.

112 Defoe, Moll Flanders.

113 Trappan'd Maiden.

114 Revel, Poor Unhappy Transported Felon.

115 Rappahannock County, mentioned in the ballad, only existed from 1656 until 1692, and Virginia refused to accept convict servants after 1671. Jennings, "Poor Unhappy Transported Felon," 182. On the other hand, Revel's fourteen-year term suggests a date after the 1718 Transportation Act.

CHAPTER THREE

1 Wareing, *Indentured Migration*, 31.

2 *CSPC, 1574–1660*, 19; Wareing, *Indentured Migration*, 31.

3 Cited in Gwynn, "Cromwell's Policy of Transportation," 616–17. See also *CSPC, 1574–1660*, Council of State, Orders "touching the transporting of vagrants, felons, &c. to the foreign plantations," 8 November 1653, 410; "a Committee to report upon … the transportation of vagrants to the foreign plantations" 15 November 1653, 410–11; "Draft of a bill … for transporting vagrants to the Western plantations, to be

recommended to Committee of Parliament appointed to consider of the poor people of the Commonwealth," 9 December 1653, 412.

4 CSPC, 1574–1660, 447–8, 493.

5 Firth and Rait, Acts and Ordinances, 104–10.

6 See G. Morgan and Rushton, Banishment, 59–80.

7 For example, "Rogues, vagabonds, idle and disorderly persons, and beggars" to be transported as magistrates see fit, "for a term not exceeding seven years" in Stock, Proceedings and Debates, v. 1; in 1662, 293, 306; in 1663, 309–10; in 1664, 320–1, 327, 351; in 1667, 351; in 1670, 353, 357. On 14 August 1656, the Council of State ordered that "lewd and dangerous persons, rogues, vagrants, and other idle persons, who have no means of livelihood, and refuse to work" be transported to the plantations. CSPC, 1574–1660, 447. See also G. Morgan and Rushton, Banishment, 24 on the turn to seven-year terms, first utilized in the case of Irish rebels.

8 Act against such who shall refuse to depone against delinquents, Edinburgh, August 1670. See also Stock, Proceedings, 448. Scotland had a long precedent of banishing people accused and convicted of crimes, as well as of particularly harsh punishments. See also the similar findings of 114 of 116 women respited and 34 of 74 men of "non-clergyable offenses" at the Old Bailey between 1663–89. G. Morgan and Rushton, Banishment, 29–42.

9 Baker, "Criminal Courts," and "English Criminal Jurisprudence"; Bellamy, Criminal Trial.

10 Fogleman, "Slaves, Convicts, and Servants," 44; Grubb, "Transatlantic Market," 113; Tomlins, Freedom Bound, 35; Games, "Migration," 41.

11 See Smith, "Transportation of Convicts," 233–4. Although transportation was preferable to death, it was not necessarily better than other lesser punishments, so the 1718 law changed some prisoners' plea strategies. For example, in 1762, John James, who had stolen four fowls and a petticoat, begged for "some corporal punishment instead of transportation," LMA, MJ/SP/1762/05/041.

12 Pickering, Statutes, v. 8, 505–9; Wareing, Indentured Migration, 33, 135, 241–3; Griffiths, Lost Londons, 286–8.

13 Zaller, "Debate on Capital Punishment," 126, 133–4; G. Morgan and Rushton, Criminal Transportation, 9–12, 43–5; Ekirch, "Bound for America"; Herrup, Common Peace; Kesselring, Mercy and Authority, 7; Hindle, State and Social Change, 120; Braddick, State Formation; Wrightson, "Two Concepts of Order."

14 Donne, Major Works, 321.

15 Cited in G. Morgan and Rushton, Banishment, 23.

16 On mercy and the state, see Kesselring, *Mercy and Authority*, especially chapter 1, 1–23.
17 In Smith, "Transportation of Convicts," 233–4.
18 G. Morgan and Rushton, *Banishment*, 19.
19 For the eighteenth century, see K. Morgan, "English and American Attitudes," 417–19, 424–6.
20 Kesselring, *Mercy and Authority*, 7; Braddick and Walter, *Negotiating Power*; Griffith et al., *Experience of Authority*; Harris, *Politics of the Excluded*; G. Morgan and Rushton, *Banishment*, 26.
21 See Briggs, *Crime and Punishment*, 74; G. Morgan and Rushton, *Banishment*, 17; Baker, "Criminal Courts," 41–2. See also *OBP*, t16760510-2, 10 May 1676; reduced punishment of branding *OBP*, s16781211e-1, 11 December 1678.
22 On eighteenth-century attitudes toward the harshness of labour for convict indentured servants, see K. Morgan, "English and American Attitudes," 420–1.
23 *OBP*, t16740429-5.
24 LMA, MJ/SP/T/02/001.
25 *OBP*, OA16760830.
26 G. Morgan and Rushton, *Eighteenth Century*, 21, 27.
27 *OBP*, t16761011-12.
28 Stock, *Proceedings*, 351.
29 *CSPC*, *1675–1676*, 78. On this case and on banishment for religious activity in general, see also G. Morgan and Rushton, *Banishment*, 22, 43–58.
30 *CSPC*, *1675–1676*, 79.
31 Floyd had been convicted of enticing children far from home and then robbing them. *OBP*, t16740717-6.
32 Stock, *Proceedings*, 176, 204; Smith, "Transportation of Convicts," 235.
33 *CSPC*, *1675–1676*, 57.
34 Ibid., 75.
35 *Calendar of State Papers Domestic, 1660–1685*, 509.
36 LMA, MJ/SP/1691/02/010.
37 *CSPC*, *1574–1660*, 281–2. See also similar incidents in *CSPC 1574–1660*, 410, 412, 447; *CSPC*, *1675–1676*, 81, 82. In 1690, Rebecca Larkin, imprisoned on a charge of theft, asked to be immediately tried or released from Newgate because "shee is very poor, and unable to bear the charge of long imprisonment here." Edward Abbott, who had paid off his wife's fine, but was still imprisoned in Newgate himself, petitioned for his fine to be remitted, otherwise he "will be in danger of perishing in prison." LMA, MJ/SP/1691/02/010. See also MJ/SP/1691/02/005; MJ/SP/1691/02/006; MJ/SP/1691/02/007.

38 *CSPC, 1675–1676,* 346–7, 350.

39 Harding, *Imprisonment*; Pendry, *Elizabethan Prisons*; Coldham, *Emigrants in Chains,* 19–29.

40 K. Morgan, "English and American Attitudes," 426.

41 G. Morgan and Rushton, *Banishment,* 28.

42 Not only was this a significant sum but also the colony typically engaged in transactions in pounds of tobacco, so the emphasis on cash money was probably also intended as a discouragement. *General Assembly, 1694–1698, 1711–1729,* MAO, v. 38, 320.

43 Beckles, *White Servitude,* 53, 56; Smith, "Transportation of Convicts," 233.

44 17 September 1649, Stock, *Proceedings,* 211.

45 Rogers, *Ireland,* 46.

46 Smith, *Colonists in Bondage,* 163.

47 15 June 1654, Irish Record Office, A/90, 50, 708, in Gardiner, *History of the Commonwealth,* v. 4, 111–12.

48 Stock, *Proceedings,* 247–9.

49 *CSPC 1574–1660,* 428. See also Beckles, *White Servitude,* 53.

50 Beckles, *White Servitude,* 52–3, 55; Sheppard, *The "Redlegs" of Barbados,* 29; Pitman, *A Relation,* 435–9.

51 Beckles, *White Servitude,* 5, 52–6, 165–6.

52 A few examples include "The humble overtures of divers persons nearly concerned in the present posture and condition of the island of Barbados" (1655), TNA CO 1/69, No. 2, as well as *CSPC, 1574–1660,* 19, 440, 443, and *CSPC, 1675–1676,* 304. Also see Wareing, *Indentured Migration,* 28–30.

53 For instance, a prisoner in Newgate who was recommended to be pardoned and discharged to enlist as a soldier in the "Caribdee Islands" in 1696. LMA, LSP/1696/02.

54 To give some idea of the reason for urgency, in 1676, a report showed that there were 3,582 English persons living in the Caribbean altogether, as opposed to 9,720 French able to bear arms. Wells, *Population of the British Colonies,* 24.

55 *CSPC 1574–1660,* 429–30.

56 April 1656. Ibid., 440, 443.

57 Ibid., 429–30, 448. Smith, "Transportation of Convicts," 240–1; Wareing, *Indentured Migration,* 51, 79–80, 89, 308.

58 *CSPC, 1574–1660,* 431. On populating Jamaica with whites, see *CSPC 1574–1660,* 429–30. For further attempts to transport people to Jamaica in 1656, see *CSPC 1574–1660,* 448.

59 *CSPC, 1574–1660,* 431.

60 Henry Cromwell in Birch, *Thurloe Papers,* v. 4, 23, 40; Gardiner, *History of*

the Commonwealth, v. 4, 218-20. At various places, Cromwell refers to the youths as both "boys" and "girls" and "men" and "women." In addition, he suggests numbers that range between 1,000, 1,500, and 2,000 for the males. At that time, Henry Cromwell was nominally assistant to the Lord Deputy of Ireland, but was actually executing the bulk of governance himself.

61 Gardiner, *History of the Commonwealth*, v. 4, 218–20; Birch, *Thurloe Papers*, v. 4, 23, 40.

62 Gardiner, *History of the Commonwealth*, v. 4, 219; Smith, *Colonists in Bondage*, 169. It was also not feasible to transport unwilling Scots, Rogers, *Ireland*, 47.

63 Smith, *Colonists in Bondage*, 170.

64 Cromwell in Birch, *Thurloe Papers*, v. 4, 23, 40.

65 Beckles, *White Servitude*, 47.

66 CSPC, *1675–1676*, 346–7.

67 Wareing, *Indentured Migration*, 90.

68 A 1666 Maryland lawsuit to recover unpaid expenses established the Atlantic passage money for sixty-nine servants at 850 pounds of tobacco each for a total of 58,650 pounds of tobacco, equal to £344 or just under £5 per servant. *Provincial Court*, MAO, v. 57, 416, and see also editor's comments, liii; John Hammond estimated travel costs for free travellers at £6, Hammond, *Leah and Rachel*, See also Waring, *Indentured Migration*, 126–8, 139–40, 196.

69 Pickering, *Statutes*, 505–9; Wareing, *Indentured Migration*, 33, 135, 241–3.

70 Orders of the Council of State: "Concerning the transportation of 1,200 men from Knockfergus, in Ireland, and Port Patrick, in Scotland, to Jamaica." 22 May 1656, CSPC, *1574–1660*, 440–1.

71 On Noell, see Anna Suranyi, "Indenture, Transportation, and Spiriting," which arose from a conference paper given at Unfree Labor, the Atlantic Empires, and Global Capitalism Conference, Loyola University Chicago, 11 June 2010, and also Menard, *Sweet Negotiations*, 44, 54, 59, 93, 146; Andrews, *British Committees*, 49–51; Sheridan, *Sugar and Slavery*, 90–2; Beckles, *White Servitude*, 35; and also the *Oxford Dictionary of National Biography*.

72 On Povey, see Andrews, *British Committees*, 51–6; Beckles, *White Servitude*, 35; and *The Dictionary of National Biography*.

73 For Thomson and the others, see Menard, *Sweet Negotiations*, 55, 59, and also the *Dictionary of National Biography*.

74 On Haveland, see Wareing, *Indentured migration*, 111, 114–25, 188–91, 206, 211–16, 232–4, 237–8. Although often prosecuted, Haveland rose to

High Bailiff of St Katherine largely on the basis of his spiriting wealth.

75 See Johnson, "Transportation of Vagrant Children," 142, for some discussion of young street children being detained by the authorities without surety of vagrancy.

76 Balak and Lave, "Dismal Science of Punishment," 883–4, 897–9.

77 Grubb, "Transatlantic Market"; Grubb, "Market Evaluation."

78 Johnson, "Transportation of Vagrant Children," 150.

79 Grubb, "Transatlantic Market"; Grubb, "Market Evaluation."

80 *CSPC, 1574–1660,* 19; See also Wareing, *Indentured Migration,* 169.

81 *CSPC, 1574–1660,* 411, 15 November 1653; *CSPC, 1661–1668,* 555; see Wareing, *Indentured Migration,* 148.

82 *The grand kidnapper at last taken.*

83 Ashbridge, *Quaker Grey,* 17. Ashbridge was about nineteen years old at the time.

84 *CSPC 1574–1660,* 457. See also Wareing, *Indentured Migration,* 70.

85 Cited in G. Morgan and Rushton, *Banishment,* 16–17. Also see a case of prosecution in America and West Indies, *CSPC, 1675–1676,* 516–24.

86 *CSPC, 1675–1676,* 521.

87 John Wareing, *Indentured Migration,* 5, 170.

88 See Beckles, *White Servitude,* 50–2.

89 Wareing, *Indentured Migration,* 25–6, 170, 176–80, 184–95.

90 On Haveland, see Wareing, *Indentured Migration,* 111, 114–25, 188–91, 206, 211–16, 232–4, 237–8.

91 See Wareing, "Preventative and Punitive Regulation"; Wareing, *Indentured Migration,* 171–89 and following.

92 Beckles, *White Servitude,* 50.

93 *An Ordinance of the Lords and Commons;* Firth and Rait, *Acts and Ordinances,* 681.

94 Firth and Rait, *Acts and Ordinances,* 912.

95 In Galenson, *White Servitude,* 189–90.

96 *CSPC, 1675–1676,* 138.

97 Quoted in Wareing, "Preventative and Punitive Regulation," 296.

98 *At the Court at Whitehall;* also in Galenson, *White Servitude,* 190–2.

99 Luttrell, *Brief Historical Relation,* v. 1, 232, 244, 375.

100 For 1647, see Stock, *Proceedings,* 185–6; Firth and Rait, *Acts and Ordinances,* 912–13. Also debated in Stock, *Proceedings,* in 1662, 303; in 1670, 357–9, 361, 366; in 1671, 375, 382; in 1673, 397–8, 400–1. An act against this was passed in 1671. *CSPC, 1675–1676,* 521. See also Wareing, "Preventative and Punitive Regulation"; Wareing, *Indentured Migration,* 5, 112–25, 171, 193–5, 205; Beckles, *White Servitude,* 50.

101 *CSPC, 1661–68*, 220–2. See also Wareing, "Preventative and Punitive Regulation," 294–5.

102 Wareing, "Preventative and Punitive Regulation," 295.

103 The full title of the law was An Act for the good Governing of Servants, and Ordering the Rights between Masters and Servants. See Beckles, *White Servitude*, 82; Hall, *Acts, Passed in Barbados*, 36.

104 *Upon a complaint and rumour*. See also Wareing, *Indentured Migration*, 180.

105 Grubb, "Fatherless and Friendless."

106 Henry Whalley, *The True Informer*, no. 3, p. 28 (1645), in Wareing, *Indentured Migration*, 32.

107 See Wareing, *Indentured Migration*, 34, for a discussion of the word "slave" in critiques of indentured servitude.

108 Stock, *Proceedings*, 209 –11, 222, 241. See also Wareing, *Indentured Migration*, 3.

109 Stock, *Proceedings*, in 1670, 354–5, 359–10; in 1674, 404–5; in 1675, 405–9; in 1676, 410; in 1679, 417.

110 Ibid., 248–53, 263; House of Commons, *Journals*, v. 7, 620; Rivers, *Englands Slavery*; Burton, *Diary*, 25 March 1658–9, 254–73. On this debate, see also Suranyi, "Indenture, Transportation, and Spiriting"; Shaw, *Everyday Life*, 19–26; Handler and Reilly, "Contesting 'White Slavery," 38–9.

111 Stock, *Proceedings*, 252, 263.

112 Burton, *Diary*, 25 March 1658–9, 257; Stock, *Proceedings*, 250.

113 The high cost is more like a ransom than the cost of a normal indenture contract. The normal price for servants in North America during the eighteenth century was closer to £15. Abbot Emerson Smith discussed security payments of £100 required in St Christopher for convicts, and something similar may have occurred in this case. Smith, "Transportation of Convicts," 240–1. Henry Pitman also described a bond for £120 that a merchant fraudulently claimed would allow for the release of Pitman and his brother once they reached Barbados, Pitman, *A Relation*, 436.

114 Stock, *Proceedings*, 250; Burton, *Diary*, 258–9.

115 For example, Burton, *Diary*, 263, 270.

116 Burton, *Diary*, 263, 270. Vane, like others, clarified that he did "detest and abhor" the Cavalier cause. See also Sir Arthur Haselrig's comment on the same page, "I shall never plead for a Cavalier in this House, but for the liberty of an Englishman, and for the laws." 270.

117 Ibid., 256–73.

118 Stock, *Proceedings*, 257.

119 Burton, *Diary*, 269.

120 See discussion of Calvin's Case below, n123.

121 Burton, *Diary*, 269.

122 Stock, *Proceedings*, 257; Burton, *Diary*, 273. See also Beckles, "Concept of 'White Slavery,'" 580 and following. In addition, the ethics of the practice of banishment was also debated in Parliament in 1657. See G. Morgan and Rushton, *Banishment*, 24–5.

123 Bilder, *Transatlantic Constitution*, 34–40; Price, "Natural Law," 73–4, 95, and throughout; Wheeler, "Calvin's Case"; Tomlims, *Freedom Bound*, 82–92; Kettner, *Development*, 41, 45; Muller, *Subjects and Sovereign*, 21–8; Hulsebosch, "Ancient Constitution," 454–8, 462.

124 Handler and Reilly, "Contesting 'White Slavery'"; Rogers, *Ireland*, 45–6; Block and Shaw, "Subjects without an Empire."

125 See the discussion of transportation policies and practices for rebels, including the Irish as well as the English, in G. Morgan and Rushton, *Banishment*, 59–89; Beckles, "Riotous and Unruly Lot,'" 506–7.

126 Stock, *Proceedings*, 241n23. Although some landowners were expelled westward, Irish Catholic tenants remained on their estates to serve the new Protestant landlords.

127 Beckles, *White Servitude*, 38. From 1700–1780, about 70 per cent of migrants from the British Isles were Irish or Scottish. Games, "Migration," 38.

128 Gardiner, *History of the Commonwealth*, v. 4, 110.

129 Ibid., 110–11; Prendergast, *Cromwellian Settlement*, 245.

130 Beckles, *White Servitude*, 62–3; Smith, *Colonists in Bondage*, 63–4. The majority of the servants in the hold of Captain Anthony's ship had apparently contracted for servitude.

131 Gardiner, *History of the Commonwealth*, v. 4, 110–11.

132 Prendergast, *Cromwellian Settlement*, 246. The warrants were for the detention of vagrants – thus the search was for servants who had been seized but were previously employed or supported by families.

133 Order by the Deputy and Council, 6 July 1655, Irish Record Office, A/5, 5, 188, in Gardiner, *History of the Commonwealth*, v. 4, 111.

134 Cited in Prendergast, *Cromwellian Settlement*, 246; Smith, *Colonists in Bondage*, 168.

135 Gwynn, "Cromwell's Policy," 622–3. See also Smith, *Colonists in Bondage*, 163–9 on fraud among shippers and magistrates in shipping supposed vagrants from Ireland to servitude overseas, and governmental attempts to curtail it.

136 Newman, *New World*, 81–2.

137 Handler and Reilly, "Father Antoine Biet," 36; Handler and Reilly "Contesting 'White Slavery,'" 36, 39.

138 In Billings, *Old Dominion*, 133.

139 Beckles, "Riotous and Unruly Lot," 509–12, and Beckles, "Colours of Property," 44; Handler and Reilly, "Father Antoine Biet," 37–41.

140 Discussed in Handler, "Slave Revolts," Beckles, "Riotous and Unruly Lot," 515–21; Beckles, *White Servitude*, 100, 107–13; G. Morgan and Rushton, *Banishment*, 63–4; Block and Shaw, "Subjects without an Empire"; Gwynn, "Documents," 243–5.

141 *The humble overtures.*

142 *CSPC, 1675–1676*, 304.

143 Ibid., 516. See also p. 105, as well as Beckles, *White Servitude*, 69; Rogers, *Ireland*, 40.

144 *CSPC, 1675–1676*, 445. See also Beckles, *White Servitude*, 38–9, 123.

145 Beckles, "Riotous and Unruly Lot," 517–18; Gwynn, "Documents," 337–9.

146 Hening, *Statutes*, v. 1, 411, 471.

147 Ibid., 257.

148 Ibid., 538–9.

149 Cromwell in Birch, *Thurloe Papers*, v. 4, 23, 40; Gardiner, *History of the Commonwealth*, v. 4, 218–20.

150 Shaw, *Everyday Life*, 2–3.

CHAPTER FOUR

1 See *OED*, "indenture."

2 The binding nature of contracts on both parties was solidified in English law in the 1602 case *Slade, v. Morely*, which was ostensibly about debt, but established the right to penalties and legal remedies on behalf of the plaintiff. Ibbetson, "Sixteenth Century Contract Law"; Biernacki, "Cultural Coherence."

3 Biernacki, "Cultural Coherence," 292.

4 Kahn, *Wayward Contracts*.

5 *At the court at Whitehall.*

6 LMA, CLA/024/10/266 MC/GB 266.

7 On the printing and sale of indenture forms, see Gowing, "Girls on Forms," 455–6; Wareing, *Indentured Migration*, 44–6.

8 Wareing, *Indentured Migration*, 44–5, 93, 203, 266–71. The other two versions differed in some small details from the indenture of William Smith following these pages.

9 In Billings, *Old Dominion*, 151.

10 Ibid., 151.

11 *Provincial Court*, MAO, v. 49, 83. See also on this case, Daniels, "Liberty to Complaine," 245.

12 *Provincial Court*, MAO, v. 49, 83–4.

13 *Provincial Court*, MAO, v. 57, xlvii, 79–80, 110, 117, 129. Utie and his attorney failed to show up in court for three subsequent hearings, likely because they realized that there was little chance of contesting the indenture document.

14 On Haveland's spiriting activities, see Wareing, *Indentured Migration*, 111, 114–25, 188–91, 206, 211–16, 232–4, 237–8.

15 FSL manuscript V.b.16 (32), image 147360 and V.b.16 (31), 147358.

16 The classic work describing the early modern European marriage pattern is Wrigley et al., *English Population History*, especially chapter 6, "Nuptiality."

17 I thank Muriel McClendon for her advice on this question.

18 Family members travelling together were rare, and it was not unusual for them to be split up; there are some cases discussed in this book. For some families travelling into indenture together into late seventeenth-century Pennsylvania, see Sharon Salinger, *To Serve Well*, 29.

19 See editor's comments, *Provincial Court*, MAO, v. 65, xxxiii.

20 In Billings, *Old Dominion*, 151.

21 Carr, "Emigration," 282–5.

22 Hening, *Statutes*, v. 1, 257.

23 *General Assembly*, MAO, v. 1, 40, 80, 97.

24 *Provincial Court*, MAO, v. 4, 360.

25 *General Assembly*, MAO, v. 2, 525.

26 Bacon, *Laws of Maryland*, 264, 667–8. See also Peyrol-Kleiber, "Starting Afresh."

27 Handler and Reilly, "Contesting 'White Slavery,'" 32–3.

28 Beckles and Downes, "Economics of Transition," 241–3; Abramitzky and Braggion, "Migration and Human Capital," 882–905; 896–7.

29 27 July 1669 and August 1672, CSPC, *1669–1674*, 31, 209, 398; May 1672, CSPC, *1675–1676*, 145.

30 Hazard, *Pennsylvania Archive*, v. 1, 27, 37.

31 Ames, *Court Records of Accomack-Northhampton*, v. 1, 67.

32 Walter, *Norfolk County Court Records*, 9.

33 Ibid., 134, 142 in Billings, *Old Dominion*, 150.

34 *Courts of Kent, Talbot, and Somerset Counties,* MAO, v. 54, 163. Morgan had identified a specific tract "on the e[a]sterne Shore, adjoyninge to his land on the south e[a]st side of River Wye."

35 Pagan, *Anne Orthwood's Bastard,* 21.

36 CSPC *1669–1674,* 31; CSPC, *1675–1676,* 145.

37 *General Assembly,* MAO, v. 1, 496. See also *Provincial Court,* MAO, v. 65, xxxiii–iv.

38 *Courts of Kent, Talbot, and Somerset Counties,* MAO, v. 54, 124–5.

39 Ibid., 247, and also 152.

40 *Provincial Court,* MAO, v. 41, 335–6.

41 BNA, *Deeds of Barbados,* RB3/2, 1640–42, 1647, 1654 ..., 18–19.

42 *Provincial Court,* MAO, v. 57, lii, 579.

43 Ibid., lii–iv, 580, 601–3. Hog stealing was a serious offense, for which penalties had been laid out in the 1666 "Act Against Hoggstealers," which was invoked by the court.

44 Ibid., lii, 254. As in many documents, the contract is referred to as a "condicon" here.

45 Servants who hired themselves out within the colonies were sometimes regarded by the law as hired rather than indentured servants, a status with greater rights. See Tomlins, "Early British America."

46 *Provincial Court,* MAO, v. 41, 264.

47 Ibid., 226.

48 *Provincial Court,* MAO, v. 49, 73.

49 *Provincial Court,* MAO, v. 57, 208–10, and editor's comments, liii.

50 *Provincial Court,* MAO, v. 41, 259.

51 BNA, *Deeds of Barbados,* RB3/3 1648–67, 10, 20.

52 For example, in the BNA, *Deeds of Barbados,* RB3/3 1648–67, 782, 807, 869.

53 *Provincial Court,* MAO, v. 49, 363.

54 *Provincial Court,* MAO, v. 41, 135. The appraisals for this particular will tend to be very low in value, not only for the servants but also for all the goods enumerated in the list.

55 *Courts of Kent, Talbot, and Somerset Counties,* MAO, v. 54, 102.

56 *Provincial Court,* MAO, v. 49, 240–1. The new appraisal accords better with typical servant prices.

57 Daniels, "Liberty to Complaine," 219–49. See also Hay, "England, 1562–1875," 76–9; Christopher Tomlins, "Early British America," 120; Amussen, *Caribbean Exchanges,* 17–18.

58 Daniels, "Liberty to Complaine," 228–30.

59 *Provincial Court*, MAO, v. 65; editor's preface, xxxiii: "Always they were presented by way of petition, for servants had not the capacity to present them at law."

60 Hammond, *Leah and Rachel.*

61 *Acts and Statutes of Barbados*, 111; Handler, "Custom and Law," 13–14; Beckles, *History of Barbados*, 86–8; Beckles, "Riotous and Unruly Lot," 514–15. Jenny Shaw, in conversation, recalls seeing a handful of successful servant complaints, and a larger number of successful complaints by masters and mistresses, before the Barbados Council rather than in the courts, in the Lucas Manuscript, on microfilm in the Barbados Department of Archives.

62 Rackrow, "Right to Counsel," 4, 16–20; [n.a.], "Right to Counsel," 1326–8; Carson, "Right to Counsel," 625–7, 630, 634; Bilder, *Transatlantic Constitution*, 17, 26.

63 *Charles County Courts*, MAO, v. 60, 496.

64 By the end of the seventeenth century, the population had just reached 32,000. Wells, *Population of the British Colonies*, 146.

65 *Provincial Court*, MAO, v. 65, 279.

66 Ibid., 236, 255, 260, 269, 270, 283, 640 (1675).

67 Beitzell, *Cheseldyne Family*, 21.

68 *Proceedings of the County Courts of Charles County 1666–1674*, MAO, v. 60, 233–4. On this case (as Elizabeth Haselton), see also Daniels, "Liberty to Complaine," 236.

69 Even in England, runaway servants who had contracted with their masters, such as rural labourers, were seen as lawbreakers. Hay, "England, 1562–1875," 76, 82, 92–3.

70 *Charles County Courts*, MAO, v. 60, 233–5.

71 Ibid., preface, xvi.

72 *Provincial Court*, MAO, v. 49, 215, 220, 237–8, 261, 265, 315, 380–1. This case originated in the Calvert County Court.

73 Ibid., 238.

74 Nicculgutt may have married during these proceedings, as in some of the later depositions she is called Jone Maglanna or Moglanna.

75 January 1685, *York County Deeds*, Book 7.

76 December 1703, *York County Deeds*, Book 12.

77 February 1704, *York County Deeds*, Book 12.

78 *Provincial Court*, MAO, v. 41, 476.

79 *Somerset County Courts*, MAO, v. 191, 126.

80 *Provincial Court*, MAO, v. 49, 493–4.

81 Amussen, *Caribbean Exchanges*, 17–18.

82 *Provincial Court*, MAO, v. 49, 137.

83 *Provincial Court*, MAO, v. 65, 177–8.

84 *Provincial Court*, MAO, v. 68, 107–8.

85 *Courts of Kent, Talbot, and Somerset Counties*, MAO, v. 54, 515,

86 Ibid., 249,

87 Daniels, "Liberty to Complaine," 246–7,

88 *Somerset County Counts*, MAO, v. 106, 33.

89 *Provincial Court*, MAO, v. 49, 103.

90 Ibid., 103–4.

91 Ibid., 103–4, 140.

92 Ibid., 140–1.

93 Ibid., 141. On this case, see also Daniels, "Liberty to Complaine," 246.

94 *Provincial Court*, MAO, vol. 49, xix, 192, 236.

95 After he became free, Gunby was involved in a number of further law-suits in which he sued various individuals over debts, mainly in the early 1690s. Oddly, as in the indenture case, he often lost suits because he subsequently did not show up in court. See *Somerset County Courts*, MAO, v. 535, 9, 12, 21, 152; *Provincial Court*, MAO, v. 57, 16. Gunby was also summoned at least once for nonpayment of debt: *Somerset County Courts*, MAO, v. 406, 147–8. Yet Gunby did gain some success in life. When he died in 1695, he left a small estate with yet another suit for debt (37 shillings) placed upon it. *Somerset County Courts*, MAO, v. 535, 131.

96 *Provincial Court*, MAO, v. 41, 477.

97 Ibid., 477–8.

98 Ibid., 478. Although this testimony is unfavourable to Mecane's claim, in the rest of his statement, Salstceme implicitly criticized the practice of indenturing young boys, as is discussed in chapter 7.

99 Hening, *Statutese*, v. 2, 116.

100 Ibid., 296.

CHAPTER FIVE

1 G. Morgan and Rushton, *Criminal Transportation*, 56–9; Beckles, *White Servitude*, 65–7; Coldham, *Emigrants in Chains*, 100–12; Salinger, *To Serve Well*, 92–6; on the Middle Passage, see Smallwood, *Saltwater Slavery*; Rediker, *The Slave Ship*; O'Malley, *Final Passages*; and for non-European indentured servants in later centuries, Rediker, Pybus, and Christopher, *Many Middle Passages*.

2 Hammond, *Leah and Rachel*; Alsop, *A Character*, 462, 501.

3 See reference to "not above ten men and boys living, of the whole number of servants taken to Virginia in the *Seaflower*." CSPC, *1574–1660*, 36. See also the discussion of servant death rates in Johnson, "Transportation of Vagrant Children," 147–8. On the *Seaflower*, see CSPC, *1574–1660*, *passim*, and also Newton, *Colonizing Activities*, 90–1, 94, 98–9, 108, 111–13, 115, 118, 129, 135. The ship is also mentioned in the Richard Frethorne letters.

4 Coad, *Memorandum*, 23–9. His passage home a few years later was much stormier, 135–8.

5 Stock, *Proceedings*, 253.

6 Cooke, *Sot-weed Factor*, 1.

7 Harrower, "Diary," 73–8.

8 Moraley, *Infortunate*, 23–7.

9 Hening, *Statutes*, v. 1, 435.

10 Salinger, *To Serve Well*, 97.

11 Ligon, *History of Barbados*, 44.

12 Ashbridge, *Quaker Grey*, 21.

13 Wareing, *Indentured Migration*, 76–9.

14 Wells, *Population of the British Colonies*, 146; Billings, *Old Dominion*, 133. Handler, "Custom and Law," 2.

15 Abramitzky and Braggion, "Migration and Human Capital"; Beckles and Downes, "Economics of Transition," 241–3.

16 Frethorne, "Letters," 41–2, 59–60. On the harsh conditions in Virginia at this time, see Billings, *Old Dominion*, chapter 1, especially 12–13. The book also includes a copy of Frethorne's letter.

17 Frethorne, "Letters," 58–60.

18 Stock, *Proceedings*, 249 and Burton, *Diary*, 256–7.

19 Handler, "Father Biet," 65–7. See also Beckles, *White Servitude*, 96–7.

20 Pitman, *Relation*, 443.

21 von Uchteritz, "German Indentured Servant," 93–5.

22 Ligon, *History of Barbados*, 44–5.

23 Ibid., 115. Also see Beckles, *White Servitude*, 97.

24 Ligon, *History of Barbados*, 44.

25 *Trappan'd Maiden*.

26 Revel, "Poor Unhappy Transported Felon."

27 "Decisions of the General Court," 234–5.

28 Hening, *Statutes*, v. 1, 217.

29 Carr, "Emigration," 276–80.

30 Ashbridge, *Quaker Grey*, 21–4.

31 Sprigs, "Letter."

32 *Somerset County Courts*, MAO, v. 87, 134–5, 145.

33 Menard, "From Servant to Freeholder," 50.

34 *Somerset Count Courts*, MAO, v. 535, 8; other examples in *Charles County Courts*, MAO, v. 60, 53, 573.

35 Gwynn, "Documents," 233. See other examples: BNA, RB 6/13, ff 44–5; RB 6/14, ff. 82–4; Beckles, *White Servitude*, 143.

36 *Charles County Courts*, MAO, v. 60, 221, 497.

37 Ibid., 518.

38 Ibid., 417.

39 *Provincial Court*, MAO, v. 41, 476–8.

40 Hay and Craven, *Masters, Servants, and Magistrates*, 19; Douglas Hay, "England, 1562–1875," 66.

41 Hening, *Statutes*, v. 1, 401.

42 Ibid., v. 2, 109–10.

43 *Acts and Statutes of Barbados*, 19–20.

44 *Somerset County Courts*, MAO, v. 535, 26; *Somerset County Courts*, MAO, v. 406, 187–8.

45 *Provincial Court*, MAO, v. 717, 93–4.

46 *Provincial Court*, MAO, v. 67, 42, 135, 181, 294–5.

47 September 1689, *York County Deeds*, Book 8.

48 Corbett probably had little time left to serve, as the disparity between the 250 pounds of tobacco equivalence to his remaining time compared to the 2,000 pounds of tobacco in exchange for two further years indicates, as does the judgment discussed next, which implies that his original time had expired a year and a half later by the time of the second court proceeding.

49 *Provincial Court*, MAO, v. 57, xlvii, 182, 368–9.

50 Ibid., xlivii, 492.

51 Ibid., xlvii, 182.

52 *Charles County Courts*, MAO, v. 60, 433.

53 In the Acts of the Maryland Assembly, 1716: "be itt also enacted … that every indenture [contract] made by any servant during the time of his service by former indenture or judgm[en]t of the County Court according to the tenor of this act shall be void and not any ways oblidge any servant for longer time then by his first indenture or judgment of the court." *General Assembly*, MAO, v. 30, 288; in Barbados, 1652, *Acts and Statutes of Barbados*, 17.

54 In 1642 and 1657, in Hening, *Statutes*, v. 1, 274–4, 445. In 1661, Hening, *Statutes*, v. 2, 118.

55 "Decisions of the General Court," 240.

56 *Provincial Court*, MAO, v. 57, li, 125.

57 *Provincial Court*, MAO, v. 57, xlvii, li, 409, 423–4.

58 Hening, *Statutes*, v. 2, 217.

59 *Provincial Court*, MAO, v. 57, li, 426.

60 *Provincial Court*, MAO, v. 49, 76–77, 86–7.

61 Ibid., 44.

62 Ibid., 498–501.

63 *Somerset County*, MAO, v. 405, 179–81.

64 Amussen, "'Being Stirred."

65 Hale, *Historia Placitorum*, v. 1, 376–83;, v. 2, 336; Coke, *Institutes*, v. 3, 20; Dalton, *Country Justice*, 336–7. However, husbands killing wives or masters killing servants was murder, because "the reason of this difference, is, for that the one is in subjection and oweth obedience, and not the other." Hale, *Historia Placitorum*, v. 2, 337. See also Walker, *Crime, Gender, and Social Order*, 137–44; Ben-Amos, *Adolescence and Youth*, 7; Mendelson and Crawford, *Women in Early Modern England*, 44.

66 Jurist William Blackstone wrote that a husband was allowed to give his wife, children, and servants "moderate correction," but "confined within reasonable bounds," *Commentaries*, vol. 1, 430–2; Hay, "England, 1562–1875," 78; for legislation on rape that omits mention of marital rape, see Dalton, *Country Justice*, 392–3; Hale, *Historia Placitorum*, v. 2, 291.

67 Tomlins, "Early British America, 122.

68 BNA, *Deeds of Barbados*, RB3/1: 1640–45, 17.

69 Sharpe, "Domestic Homicide," 38; Walker, *Crime, Gender, and Social Order*, 134–8; however, Krista Kesselring finds the manslaughter defence for husbands killing wives to be mainly post-seventeenth century: "No Greater Provocation?"

70 Mendelson and Crawford, *Women in Early Modern England*, 104.

71 Hening, *Statutes*, v. 1, 440.

72 Ibid., 538.

73 Ibid., v. 2, 118.

74 Ibid., 118–19.

75 See Kesselring, *Mercy and Authority*, 98–9.

76 Ibid., 102. Notably these verdicts also saved defendants from the "especially grisly deaths" for convictions of petit treason. See, for example, OBP, t16760114-6 in 1675.

77 *Provincial Court*, MAO, v. 49, 290, 303–7, 311–14, 332–3.

78 Ibid., 290, 308–12, 351, 401.

79 Ibid., 303.

80 Ibid., 304. Testimonies of Edward Ladd and Thomas Wyniard.

81 Ibid., 304–5. This witness, Susanna Leeth, was the servant to another master, and was working nearby.

82 Ibid., 305–7. Testimonies of William Gunnell, Lawrence Organ, Thomas Miles, and Robert Loyde, the last a surgeon who viewed the body and stated that one sore he observed was one that he had previously tried to cure, but that he also observed evidence of "two stroakes."

83 Ibid., 312–13.

84 Ibid., 308. However, the medical knowledge of the jury and even of the dissecting surgeon who was presumably instructing them was probably questionable.

85 Ibid., 308–10.

86 Ibid., 311–12.

87 Ibid., 351.

88 Ibid., 401.

89 *Provincial Court*, MAO, v. 57, xlvii, 352, 354–6, 363–4, 380.

90 Ibid., xxvi. According to the editor, of fourteen murder trials in the Maryland Provincial Court from 1666–1670, there were only four convictions, with two of the convicted murderers escaping the death penalty by claiming benefit of the clergy, one hanged, and one possibly pardoned. The other ten accused were adjudged either to have killed by "misadventure" or were cleared.

91 Ibid., 356.

92 *Court of Chancery*, MAO, v. 51, 121–3.

93 Ibid., 124–7.

94 Ibid., 128–9.

95 Ibid., 129–30; on this case, see also *Provincial Court*, MAO, v. 49, 166–8, 233–5, 453, 496, 538–46, 555.

96 In England, verdicts of killing by "misfortune" were more likely when the victims were women or children. Walker *Crime, Gender, and Social Order*, 136.

97 *Provincial Court*, MAO, v. 41, 478–80.

98 *Provincial Court*, MAO, v. 49, 215–16. Suicide was considered a sin.

99 Ashbridge, *Quaker Grey*, 24.

100 In Billings, *Old Dominion*, 160.

101 *Provincial Court*, MAO, v. 10, 534–45, 557. On cruentation, the belief in a corpse bleeding in the presence of the murderer, see Davis and Matteoni, *Executing Magic*, 21–3; Gaskill, "Reporting Murder," 8–13.

102 *Provincial Court*, MAO, v. 41, 499–505. The surname is spelled "Brodnox" here and "Bradnox" in the case I discuss subsequently, but this is clearly the same couple.

103 *Courts of Kent, Talbot, and Somerset Counties*, MAO, v. 54, 224–5, and see also 167–9, 178–80, 213, 234. See also *Provincial Court*, MAO, v. 41, 482, 525.

104 *Provincial Court*, MAO, v. 69, 413–14.

105 *Provincial Court*, MAO, v. 41, 67.

106 Walter, *Norfolk County Court Records*, 189. The court records indicate some weekly meetings, but equally often took breaks of up to two months; the average seems to have been about a meeting every month. Jane Latham does not appear again, and the resolution of the case is unknown.

107 *Somerset County Courts*, MAO, v. 106, 196, 122.

108 Hening, *Statutes*, v. 2, 35.

109 *Provincial Court*, MAO, v. 49, 318–19.

110 Walter, *Norfolk County Court Records*, 110, 113, 119–20, and also in Billings, *Old Dominion*, 152.

111 *Courts of Kent, Talbot, and Somerset Counties*, MAO, v. 54, 126–7.

112 *Provincial Court*, MAO, v. 70, 40. Elias Nuthall had himself been a servant in Virginia. In 1665, his brothers arranged to trade another servant, Elizabeth Bradshaw, to redeem him. *Council of Maryland*, MAO, v. 5, 103.

113 *Charles County Courts*, MAO, v. 60, 233–5.

114 August 1712, *York County Deeds*, Book 14.

115 December 1712, *York County Deeds*, Book 14.

116 *Provincial Court*, MAO, v. 41, 296.

117 BNA, *Deeds of Barbados*, RB3/1: 1640–45, 17.

118 On defamation in early modern England, see Harding, "Families," 23–4; Sharpe, *Defamation and Sexual Slander*; Gowing, "Gender and Language of Insult."

119 *Provincial Court*, MAO, v. 57, 119–22, and editor's comments, xlvii.

120 Ibid., 358 and 126–7.

121 E. Morgan, *American Slavery*, 153.

122 Walter, *Norfolk County Court Records*, 9.

123 *Courts of Kent, Talbot, and Somerset Counties*, MAO, v. 54, 478.

124 Walter, *Norfolk County Court Records*, 8.

125 *Provincial Court*, MAO, v. 69, 116, 222.

126 *Provincial Court*, MAO, v. 41, 417–18.

127 *Provincial Court*, MAO, v. 49, 331–2.

128 It was not recorded whether Crow showed a contract or relied on records showing her arrival by custom of the country. *York County Deeds*, Book 7.

129 *Provincial Court*, MAO, v. 69, 123–4, 207–8.

130 Ibid., 122–3.

131 *Provincial Court*, MAO, v. 57, lii, 579. See also Daniels, "Liberty to Complaine," 247.

132 *Charles County Courts 1666–1674*, MAO, v. 60, 179, 492–3.

133 Daniels, "Liberty to Complaine," 247.

134 *Provincial Court*, MAO, v. 41, 6–7, 67.

135 Ibid., 67. While "deft" often appears in court records as an abbreviation for "defendant," here the clerk appears to have indulged in a pun. The OED testifies to the early modern use of the word "deft" to mean "dexterous" or "clever." Frame's contention is similar to that made by Francis Gunby in his business dealings with Petronella Chivers earlier in this chapter, except that Frame was successful in her claim.

136 *Provincial Court*, MAO, v.41, 67.

137 *Somerset County*, MAO, v. 535, 26, 74.

138 *York County Deeds*, Book 14.

139 *Provincial Court*, MAO, v. 4, 470–1.

140 January 1711, May 1712, *York County Deeds*, Book 14.

141 For example, *Provincial Court*, MAO, v. 65, 95, 179, 511 and *Charles County Courts* MAO, v. 60, 416–17.

CHAPTER SIX

1 On indentured women, see Suranyi, "Willing to Go"; Wood, "Servant Women and Sex"; Salinger, "'Send No More Women'"; and Grubb, "Servant Auction Records"; and in passing in Carr and Walsh, "Planter's Wife"; Brown, *Good Wives*; Gowing, "Girls on Forms," and other works.

2 See Mendelson and Crawford, *Women in Early Modern England*, 42–58.

3 Daniels, "Liberty to Complaine," 233, 240–1.

4 *CSPC 1574–1660*, 457.

5 Ashbridge, *Quaker Grey*, 11, 13–14, 26.

6 On female poverty in the early modern era, see Willen, "Women in the Public Sphere," 561–9; Mendelson and Crawford, *Women in Early Modern England*, 256–300.

7 On the patriarchal structure of early modern society and households, see Brown, *Good Wives*, chapter 1; Gowing, *Gender Relations*; Mendelson and Crawford, *Women in Early Modern England*, 5–6, 15, 71–4, 301–2.

8 On coverture laws: Erikson, *Women and Property*; Joan Hoff, *Law, Gender, and Injustice*; Ulrich, *Good Wives*; Mendelson and Crawford, *Women in Early Modern England*, 37–9; Gowing, *Gender Relations*, 45–6, 57, 76, 171;

Norton, "Either Married," 27–35; primary sources include Blackstone, *Commentaries*, v. 1, 430; *Lawes Resolutions of Womens Rights*.

9   *Provincial Court*, MAO, v. 41, 499–505.

10 Salmon, *Women and the Law of Property*, 3–9. However, public participation by women decreased in the eighteenth century. Offutt Jr, "Limits of Authority," especially 377–85.

11 Sturtz, "'As Though I Was Pr[e]sent.'"

12 Mendelson and Crawford, *Women in Early Modern England*, 96–7, 265, 292–8.

13 Brown, *Good Wives*, 99, 186, and OED.

14 *Provincial Court*, MAO, v. 49, 380. There are many other examples, such as passing references to a servant woman as a wench in the case about Jeffrey Haggman's murder, 305–6, or in a dispute about which master owned servant Mary Maxwell, *Somerset County Courts*, v. 191, 158.

15 Gardiner, *History of the Commonwealth*, v. 4, 113; Wareing, *Indentured Migration*, 52.

16 Carr, "Emigration," 273–6; Carr, "The Planter's Wife," 546, 550–1. See also Salinger, "'Send No More Women,'" 42.

17 Hammond, *Leah and Rachel*.

18 Alsop, *Character*, 467.

19 See CSPC, *1574–1660*, for 1634 and 1660, "To send over women for planters wives Newgate and Bridewell to be spared as much as may be and poor maids instead with which few parishes in England are unburdened sent over," 491–2. See also Spanish ambassador describes women sent to Virginia to be married, CSPC, *1675–1676*, 47–53; Pagan, *Anne Orthwood's Bastard*, 14–15.

20 See for example CSPC, *1574–1660*, v. 4, 110, 219–20; Ransome, "Wives for Virginia"; Wood, "Servant Women," 96–7.

21 Brown, *Good Wives*, 80–2.

22 November 1660, CSPC *1574–1660*, 491–2.

23 Menard. "From Servant to Freeholder," 54, 56–7; Carr, Menard, and Walsh, *Robert Cole's World*, 142, 315, 262.

24 Gender ratios among whites were particularly uneven in the Caribbean, where most women travelled with their husbands, and colonial assemblies' attempts to entice single women mostly fell flat, as in seventeenth-century Jamaica. The Council of Trade and Plantations specifically sought to import more "white women" in 1715. Mair, *Women in Jamaica*, 20, 37.

25 Gardiner, *History of the Commonwealth*, v. 4, 110.

26 Ibid., 218n2.

27　Ibid., 218–20.

28　Mair, *Women in Jamaica*, 39–40.

29　Hammond, *Leah and Rachel*.

30　*OBP*, OA16760517. On eighteenth-century criminal gangs paying off their associates' indentures in the colonies, see G. Morgan and Rushton, "Running Away," 74. Seventeenth-century London criminal gangs are discussed in Griffiths, *Lost Londons*, 157–71.

31　*OBP*, OA16760517.

32　*OBP*, OA16760517. See also Morgan and Rushton, *Banishment*, 27–8 and following, on Longman.

33　See Matthew Hale, *Historia Placitorum*, v. 2, 412–13; Mendelson and Crawford, *Women in Early Modern England*, 284; Briggs, *Crime and Punishment*, 74; Morgan and Rushton, *Banishment*, 17; Baker, "Criminal Courts," 41–2. See also *OBP*, t16760510-2, 10 May 1676; reduced punishment of branding *OBP*, s16781211e-1, 11 December 1678.

34　*OBP*, t16740717-6.

35　Upon "judgment, she pleaded she was with child, and thereupon a jury of matrons were impannelled to inspect her, who returned upon their oaths that they did not find that she was quick with child, so she was set by for execution with the rest of the condemned persons." *OBP*, s16750707-1.

36　Humphries, "Mary Carleton"; Carleton, *The Case of Madam Mary Carleton*.

37　Ó Danachair, *Newgate Calendar*, v. 1, 180–90.

38　*OBP*, OA16841219; O16841210-3, s16841210-1.

39　See Briggs, *Crime and Punishment*, 74; G. Morgan and Rushton, *Banishment*, 17; Baker, "Criminal Courts," 41–2. See also *OBP*, t16760510-2.

40　*OBP*, t16760510-2, 10 May 1676.

41　*OBP*, s16781211e-1, 11 December 1678.

42　Those who did not repent were seen as justifiably punished – in 1692, the Ordinary[bishop] of Newgate preached of the "woful miseries which are justly inflicted on wilful, impenitent sinners." *OBP*, OA16921026, 26 October 1692.

43　See Hale, *Historia Placitorum* , v. 2, 412–13.

44　Mendelson and Crawford, *Women in Early Modern England*, 284.

45　*OBP*, Ordinary's Account, 23 October 1685. Reference Number: OA16851023. On the veracity of Ordinary's Accounts in general, see Peter Linebaugh, "The Ordinary of Newgate and His *Account*," in Cockburn, *Crime in England*, 246–69, here 246–9.

46　A widely used legal manual stated: "If a woman at the time of the supposed rape, do conceive with child by the ravisher, this is no rape; for a woman cannot conceive with child except she doth consent," Dalton, *Country Justice*, 392. See also Mendelson and Crawford, *Women in Early Modern England*, 47; Crawford, "Sexual Knowledge," 86–7.

47 Hale, *Historia Placitorum*, v. 2, 412–13.

48 Ibid.

49 See Ordinary's Account, 19 December 1677, *OBP*, OA16771219, and elsewhere in the Old Bailey proceedings.

50 Ordinary's Account, 23 October 1685, *OBP*, OA16851023. The jury of women were "sworn" in like a jury in a legal case: see s16871207-1.

51 These statistics were generated with the use of the *Old Bailey Proceedings Online* statistics engine, version 6, consulted on 10 August 2011.

52 Krista Kesselring shows similar figures of 25 per cent of women being found pregnant in the Tudor era, though she argues that the pregnancy reprieve was not necessarily followed by a general pardon, but often merely postponed execution. Kesselring, *Mercy and Authority*, 212–14. Notably, she shows that in the county courts the percentage was higher: around 40 per cent – in Sussex, an unbelievable 60 per cent. It was roughly compatible, she notes, with the number of men receiving benefit of clergy. See also Oldham, "Pleading the Belly." In general, the rate of assumed pregnancy for women in these records, many of whom were unmarried, and perhaps of unlikely ages, is comparable to the rate of fertility for young married women. On fertility rates, see Wrigley et al., *English Population History*, chapter 7, "Fertility."

53 Hale, *Historia Placitorum*, v. 2, 412–13.

54 Gaskill, *Crime and Mentalities*, 126–34, 154.

55 *OBP*, t16771212-7.

56 *OBP*, OA16771219. For another case of respite for pregnancy, see *OBP*, t16780703-5.

57 Baker, "Criminal Courts and Procedure," 44.

58 Beattie, "Crime and the Courts," 182.

59 *OBP*, t16780411-8 April 1678. See also t16790226-5 in 1679.

60 *OBP*, t16760114-6 1676.

61 See, for example, *OBP*, t16760114-6 in 1675. Lest we think this is a problem of the past, recent analyses show sentences of murder during self-defence favour men over women: Franks, "Real Men Advance"; Murphy, "'Stand Your Ground' Laws."

62 Beattie, "Crime and the Courts," 170–4.

63 Ibid., 182. Beattie argues that women were more likely to be acquitted of capital crimes, more likely to be reprieved if convicted, and more

likely to be given a reduced sentence such as whipping. See also similar findings in G. Morgan and Rushton, *Banishment*, 26–8; on the other hand, Garthine Walker argues that women were less likely to be reprieved for capital crimes than men. Walker, *Crime, Gender, and Social Order*, 136. The disparity may be due to differences between various courts or jurisdictions, or inadequate records.

64 Walker, "Women, Theft, and Stolen Goods," 82.

65 Beattie, "Crime and the Courts," 163, 172; Mendelson and Crawford, "Women in Early Modern England," 46–7.

66 Mendelson and Crawford, *Women in Early Modern England*, 46.

67 See the case of "Cambridge Mall" for pickpocketing in OBP t16941010-13, and the handing down of sentences, OBP s16941010-1. This assumes that the individuals referred to as "W.I." and "G.C." were male.

68 Ordinary of Newgate's Account, 27 May 1718, OBP OA17180527.

69 For a detailed statistical analysis, see Grubb, "Transatlantic Market," 113.

70 It is difficult to compare the results of these cases to the outcomes for men. Of 2,477 cases involving capital punishment, the outcomes for 2,437 or 98.4 per cent are not recorded. These statistics were generated with the use of the *Old Bailey Proceedings Online* statistics engine, version 6, consulted on 10 August 2011.

71 G. Morgan and Rushton, *Criminal Transportation*, 46–51.

72 See Beattie, "Crime and the Courts," 182.

73 In general, male work was believed to be of greater importance than female labour. See Mendelson and Crawford, *Women in Early Modern England*, 258–60, 263, 266, and also "A complaint from Pennsylvania about the duty of 10 per cent levied on women-servants and guns transported thither," 1 March 1698, CSPC, *1697–1698*, 155.

74 Grubb, "Transatlantic Market," 112.

75 On the gendered division of labour in England, see Kussmaul, *Servants in Husbandry*, 4, 70; Meldrum, *Domestic Service*, table 2.2; Clark, *Working Life of Women*, especially 42–92 on rural labour; Mendelson and Crawford, *Women in Early Modern England*, 256–307; Whittle, "Housewives and Servants"; and the discussion of precursors to indentured servitude in chapter 2 of this book. On women's work in the colonies, see Carr, "Planter's Wife," 547.

76 Hammond, *Leah and Rachel*.

77 Revel, "Poor Unhappy Transported Felon."

78 Brown, *Good Wives*, 86–8.

79 *Trappan'd Maide.*

80 Cooke, *Sot-weed Factor*, 7.

81 Newman, *New World*, 92.

82 On income disparities in England, see Mendelson and Crawford, *Women in Early Modern England*, 266.

83 15 June 1654, Irish Record Office, A/90, 50, 708, in Gardiner, *History of the Commonwealth*, v. 4, 111–12.

84 On the value of clothing as an investment, see Brown, *Good Wives*, chapter 9; Rosenthal, "Cultures of Clothing," 460–2; Fontaine, *Alternative Exchanges*, chapters 1–5; in passing in Spence, *Women, Credit, and Debt*, especially 63–8; Reinke-Williams, "Women's Clothes and Female Honour."

85 *CSPC, 1675–1676*, 145.

86 Ibid.

87 27 July 1669, *CSPC 1669–1674*, 31.

88 May 1671, *CSPC, 1669–1674*, 209.

89 31 August 1672, *CSPC, 1669–1674*, 398.

90 Act Relateing to Servants and Slaves, 1676, *General Assembly*, MAO, v. 2, 525. See also *General Assembly*, MAO, v. 1, 80.

91 Bacon, *Laws of Maryland*, 264, 667–8. See also Peyrol-Kleiber, "Starting Afresh."

92 Galenson, "Market Evaluation," 446–67, 453–4.

93 See also Wood, "Servant Women," 98.

94 Daniels, "Liberty to Complaine," 238, 240–1.

95 Ames, *Court Records of Accomack-Northhampton*, v. 1, 79.

96 On the abuse women servants in England often faced, see Mendelson and Crawford, *Women in Early Modern England*, 106–8, 268; Meldrum, "London Domestic Servants"; on rape in the colonies, see Block, *Rape and Sexual Power*; on the gang rape of a hired woman servant on shipboard, see Coldham, *Emigrants in Chains*, 110–11.

97 Hale, *Historia Placitorum*, v. 2, 291. Rape remained a felony even if consent or marriage occurred after the fact, but marital rape was not conceived of. Dalton, *Country Justice*, 392–3.

98 However, few of the reported victims would have been servant women. Offutt, "Limits of Authority," 380–1.

99 Ashbridge, *Quaker Grey*, 21–4. She mentioned an uncle in Pennsylvania, 16.

100 *Records of the Suffolk County Court*, 807.

101 *Provincial Court*, MAO, v. 41, 270–5. See also *Courts of Kent, Talbot, and Somerset Counties*, MAO, v. 54, 69 for a complaint three years previously by Gould against Owens. It seems likely that Owens had raped Gould, but she may have been previously infected with syphilis, which has

variable long-term effects. On this case, see also Daniels, "Liberty to Complaine," 238–9.

102 *Courts of Kent, Talbot, and Somerset Counties*, MAO, v. 54, 122.

103 In Billings, *Old Dominion*, 164. Also see Brown, *Good Wives*, 193–4, 207–9.

104 For example, see Gowing, "Language, Power and the Law"; Gowing, *Domestic Dangers*.

105 For a discussion of servant women's risk of rape or seduction in England, see Mendelson and Crawford, 107–8.

106 *Provincial Court*, MAO, v. 49, 115–18.

107 *General Assembly*, MAO, v. 1, 515–16, 518–20.

108 Ames, *Court Records of Accomack-Northhampton*, v. 1, 82–3. See also E. Morgan, *American Slavery*, 152.

109 *Provincial Court*, MAO, v. 10, 456–8. There were at least three witnesses against her, but they were repeating hearsay from another servant who had since died.

110 In Rappahannock County Virginia from 1692–1720, the majority of bastardy cases were brought against indentured women by masters hoping to recoup the loss of their servants' labour. G. Morgan, "Law and Social Change," 470.

111 See Wood, "Servant Women and Sex"; Carr, "Planter's Wife," 548–9; Norton, "Either Married," 35–6.

112 Wood, "Servant Women," 102–3; Carr, "Planter's Wife," 548.

113 Wood, "Servant Women," 99. Also see *Acts and Statues of Barbados*, 33, which imposed steep additional servitude requirements for servants who married without permission.

114 Hening, *Statutes*, v. 1, 438.

115 Ibid., v. 2, 114–15; Wood, "Servant Women," 101.

116 Walter, *Norfolk County Court Records*, 107.

117 Brown, *Good Wives*, 97–8, 102.

118 *Provincial Court*, MAO, v. 65, 27, 29–30.

119 Lewis was an unsavory individual who was frequently in court and years later murdered his servant. *Provincial Court*, MAO, v. 65, 17, 21, 23, 39–40, 43–4. He was probably not a gentleman, as they were not subject to corporal punishment. *General Assembly*, MAO, v. 1, 184.

120 For the English context, see Mendelson and Crawford, *Women in Early Modern England*, 148, 296. The 1661 Virginia law did mandate that the father pay for the child's maintenance.

121 Hening, *Statutes*, v. 2, 165.

122 *Somerset County Courts*, MAO, v. 535, 71.

123 Hening, *Statutes*, v. 2, 167; See Woods, "Servant Women," 99–100; Mendelson and Crawford, 107.

124 Brown, *Good Wives*.

125 Wood "Servant Woman," 101,

126 Betty Wood found that in four Maryland counties, from 1670–1700, of ninety-eight women, sixty-six named the father. Ibid., 104–5.

127 Daniels, "Liberty to Complaine," 239.

128 Mendelson and Crawford, *Women in Early Modern England*, 47; Crawford, "Sexual Knowledge," 86–7.

129 On this, see Wood, "Servant Women," 101–2, 104.

130 Ibid., 106.

131 *Courts of Kent, Talbot, and Somerset Counties*, MAO, v. 54, 211.

132 *General Assembly*, MAO, v. 1, 373–4, 428, 433, 441–2, 468; For the 1662 law, see Bacon, *Laws of Maryland*, 703.

133 Bacon, *Laws of Maryland*, 703. See also *General Assembly*, MAO, v. 30, 290 and An Acte Concerning those Serv[an]ts that have Bastards (1662), *General Assembly*, MAO, v. 1, 441–2.

134 She appeared the following year claiming her freedom dues from another master. *Somerset County Courts*, MAO, v. 535, 26, 77; *Somerset County Courts*, MAO, v. 406, 182–4, 229–30.

135 *Courts of Kent, Talbot, and Somerset Counties*, MAO, v. 54, 513, 518; see 508 for mention of Rowle as a constable.

136 Ibid., 513, 519. Twotley or Twotle or Towkle had two further children, in 1673 and 1675, the name of their mother(s) not listed, 607.

137 Walter, *Norfolk County Court Records*, 2.

138 On Deaverley's case, see the *Somerset County Courts*, MAO, v. 405, 182. Peter Bodkin's involvement in other cases can be seen in same volume, 157, 159, 191, and for Dent, who was an attorney, 197, 227.

139 *Somerset County Courts*, MAO, v. 406, 91.

140 Bacon, *Laws of Maryland*, 703.

141 In Billings, *Old Dominion*, 161–4. On this case, see also Pagan, *Anne Orthwood's Bastard*.

142 The midwife had threatened Orthwood with "answer at the dreadful Day of Judgment when all harts shal be opened and all secrets made knowne, to speake who was the father of the child." In Billings, *Old Dominion*, 163.

143 In Billings, *Old Dominion*, 162.

144 Pagan, *Anne Orthwood's Bastard*, introduction.

145 *Somerset County Courts*, MAO, v. 87, 310.

146 *Somerset County Courts*, MAO, v. 191, 95–6, 112.

147 Offutt, "Limits of Authority," 380.

148 *Acts and Statutes of Barbados*, 19.

149 *Somerset County Courts*, MAO, v. 191, 95.

150 *General Assembly*, MAO, v. 1, 442; Wood, "Servant Women," 101–2; Pagan, *Anne Orthwood's Bastard*, 5; on the strength of a promise of marriage in English law, see Harding, "Families," 18–19; Mendelson and Crawford, 119; Gowing, *Gender Relations*, 33–5.

151 Bacon, *Laws of Maryland*, 703. See also *General Assembly*, MAO, v. 30, 290 and An Acte Concerning those Serv[an]ts that have Bastards (1662), *General Assembly*, MAO, v. 1, 441–2.

152 *Courts of Kent, Talbot, and Somerset Counties*, MAO, v. 54, 205, 206, 211.

153 *Charles County Courts*, MAO, v. 60, 141–2.

154 There was no mention of whipping Carre, perhaps because Hassards acknowledged paternity and he was possibly not a servant. There is also no mention of what compensation was made to Carre's master, Randall Revell, and she may have been a hired rather than indentured servant. *Somerset County Courts*, MAO, v. 86, 27, 51, 67, 128; *Somerset County Courts*, MAO, v. 87, 26, 67. The case of Mary Perymane, the servant who had sought to return to the Revell household and Mrs Revell, mentioned earlier, suggests some consideration for servants among the Revells. *Somerset County Courts*, MAO, v. 87, 134.

155 *Somerset County Courts*, MAO, v. 535, 77, 82; *Somerset County Courts*, MAO, v. 406, 184, 230.

156 *Courts of Kent, Talbot, and Somerset Counties*, MAO, v. 54, 513, 518.

157 *Provincial Court*, MAO, v. 41, 26–7, 91, 175–6.

158 Ibid., 27.

159 Ibid., 176.

160 Ibid., 91.

161 Ibid., 176.

162 There were few such marriages. One famous case was the marriage of a woman called Irish Nell in 1681 in Maryland. Hodes, *White Women, Black Men*, 19–22, 29–35.

163 Pitman, *A Relation*, 442.

164 Hening, *Statutes*, v. 3, 447–63.

165 *General Assembly*, MAO, v. 30, 288–9.

166 Handler, "Custom and Law," 9.

167 *Kent County Court*, MAO, v. 567, 184–5, 459, 473. Her punishment was initially nine lashes and 290 pounds of tobacco, but was increased at a later hearing.

168 Ibid., 185–6.

169 Ibid., 186–7.

170 Ibid., 179–80. Morsall was the local constable, 297. That same year he was also fined for "keeping company," a euphemism for sexual inter-course, with Rosemond Thompson. There was no bastard begotten in this case, and the fine was discharged. 406.

171 Ibid., 474–5.

172 Ibid., 475–8.

173 Ibid., 478–83. For more bastardy cases, see 71–2, 210–13, 353–4, 385–8, 399–406, 453, 567–8; *Provincial Court*, MAO, v. 57, liii, 310, and many others.

174 Bastardy and refusing to name father: Elizabeth Yellowe, 1648; Anne Watkins, 1650, Walter, *Norfolk County Court Records*, 9, 135; servant woman: running away and stealing canoe, 1698, CSPC, *1697–1698*, 444; Margaret Riggs: returning early from transportation and stealing, 1677, OBP OA16771219; Elizabeth Hewett: for not transporting herself after a court order, 1677, OBP OA16771219; returning early from transporta-tion and theft: "A notorious criminal," 1677, OBP t16771212-6; refusing to name criminal associates: "A servant-wench," 1677, OBP t16770906-8; a woman pressed to death for refusing to plead unless criminal associ-ates released first, despite non-capital offense, 1676, OBP t16770906-8.

CHAPTER SEVEN

1 Wareing, *Indentured Migration*, 152, 156–8.

2 For example, a Virginia report stating "not above ten men and boys liv-ing, of the whole number of servants taken to Virginia in the Seaflower." CSPC, *1574–1660*, 36; causes of death included shipboard mortality, disease, and Indian attacks. Richard Frethorne's colony was supplied by the *Seaflower*. Frethorne, 41, 62. George Sandys, Virginia Company treasurer, wrote uneasily in 1623, that "if the Seaflower com not quickly in, there will hardly be found a preservation from famin." The *Seaflower* was unable to relieve the colony because it blew up near Bermuda "by firing of her owne powder." Kingsbury, *Records of the Vir-ginia Company*, 4, 92, 109. See also Johnson, "Transportation of Vagrant Children," 146–9; Wareing, *Indentured Migration*, 31.

3 On child vagrancy in early modern Europe, see Cunningham, *Children and Childhood*, chapter 5.

4 See the OED: "Originally, to steal or carry off (children or others) in order to provide servants or labourers for the American plantations;

hence, in general use, to steal (a child), to carry off (a person) by illegal force."

5 One of the earliest works, Ariès, *Centuries of Childhood*, posited the lack of a notion of childhood in the medieval and early modern era, although he did admit some indulgence toward children, while Stone, *Family, Sex, and Marriage*, described family relations as distant. More recently, Brewer emphasizes many ways that children were viewed as adults by the law in *By Birth or Consent*.

6 Historiography from the 1980s, including Pollock, *Forgotten Children*; Houlbrooke, *English Family*; Ozment, *When Fathers Ruled* emphasized a more emotional and loving connection between parents and children, while MacFarlane, *Marriage and Love in England*, showed that loving relationships did prevail, but that families also made economically shaped decisions about how to raise their children. More recently, see Cunningham, *Children and Childhood*.

7 Chapters 3 and 4 of Cunningham, *Children and Childhood*, discuss developing ideologies of children, and the attitude that children should contribute labour to the household economy. See also Ben-Amos, *Adolescence and Youth*, 39–47.

8 Hindle, "On the Parish," 24–5; Cunningham, "Employment and Unemployment of Children." Also see the various chapters in Herndon and Murray, *Children Bound*.

9 Hindle, "'Waste' Children?"; Ewen, "Poore Soules." See Slack, *English Poor Law*, about attempts to reform the poor.

10 *CSPC, 1574–1660*, 19. See also Johnson, "Transportation of Vagrant Children"; Waring, *Indenture Migration*, 31.

11 A detailed description of these events can be found in Johnson, "Transportation of Vagrant Children," 138–44.

12 *CSPC, 1574–1660*, 23.

13 Dahlberg, "'Do Not Forget Me,'" 22.

14 Ewen, "Poore Soules," 141–3.

15 *CSPC, 1574–1660*, 37.

16 Stock, *Proceedings*, 140.

17 Grubb, "Fatherless and Friendless."

18 Hall, *Acts passed in Barbados*, 35. By 1652, it had already been stated that no English children under the age of fourteen be transported as servants, unless with their parish's consent. *Acts and Statutes of Barbados*, 16.

19 The Council of Trade and Plantations found that, of the colonies, only Barbados was willing to take "malefactors." *CSPC, 1696–1697*, 303, 341.

20 In January 1697, Jamaica merchants "were quite at a loss" because the only people they could "prevail with" to go to Jamaica were "a few poor families of more women and children than men, who would not serve their end." *CSPC, 1696–1697*, 303, 341.

21 Hindle, *On the Parish?*, 195; Lashua, "Children," 210–49.

22 Firth and Rait, *Acts and Ordinances*, 681. See also Wareing, *Indentured Migration*, 181, 185.

23 See Wareing, "Preventive and Punitive Regulation," 305 on the end of government-sanctioned mass transplantations of children.

24 *CSPC 1574–1660*, 407, 7 September 1653. The shipper, David Selleck of Boston, was a frequent contractor for government shipments of the Irish. A week after this commission, he was paid by the Irish Commissioners to ship 550 Irish vagrants into New England as indentured servants. Prendergast, *Cromwellian Settlement*, 245.

25 *CSPC 1574–1660*, 409.

26 See Wareing, "Preventative and Punitive Regulation."

27 *CSPC, 1675–1676*, 138.

28 Wareing, "Preventive and Punitive Regulation," 288–308; Wareing, *Indentured Migration*, 184–95.

29 Bayly, *True and Faithful Warning*, 7–9; Carroll, "From Bond Slave to Governor," 20–1.

30 Williamson, "French and Indian Cruelty," 216–17.

31 Quoted in Wareing, "Preventative and Punitive Regulation," 296.

32 M., "A Letter from Jamaica to London."

33 Luttrell, *Brief Historical Relation*, v. 1, 232, 244, 375.

34 *Upon a complaint and rumour.*

35 Luttrell, *Brief Historical Relation*, 183. According to the OED, this was the first known written use of the word "kidnap."

36 Probably the same John Wilmore mentioned earlier in Luttrell's narrative as associated with various political leaders and being arrested during the royal Exclusion Crisis. Luttrell, *Brief Historical Relation*, 116, 138, 147, 159, 164. Several witnesses testified that "above 500" children had been "sent away in two years" by Wilmore, and that he "had been a practiser of that trade" (kidnapping). Luttrell, *Brief Historical Relation*, 182. On this case, see also Wareing, *Indentured Migration*, 99, 161, 205, 216.

37 Luttrell, *Brief Historical Relation*, 188.

38 Ibid., 182, 188.

39 Ibid., 192.

40 Two shippers of kidnapped children, Mr Dessigny and Mr Baily, were each fined £500, and "one Haviland" was fined 500 marks (gold or silver in weight) and sentenced to the pillory "thrice." Ibid., 232, 329.

41 Ibid., 88.

42 Ibid., 188.

43 Wareing, *Indentured Migration*, 184–95.

44 Luttrell, *Brief Historical Relation*, 247.

45 Wilmore, *Case of John Wilmore*.

46 Wareing, *Indentured Migration*, 230–1.

47 *CSPC 1574–1660*, 411, 15 November 1653.

48 *CSPC, 1661–1668*, 555; see Wareing, *Indentured Migration*, 148, on this case and others.

49 *The grand kidnapper at last taken*.

50 *Provincial Court*, MAO, v. 67, 26.

51 Stock, *Proceedings*, 269.

52 On patriarchal household expectations, see Cunningham, *Children and Childhood*; Mendelson and Crawford, *Women in Early Modern England*, 5–6, 15, 71–4, 301–2; Gowing, *Gender Relations*, 29–50.

53 In Virginia: Hening, *Statutes*, v. 2, 169; in Maryland: *General Assembly*, MAO, v. 2, 147.

54 *Courts of Kent, Talbot, and Somerset Counties*, MAO, v. 54, 590–1.

55 Ibid., 431; *Provincial Court*, MAO, v. 41, 422.

56 *Charles Count Courts*, MAO, v. 60, 188.

57 Hening, *Statutes*, v. 1, 257.

58 Ibid., 441.

59 Ibid., v. 2, 114–15. From 1666, those over nineteen years of age would serve five years and those under nineteen, until age twenty-four, 240.

60 Hening, *Statutes*, v. 2, 169.

61 *General Assembly*, MAO, v. 1, 80.

62 Ibid., 1, 409.

63 *General Assembly*, MAO, v. 2, 147.

64 "An Acte lymiting servants tymes," *General Assembly*, MAO, v. 1, 409.

65 *General Assembly*, MAO, v. 2, 527.

66 Bacon, *Laws of Maryland*, 702.

67 *Courts of Kent, Talbot, and Somerset Counties*, MAO, v. 54, 356. The case was referred to the next session of the Talbot County Court.

68 *Somerset County Courts*, MAO, v. 89, 56.

69 In Billings, *Old Dominion*, 151.

70 Age determination was usually done for several servants at a time. For

examples, see in *Courts of Kent, Talbot, and Somerset Counties*, MAO, v. 54, 314, 356, 386, 426, 430–1, 438–9, 448, 454, 526, 590–1; *Provincial Court*, MAO , v. 41, 422; *Charles County Courts*, MAO, v. 53, 485, 501.

71 *Charles County Courts*, MAO, v. 60, editor's preface, xxxvi.

72 *Provincial Court*, MAO, v. 57, liii, 358.

73 *Provincial Court*, MAO, v. 41, 476–8.

74 Ibid., 478.

75 *Somerset Count Court*, MAO, v. 535, 94.

76 Bayly, *True and Faithful Warning*, 7–9; Carroll, "From Bond Slave to Governor."

77 *Provincial Court*, MAO, v. 57, xxvii, xlvi–ii, 59–69, 153; *Courts of Kent, Talbot, and Somerset Counties*, MAO, v. 54, 62, 64–5, 410.

78 9 October 1640. McIlwaine, *Minutes of the Council and General Court*, 465.

79 *Provincial Court*, MAO, v. 41, 515–16; *Provincial Court*, MAO, v. 49, xiii, 122, 137; *General Assembly*, MAO, v. 1, 463–4.

80 *General Assembly*, MAO, v. 1, 463–6, 481.

81 Ben-Amos, *Adolescence and Youth*, 43–5, 90–3; Kussmaul, *Servants in Husbandry*, 4, 24.

82 Ames, *Court Records of Accomack-Northampton*, v. 1, 15.

83 In York County Virginia: in 1690, Thomas and Ellinor Thorpe sued Robert Green on behalf of their son Gilbert; in 1692, Stephen Clarke sued his master who "through his covetous & sinister ends" had failed to teach him a trade, and Dannll Davis sued his master for the same, *York County Deeds*, Books 8 and 9. In 1705, Edward Powers and Charles Hansford also complained of this, as well as "imoderate correction," *York County Deeds*, Book 12. In 1714–15, Hugh Norvell sued his son's master for "ill usage" and "neglecting to instruct his apprentice," and Bridgett Minitree complained of "hardships" imposed on her son and his lack of training, *York County Deeds*, Book 14.

84 *Somerset County Courts*, MAO, v. 89, 56, 63.

85 Ibid., 66.

86 On the effects of parental loss, see Ben-Amos, *Adolescence and Youth*, 48–54. On the high levels of parental mortality, see Harding, "Families," 31–3; Carr, Menard, and Walsh, *Robert Cole's World*, chapter 1, 153–8, 176.

87 Herndon and Murray, *Children Bound*.

88 Ibid., 9–10.

89 Russo and Russo, "Responsive Justices," 154.

90 In Billings, *Old Dominion*, 380.

91 Russo and Russo, "Responsive Justices," 155.

92 Herndon and Murray, *Children Bound*, 13–16; Hindle and Murray, "Recreating Proper Families," 32; Russo and Russo, "Responsive Justices," 161–3.

93 *Somerset County Courts*, MAO, v. 406, 2; *Somerset County Courts*, MAO, v. 535, 8–9.

94 *Charles County Courts*, MAO, v. 60, 106.

95 Ibid., 142.

96 In Billings, *Old Dominion*, 381.

97 Carr, Menard, and Walsh, *Robert Cole's World*, 242–67.

98 On duration of breast-feeding, see McLaren, "Marital Fertility"; Davenport, "Infant-feeding Practices," 178, 182–6; Wrigley et al., *English Population History*, 447; Treckel, "Breastfeeding," 35–8; Fildes, *Breasts, Bottles and Babies*, 352–70. On fertility rates, see Wrigley et al., *English Population History*, 508.

99 MHS, Peter Collamore papers, Ms. N-1012.

100 *Somerset County Courts*, MAO, v. 535, 80.

101 On parishes in England paying women to care for indigent infants, see Willen, "Women in the Public Sphere," 569.

102 *Somerset County Courts*, MAO, v. 405, 182; *Somerset County Courts*, MAO, v. 406, 91.

103 Both the court and Bishopp refer to the infant only as the "basterd child" of Deaverley. *Somerset County Courts*, MAO, v. 535, 16, 21; *Somerset County Courts*, MAO, v. 405, 182; *Somerset County Courts*, MAO, v. 406, 87, 89, 91, 97, 154.

104 *Somerset County Courts*, MAO, v. 87, 537.

105 Williamson, "French and Indian Cruelty," 216–17.

106 In Billings, *Old Dominion*, 381. "Natural" implied illegitimacy, but also had a similar connotation to the term "biological" today.

107 MHS, "Witness for Thomas Hathaway's indenture of James Bryant," Miscellaneous Manuscripts, 9 October 1721.

108 *Somerset County Courts*, MAO, v. 191, 96–7. The outcome of this case is not recorded, but as the text of the indenture was copied into the court records and did not include any mention of the child, it seems likely that Cunningham's indenture was not voided.

109 *Courts of Kent, Talbot, and Somerset Counties*, v. 54, 195. Dabb won 750 pounds of tobacco from Reede, but remained responsible for the court costs. Perhaps Reede was the father of the child, but he was also accused of getting another woman servant with child shortly thereafter, 233.

110 *Provincial Court,* MAO, v. 65, 275–6. The clerk must have been having a bad day, because although the individuals in the case are clearly identified, the plaintiff is variously named Isabella, Elizabeth, and Isabell with her surnames both as Goodale and Gibbs. Spelling of names was often inconsistent and could cause real legal problems, such as in the case of Thomas Kerey, whose right to 300 acres was in question because his title had been filed under the alternate spelling of Carey. The title was only resolved after "the Records being searched" at Kerey's request revealed the "mistake," Ibid., 60.

111 FSL manuscript V.b.16 (32), image 147360 and V.b.16 (31), 147358.

112 See Wood on this case and on Hannah Holland's mother. "Servant Women," 106–8.

113 *Somerset County Courts,* MAO, v. 106, 167. The case was complicated by the fact that Hannah Holland had initially been indentured to another master, John Kirk/Kirke, who had then sold her to her current master. Her father Dennis Holland had also been a servant.

114 Ibid., 197.

115 *Somerset County Courts,* MAO, v. 406, 108; *Somerset County Courts,* MAO, v. 535, 17.

116 *Somerset County Courts,* MAO, v. 406, 48.

117 *Somerset County Courts,* MAO, v. 406, xi, 126–7; *Somerset County Courts,* MAO, v. 535, 5, 12, 19.

118 *Somerset County Courts,* MAO, v. 535, 89; *Somerset County Courts, 1693–1694,* MAO, v. 407, 139.

119 *Somerset County Courts,* MAO, v. 106, 197.

120 *Somerset County Courts,* MAO, v. 535, 31; *Somerset County Courts,* MAO, v. 406, 241–2. It's unclear whether these children were placed in an indenture arrangement, but the freedom dues and mandate to educate the boy suggest that Dregers expected to gain from their presence in the household.

121 *Somerset County Courts,* MAO, v. 406, 7.

122 Ibid., 7–8; *Somerset County Courts,* MAO, v. 535, 8.

123 *York County Deeds,* Book 9.

CHAPTER EIGHT

1 See E. Morgan, *American Slavery,* 250–70; Rice, *Tales from a Revolution,* especially 14–16, 90, 119, 195–6, 220–1; Nash, *Red, White & Black,* 110–15.

2 Pestana, *English Atlantic,* 203–4.

3 Billings, *Old Dominion*, 168–89; Wolfe, "Gloucester County Conspiracy";
   Breen, "Changing Labor Force"; McIlwaine, *Minutes of the Council and
   General Court*, 511; "Virginia Colonial Records," 38–43.
4 In Billings, *Old Dominion*, 147, 170; Zacek, "John Nickson."
5 Beckles, *White Servitude*, 98–114; Gwynn, "Documents," 234.
6 Ligon, *History of Barbados*, 45, 51.
7 Dalton, *Country Justice*, 336–7; Ben-Amos, *Adolescence and Youth*, 7.
8 *Provincial Court*, MAO, v. 65, 2–8.
9 *Provincial Court*, MAO, v. 57, liv, 610–11.
10 *Provincial Court*, MAO, v. 41, 316–17. The punishment was commensu-
   rately greater than the usual one of additional time of servitude for runaways, and Morgan was also sentenced to receive thirty lashes.
11 In Billings, *Old Dominion*, 166–7. Yet this meant also that his mistress,
   unless she sold him, which would have been difficult to do, was forced
   to keep him in proximity.
12 *York County Deeds*, Book 14.
13 In Billings, *Old Dominion*, 164–6.
14 *Provincial Court*, MAO, v. 65, 1.
15 Walter, *Norfolk County Court Records*, 13.
16 Ibid., 140.
17 *Records of the Suffolk County Court*, v. 29, 436.
18 *Records of the Suffolk County Court*, v. 30, 1063.
19 *Provincial Court*, MAO, v. 49, 441–2, 457, 493–4, 564. D'mondidier was
   also spelled Mondidier, Demondidier, and Dimondidier. Southward was
   also Sowthward and Southard, and Hasling also Haslin.
20 *Provincial Court*, MAO, v. 49, 493–4.
21 Ibid., xiii, 8–10.
22 Walter, *Norfolk County Court Records*, 7.
23 *Provincial Court*, MAO, v. 4, 358.
24 *Provincial Court*, MAO, v. 49, 194–5.
25 Seventeenth-century criminal trial records from the OBP mentioning
   early return from indenture include that of Hugh Mills, OA16780306;
   Elizabeth Hewett, for not transporting herself after a court order,
   OA16771219; "A notorious criminal," t16771212-6; also t16770711-8 and
   t16781016-3; and Thomas Moore and John Parker, mentioned earlier in
   this book, OA16760830; See also Griffiths, *Lost Londons*, 289. On
   eighteenth-century cases of returning early from indenture, see
   G. Morgan and Rushton, "Running Away."
26 Elizabeth Longman, 1677, OBP, t16770711a-4 and OA16760517.
27 G. Morgan and Rushton, *Banishment*, 21, 27.

28 *OBP*, OA16771219 and t16771212-6.

29 See, for example, *Provincial Court*, MAO, v. 65, 39, 40, 63–5, 92; *Provincial Court*, MAO, v. 69, 154–5, and many other examples in the records.

30 This is mainly based on runaway ads in periodicals, not available for the seventeenth century. See G. Morgan and Ruston, *Criminal Transportation*, 106–8; Ekirch, *Bound for America*, 195, 202; K. Morgan, "Convict Runaways," 254, 265; Beckles, *White Servitude*, 104–10. On seventeenth-century runaway servants, see Pestana, *English Atlantic*, 197–201.

31 *Provincial Court*, MAO, v. 57, l–li, 121–2. Bennett failed in his suit on a technicality because the letter he provided was ruled inadequate proof.

32 *Provincial Court*, MAO, v. 57, xlvii; Hening, *Statutes*, v. 2, 114–16; Tomlins, "Early British America," 124–6. Tomlins points out that servants with short local contracts who were not indentured could not be punished as easily for leaving their employer.

33 *General Assembly*, MAO, v. 2, 523.

34 *Provincial Court*, MAO, v. 57, l, 129–30.

35 In Billings, *Old Dominion*, 160. It is difficult to ascertain what else Ballentine could have said in court.

36 *Provincial Court*, MAO, v. 57, 1, 7, 130.

37 Revel, "Poor Unhappy Transported Felon."

38 *Provincial Court*, MAO, v. 65, 179.

39 Walter, *Norfolk County Court Records*, 129–30. Bayley had previously been punished for fornication, 107.

40 Hening, *Statutes*, v. 2, 266.

41 Ibid., 277–9.

42 Ibid., v. 1, 401, 404.

43 "Decisions of the General Court," 236.

44 Ibid.; McIlwane, *Minutes*, 466–7.

45 1672 Virginia, Hening, *Statutes*, v. 2, 300–1.

46 Ibid., 26, 117.

47 "Decisions of the General Court," 236–7; McIlwane, *Minutes*, 466–7; Billings, *Old Dominion*, 159.

48 Van Den Boogaart, "Servant Migration"; Christoph, "Freedmen."

49 Hening, *Statutes at Large*, v. 2, 188.

50 "Decisions of the General Court," 237–8.

51 *Somerset County Courts*, MAO, v. 535, 71, 94. The time is listed in the later record as sixty-one days.

52 *Charles County Courts*, MAO, v. 60, 45–7.

53 Ibid., 108–10. On Ralston, see also Daniels, "Liberty to Complaine," 235.

54 See *OED*, "hue and cry."
55 Moraley, *Infortunate*, 61.
56 "Advertisement."
57 On eighteenth-century runaways, see K. Morgan, "English and American Attitudes," 431.
58 *Virginia Gazette*, Issue 5, 8 October 1736.
59 *Maryland Gazette*, Issue 96, 8–15 July 1729.
60 Ibid., Issue 97, 15–22 July 1729. See the *OED* for a definition of "osnaburg."
61 *Virginia Gazette*, Issue 3, 24 September 1736.
62 Ibid., Issue 4, 1 October 1736.
63 Ibid., Issue 6, 15 October 1736.
64 Ibid., Issue 6, 15 October 1736.
65 On women's thefts of clothing to sell, see Walker, "Women, Theft and Stolen Goods," 87–91.
66 *Provincial Court*, MAO, v. 57, xlvii, lvi, 182, 368–9.
67 Ibid., lii, 374.
68 Ibid., lii, 581.
69 *Provincial Court*, MAO, v. 49, 477. The Provincial Court seemed convinced that Sprigg had voluntarily released Newell.
70 Hening, *Statutes*, v. 1, 401, 439, 440.
71 Ibid., 482.
72 Ibid., 517.
73 Ibid., v. 2, 277–9.
74 Article 1 Barbados Slave Code 1661 CO 30/2; Rugemer, "Development of Mastery and Race," 454–5; Jordan, *White Over Black*, 106–7, 154–6; Franklin, *Runaway Slaves*, 16, 45–6.
75 Hening, *Statutes*, v. 2, 21.
76 Ibid., 187–8.
77 Ibid., 273–4.
78 Ibid., 277–9.
79 Ibid., 284.
80 Ibid., 405–6.
81 There were many cases of individuals accused of "entertaining" or "detaining" servants, such as in *Charles County Courts*, MAO, v. 60, 495, 581–2.
82 *Court of Chancery*, MAO, v. 51, 81.
83 Ibid., 103–4, 176, 204, 213–14, 224, 226–7. Wahob and Waghob were possibly relations.
84 Ibid., 212, 226.
85 *Somerset County Courts*, MAO, v. 535, 14; *Somerset County Courts*, MAO, v. 406, 70.

86 *Somerset County Courts*, MAO, v. 191, 114–15, 125–6.

87 Ibid., MAO, v.191, 158; *Somerset County Courts*, MAO, v. 405, 150.

88 *Somerset County Courts*, MAO, v. 406, 114, 125–6, 164; *Somerset County Courts*, MAO, v. 535, 19.

89 *Somerset County Courts*, MAO, v. 535, 72. She was referred to in the proceedings as a "transported indentured servant," suggesting that she had not entered indenture willingly.

CHAPTER NINE

1 Menard, "From Servant to Freeholder," 54. Also see Carr, Menard, and Walsh, *Robert Cole's World*, 142, 315, 262.

2 I am grateful to Rich and Jim Kelly for sharing the genealogical records of their ancestor with me. Doughty's life is also described in Gardner, *Involuntary American*, and in Gerrard et al., *Lost Lives, New Voices*.

3 Bayly, *True and Faithful Warning*, 7–9; Carroll, "From Bond Slave to Governor."

4 *Biographical Dictionary*, MAO, v. 426, 319.

5 Menard, "From Servant to Freeholder," 39–44, 59–63. See also a number of individuals who finished their servitude and became small or moderate planters, Carr, "Emigration," 282–5; Carr, Menard, and Walsh, *Robert Cole's World*, 17, 38–9, 103, 150, 153, 174–6, 185, 207, 219, Appendix 4; Peyrol-Kleiber, "Starting Afresh."

6 *Provincial Court*, MAO, v. 69, 207.

7 *Charles County Courts*, MAO, v. 60, 20, 21, 123; *General Assembly*, MAO, v. 2, 14.

8 Beckles, *White Servitude*, 140–7, 153–9.

9 Galenson, *White Servitude*, 13–15; Grubb, "Auction of Redemptioner Servants"; Grubb, "Market Structure"; Grubb, "Redemptioner Immigration."

10 On servitude and penal punishment in Australia, see Quinlan, "Australia"; Nicholas, *Convict Workers*.

11 K. Morgan, "English and American Attitudes," 420–3; Dressler, "'Enimies to Mankind'"; Atkinson, "Free-born Englishman Transported."

12 Northrup, *Indentured Labor*; Roopnarine, *Indo-Caribbean Indenture*; Lai, *Chinese in the West Indies*; Hui, "Chinese Indentured Labour," 51–5; Campbell, *Chinese Coolie Emigration*; Rediker, Pybus, and Christopher, *Many Middle Passages*; Hay and Craven, *Masters, Servants, and Magistrates*, 28–9, 38–42, 48–9; Mohapatra, "Assam and the West Indies"; Galenson, *White Servitude*, 180–2.

13 De Barros, "Urban British Guiana"; Altink, "Slavery by Another Name"; Bolland, "Systems of Domination."

Bibliography

PRINTED PRIMARY SOURCES

Acts and Statutes of the Island of Barbados. London: Printed by Will Bentley, 1654, Early English books, 1641–1700; 1663:13.

Advertisement: "These are to give notice to all persons where these papers shall come; that a servant man belonging to Hannah Bosworth…" Boston?: 1683, ESTC: W27248.

Alsop, George. *A Character of the Province of Maryland.* Edited by John Shea. Baltimore: Maryland Historical Society, 1880 (1666).

Ames, Susie M., ed. *County Court Records of Accomack-Northhampton, Virginia, 1632–1640,* v.1. Washington, DC: American Historical Association, 1954.

Ashbridge, Elizabeth. *Quaker Grey: Some Account of the Forepart of the Life of Elizabeth Ashbridge.* London: Astolet Press, 1904 (1774).

"At the Court at Whitehall." London: Printed by John Bill, Henry Hills, and Thomas Newcomb, 1682.

Bacon, Thomas. *Laws of Maryland at Large.* Annapolis: Jonas Green, printer, 1765.

Baxter, James Phinney. *The Trelawny Papers: Documentary History of the State of Maine,* v. 3. Portland: Hoyt, Fogg, and Dunham, 1884.

Bayly, Charles. *A True and Faithful Warning unto the People and Inhabitants of Bristol.* London: 1663.

Billings, Warren M., ed. *The Old Dominion in the Seventeenth Century: A Documentary History of Virginia, 1606–1689.* Chapel Hill: University of North Carolina Press, 1975.

Birch, Thomas, ed. *Collection of State Papers of John Thurloe, 1638–1660,* v. 4. London: Fletcher Gyles, 1742.

Blackstone, William. *Commentaries on the Laws of England*, v. 1. Edited by
John Wendell and J.F. Hargrave. New York: Harper, 1850 (1765).

Blenerhasset, Thomas. *A Direction for the Plantation in Ulster*. London:
Printed by Edward Allde for John Budge, 1610, n.p.

Burton, Thomas. *Diary of Thomas Burton Esq: Volume 4, March–April 1659*.
Edited by John Towill Rutt. London: Henry Colburn, 1828.

Calendar of State Papers, Domestic: Charles II, Addenda 1660–1685. Edited by
F.H. Blackburne Daniell and Francis Bickley. London: Her Majesty's Sta-
tioner's Office, 1939.

Calendar of State Papers Colonial, America and the West Indies. vol. 1,
1574–1660 (1860); v. 5, 1661–68 (1880); v. 7, 1669–74 (1889); v. 9, 1675–76
(1893), edited by W Noel Sainsbury, and v. 15, 1696–97 (1904); v.16,
1697–98 (1905), edited by John W. Fortescue. London: Her Majesty's Sta-
tioner's Office.

Carleton, Mary. *The Case of Madam Mary Carleton, Lately Styled the German
Princess, Truely Stated*. London: Printed for Sam Speed, 1663.

Cleaver, Robert. *A godly forme of household government for the ordering of private families ... wherunto is adjoined ... the maisters dutie towards his servants, and also the servants duty towards their maisters*. London: Printed for
R. Field, 1621.

Coad, John. *A Memorandum of the Wonderful Providences of God to a Poor Un-
worthy Creature, during the Time of the Duke of Monmouth's Rebellion*. London: Longman, Brown, Green, & Longmans, 1849.

Coke, Edward. *The First Part of the Institutes of the Laws of England*. London:
Printed for J. and W.T. Clarke, 1832 (1628).

– *The Third Part of the Institutes of the Laws of England*. London: Printed for
E. and R. Brooke, 1797 (1644).

Cooke, Ebenezer. *The Sot-weed Factor, or A Voyage to Maryland, A Satyr*. London: Printed for D. Bragg, 1708.

Dalton, Michael. *The Country Justice: Containing the Practice, Duty and Power
of the Justices of the Peace...* London: Printed by William Rawlins and
Samuel Roycroft, 1690.

"Decisions of the General Court." (Virginia), 1640, reprinted in *The Virginia
Magazine of History and Biography* 5(3) (January 1898): 233–41.

Defoe, Daniel. *The Fortunes and Misfortunes of the Famous Moll Flanders*. London: Printed for W. Chetwood, 1771.

Donne, John. *John Donne: The Major Works*. Edited by John Carey. Oxford:
Oxford University Press, 2000.

Dutton, Matthew. *The Law of Masters and Servants in Ireland*. Dublin: Printed
by S. Powell for Eliphal Dobson, 1723.

Firth, Charles H., and Robert S. Rait, eds. *Acts and Ordinances of the Interregnum, 1642–1660*. London: H.M. Stationery Office, 1911.

Fit John, John. *A Diamonde most precious, worthy to be marked, instructing all maysters and servaunts, how they ought to leade their lives*. London: Printed by Hugh Jackson, 1577.

Fleetwood, William. *The Relative Duties of Parents and Children, Husbands and Wives, Masters and Servants...* London: Printed by Charles Harper, 1705.

Fosset, Thomas. *The Servants Dutie*. London: N.p., 1613.

Frethorne, Richard. "Letters." In *The Records of the Virginia Company in London*, (1622–24), v. 4, edited by Susan Kingsbury, 41–2, 58–60. Washington, DC: US Government Printing Office, 1935.

Gother, John. *Instructions for Masters, Traders, Labourers, &c.* London: N.p., 1699.

Gouge, William. *Of Domesticall Duties: Eight Treatises*. London: Printed by John Haviland for William Bladen, 1622.

The grand kidnapper at last taken or, a full and true account of the taking and apprehending of Cap. Azariah Daniel. London: Printed for James Read, near Fleet-street, (1690?).

Gwynn, Aubrey. "Documents Relating to the Irish in the West Indies." *Analecta Hibernica*, no. 4 (1932): 139–286.

Hakluyt, Richard. *A Discourse on Western Planting, Written in the Year 1584*. Cambridge, MA: John Wilson and Son, 1877 (1584).

Hale, Matthew. *Historia Placitorum Coronae or History of Pleas of the Crown*, vols. 1 and 2. Philadelphia: R.H. Small, 1847 (1736).

Hall, Richard, ed. *Acts, Passed in the Island of Barbados. From 1643, to 1762*. London: Printed for Richard Hall, 1764.

Hammond, John. *Leah and Rachel, or the Two Fruitfull Sisters, Virginia and Mary-land*. London: Printed by T. Mabb, 1656.

Handler, Jerome, ed. "Father Antoine Biet's Visit to Barbados in 1654." *Journal of the Barbados Museum and Historical Society* 32 (1967): 56–76.

Harrower, John. "The Diary of John Harrower." *American Historical Review* 6 (1900): 65–107.

Hayward, Arthur, ed. *Lives of the Most Remarkable Criminals*. New York: Dodd, Mead & Co., 1927 (1735).

Hazard, Samuel, ed. *Pennsylvania Archive*, v. 1. New York: AMS Press, 1968 (1837).

Hening, William Waller, ed. *The Statutes at Large; Being a Collection of All the Laws of Virginia from the First Session of the Legislature, in the Year 1619*, vols. 1–3. New York: R., W., and G. Bartow, 1823. Philadelphia: Thomas Desilver, 1823.

House of Commons. *Journals of the House of Commons, 1651–1659*, v. 7. London: House of Commons, 1813.

The humble overtures of divers persons nearly concerned in the present posture and condition of the island of Barbados (1655). TNA, CO 1/69, No. 2.

Instructions for Masters, Traders, Labourers, &c, Also for servants, apprentices, and youth. London: N.p., 1718.

Jus imperij & servitutis, or, The law concerning masters, apprentices, bayliffs, receivers, stewards, attorneys, factors, deputies, carriers, covenant-servants, &c. London: Printed for Richard Sare and Robert Gosling, 1707.

Kingsbury, Susan, ed. *The Records of the Virginia Company in London*, (1622–24), v. 4. Washington, DC: US Government Printing Office, 1935.

The Lawes Resolutions of Womens Rights. London: N.p., 1632.

Ligon, Richard. *A True and Exact History of the Island of Barbados.* London: Printed by Peter Parker and Thomas Guy, 1673.

Luttrell, Narcissus. *A Brief Historical Relation of State Affairs, from Sept. 1678 to Apr. 1714*, v. 1. Oxford: Oxford University Press, 1857.

M., T. "A Letter from Jamaica to London, concerning kid-napping." London[?]: (1682[?]).

Maryland Archives Online, Maryland State Archives. http://aomol.msa .maryland.gov/html/index.html.

Mather, Cotton Mather. *A good master well served. A brief discourse on the necessary properties & practices of a good servant in every-kind of servitude.* Boston: Printed by B. Green and J. Allen, 1696.

McIlwaine, Henry R., ed. *Journals of the House of Burgesses of Virginia, 1659/60–1693.* Richmond: Virginia State Library, 1914.

– *Minutes of the Council and General Court of Colonial Virginia, 1622–1632, 1670–1676.* Richmond: Virginia State Library, 1924.

Moraley, William. *The Infortunate*, 2nd ed. University Park, PA: Pennsylvania State University Press, 2005.

Ó Danachair, Donal, ed. *The Newgate Calendar*, v. 1. Ex-classics Project, 2009. www.exclassics.com/newgate/ng01.pdf, 180–90.

Old Bailey Proceedings Online, 1674–1913. Edited by Tim Hitchcock, Robert Shoemaker, Clive Emsley, Sharon Howard, and Jamie McLaughlin, et al. www.oldbaileyonline.org, version 7.0, 24 March 2012.

Palmer, William P., ed. *Calendar of Virginia State Papers, 1652–1781*, v. 1. Richmond: R.F. Walker, 1875.

Parkyns, Thomas. *A Method Proposed for the Hiring and Recording of Servants.* Nottingham: John Collyer, 1721.

Pickering, Danby. *The Statutes at Large, from the Twelfth Year of King Charles II.*

to the Last Year of King James II. inclusive, v. 8. Cambridge: Printed by John Bentham, 1764.

Pitman, Henry. *A Relation of the Great Sufferings and Strange Adventures of Henry Pitman*. In *Stuart Tracts, 1603–1693*, edited by Charles Harding Firth, 431–67. New York: Cooper Square Publishers, 1964 (1689).

Records of the Suffolk County Court, 1671–1680, v. 30. Boston: Colonial Society of Massachusetts, 1933.

Revel, James. *The Poor Unhappy Transported Felon's Sorrowful Account of His Fourteen Years Transportation, at Virginia.* York: Printed by C. Croshaw, n.d.

Rivers, Marcellus. *Englands Slavery or Barbados Merchandize*. London: N.p., 1659.

Sprigs, Elizabeth. "Letter." In *Colonial Captivities, Marches, and Journeys*, edited by Isabel Calder, 151–2. New York: Macmillan, 1935.

Stock, Leo, ed. *Proceedings and Debates of the British Parliaments respecting North America*, v. 1, 1542–1688. Washington, DC: Carnegie Institution, 1924.

Thomas, Thomas. *Dictionarium Linguae Latinae et Anglicanae*. Menston, England: Scolar Press, 1972 (1587).

The Trappan'd Maiden or Distressed Damsel. (Printed for W. O[nley]. and A. M[ilbourn]. and sold by C. Bates, in Pye-corner, (1700?).

Upon a complaint and rumour that there were diverse little children taken up, and shipped aboard of some ship or ships to be transported for the plantations. London: Great Britain Admiralty, 1650.

"Virginia Colonial Records (Continued)." *The Virginia Magazine of History and Biography* 15(1) (July 1907): 30–43.

von Uchteritz, Heinrich. "A German Indentured Servant in Barbados in 1652." Edited by Alexander Gunkel and Jerome S. Handler. *Journal of the Barbados Museum and Historical Society* 33 (1970): 93–5.

Walter, Alice G., ed. *Lower Norfolk County, Virginia Court Records: Book "A," 1637–1646 & Book "B," 1646–1651/2*. Baltimore: Genealogical Publishing Company, 2002.

Wilmore, John. *The Case of John Wilmore, Truly and Impartially Related*. London: Printed for Edward Powell, 1682.

Williamson, Peter. *French and Indian Cruelty: Exemplified in the Life and Various Vicissitudes of Fortune of Peter Williams* (1757). In *Held Captive by Indians: Selected Narratives, 1642–1836*, edited by Richard VanDerBeets, 216–17. Knoxville: University of Tennessee Press, 1994.

York County Deeds, Orders, and Wills. Books 1–12, 1633–1706. Library of Virginia, York County Microfilms, Reels 1–5.

SECONDARY SOURCES

Abramitzky, Ran, and Fabio Braggion. "Migration and Human Capital: Self-Selection of Indentured Servants to the Americas." *Journal of Economic History* 66(4) (December 2006): 882–905.

Altink, Henrice. "Slavery by Another Name: Apprenticed Women in Jamaican Workhouses in the Period 1834–81." *Social History* 26(1) (2001): 40–59.

Amussen, Susan. "'Being Stirred to Much Unquietness': Violence and Domestic Violence in Early Modern England." *Journal of Women's History* 6(2) (Summer 1994): 70–89.

– *Caribbean Exchanges: Slavery and the Transformation of English Society, 1640–1700*. Chapel Hill: University of North Carolina Press, 2007.

– *An Ordered Society: Gender and Class in Early Modern England*. Oxford: Basil Blackwell Ltd, 1988.

– "Social Hierarchies." In *The Elizabethan World*, edited by Susan Doran and Norman Jones, 271–84. New York: Routledge, 2014.

Andrews, C.M. *British Committees, Commissions, and Councils of Trade and Plantations, 1622–1675*. Baltimore: Johns Hopkins University Press, 1908.

Ariès, Philippe. *Centuries of Childhood*. London: Jonathan Cape, 1962.

Atkinson, Alan. "The Free-born Englishman Transported: Convict Rights as a Measure of Eighteenth-Century Empire." *Past & Present* 144(1) (August 1994): 88–115.

Baker, John H. "The Refinement of English Criminal Jurisprudence, 1500–1848." In *The Legal Profession and the Common Law*, edited by John Baker, 303–24. London: Hambledon, 1986.

– "Criminal Courts and Procedure at Common Law, 1550–1800." In *Crime in England*, edited by J.S. Cockburn, 15–48. Princeton: Princeton University Press, 1977.

Balak, Benjamin, and Jonathan M. Lave. "The Dismal Science of Punishment: The Legal-Economy of Convict Transportation to the American Colonies." *Journal of Law & Politics* 18(4) (2002): 879–919.

Beattie, John. "Crime and the Courts in Surrey, 1736–1753." In *Crime in England, 1550–1800*, edited by J.S. Cockburn, 155–86. Princeton: Princeton University Press, 1977.

Beckles, Hilary. "The Colours of Property: Brown, White and Black Chattels and Their Responses on the Caribbean Frontier." In *Unfree Labour in the Development of the Atlantic World*, edited by Paul Lovejoy and Nicholas Rogers, 36–51. London: Frank Cass, 1994.

– "The Concept of 'White Slavery' in the English Caribbean during the

Early Seventeenth Century." In *Early Modern Conceptions of Property*, edited by John Brewer and Susan Staves, 572–84. London: Routledge, 1996.

– *History of Barbados*. Cambridge: Cambridge University Press, 1990.

– "'Riotous and Unruly Lot': Irish Indentured Servants and Freemen in the English West Indies, 1644–1713." *William and Mary Quarterly*, 3rd Ser., 47(4) (1990): 503–22.

– *White Servitude and Black Slavery in Barbados, 1627–1715*. Knoxville: University of Tennessee Press, 1989.

Beckles, Hilary, and Andrew Downes. "An Economic Formalization of the Origins of Black Slavery in the British West Indies, 1624–1645." *Social and Economic Studies* 34(2), (June 1985): 1–25.

– "The Economics of Transition to the Black Labor System in Barbados, 1630–1680." *Journal of Interdisciplinary History* 18(2) (Autumn 1987): 225–47.

Beier, A.L. *Masterless Men: The Vagrancy Problem in England, 1560–1640*. London: Methuen, 1985.

Beitzell, Edwin Warfield. *The Cheseldyne Family*. Washington, DC: N.p., 1949.

Bellamy, J.G. *The Criminal Trial in Later Medieval England*. Toronto: University of Toronto Press, 1998.

Ben-Amos, Ilana. *Adolescence and Youth in Early Modern England*. New Haven: Yale University Press, 1994.

Beyers, Chris. "Ebenezer Cooke's Satire, Calculated to the Meridian of Maryland." *Early American Literature* 33(1) (1998): 62–85.

Biernacki, Richard. "Cultural Coherence in Early Modern England: The Invention of Contract." *American Journal of Cultural Sociology* 2(3) (October 2014): 277–99.

Bilder, Mary Sarah. *The Transatlantic Constitution*. Cambridge, MA: Harvard University Press, 2004.

Block, Kristen, and Jenny Shaw. "Subjects without an Empire: The Irish in the Early Modern Caribbean." *Past and Present* 210 (February 2011): 33–60.

Bolland, O. Nigel. "Systems of Domination after Slavery: The Control of Land and Labor in the British West Indies after 1838." *Comparative Studies in Society and History* 23(4) (1981): 591–619.

Boulton, Jeremy. "The Poor among the Rich: Paupers and the Parish in the West End, 1600–1724." In *Londinopolis: Essays in the Cultural and Social History of Early Modern London–*, edited by Paul Griffiths and Mark S.R. Jenner, 197–225. Manchester: Manchester University Press, 2000.

Braddick, Michael J. *State Formation in Early Modern England, c. 1550–1700*. Cambridge: Cambridge University Press, 2000.

Braddick, Michael J., and J. Walter, eds. *Negotiating Power in Early Modern Society*. Cambridge: Cambridge University Press, 2001.

Breen, T.H. "A Changing Labor Force and Race Relations in Virginia 1660–1710." *Journal of Social History* 7(1) (Autumn 1973): 3–25.

Brewer, Holly. *By Birth or Consent: Children, Law, and the Anglo-American Revolution in Authority*. Chapel Hill: University of North Carolina Press, 2005.

Briggs, John. *Crime and Punishment in England*. London: University College London Press, 1996.

Brown, Kathleen. *Good Wives, Nasty Wenches, and Anxious Patriarchs*. University of North Carolina Press: Chapel Hill, 1996.

Burnard, Trevor. "European Migration to Jamaica, 1655–1780." *William and Mary Quarterly* 53(4) (October 1966): 769–96.

Campbell, Persia. *Chinese Coolie Emigration to Countries within the British Empire*. London: Frank Cass, 1971.

Carr, Lois. "Emigration and the Standard of Living: The Seventeenth Century Chesapeake." *The Journal of Economic History* 52(2) (1992): 271–91.

Carr, Lois, and Lorena Walsh. "The Planter's Wife: The Experience of White Women in Seventeenth-Century Maryland." *William and Mary Quarterly*, 3rd Series, 34(4) (1977): 542–71.

Carr, Lois, Russell Menard, and Lorena Walsh. *Robert Cole's World: Agriculture and Society in Early Maryland*. Chapel Hill: University of North Carolina Press, 1991.

Carroll, Kenneth. "From Bond Slave to Governor: The Strange Career of Charles Bayly." *Journal of the Friends Historical Society* 52 (1968): 19–38.

Carson, Hampton L. "The Right to Counsel in a Criminal Case." *The American Law Register (1852–1891)* 30(10) (1882): 625–36.

Christoph, Peter. "The Freedmen of New Amsterdam." *Journal of the Afro-American Historical and Genealogical Society* 4 (Winter 1983): 157–70.

Clark, Alice. *Working Life of Women in the Seventeenth Century*. London: Routledge, 1982 (1919).

Coers, Donald V. "New Light on the Composition of Ebenezer Cook's Sot-Weed Factor." *American Literature* 49(4) (1978): 604–6.

Coldham, Peter Wilson. *Emigrants in Chains*. Baltimore, MD: Genealogical Publishing Co., 1992.

Cooper, William. *Liberty and Slavery: Southern Politics to 1860*. Columbia: University of South Carolina Press, 2001.

Crawford, Patricia. "Sexual Knowledge in England, 1500–1750." In *Sexual Knowledge, Sexual Science*, edited by Roy Porter and Mikulas Teich, 82–106. Cambridge: Cambridge University Press 1994.

Cunningham, Hugh. *Children and Childhood in Western Society since 1500.* Hoboken: Taylor and Frances, 2014.

– "The Employment and Unemployment of Children in England, c. 1680–1851." *Past and Present,* 126 (1990): 115–50.

Dahlberg, Sandra. "'Do Not Forget Me': Richard Frethorne, Indentured Servitude, and the English Poor Law of 1601." *Early American Literature* 47(1) (2012): 1–30.

Daniels, Christine. "'Liberty to Complaine': Servant Petitions in Maryland, 1652–1797." In *The Many Legalities of Early America,* edited by Christopher Tomlins and Bruce Mann, 219–49. Chapel Hill: University of North Carolina Press, 2001.

Davenport, Romola Jane. "Infant-feeding Practices and Infant Survival by Familial Wealth in London, 1752–1812." *The History of the Family* 24(1) (2019): 174–206.

Davis, David Brion. *Inhuman Bondage: The Rise and Fall of Slavery in the New World.* Oxford: Oxford University Press, 2006.

Davis, Owen, and Francesca Matteoni. *Executing Magic in the Modern Era: Criminal Bodies and the Gallows in Popular Medicine.* Cham, Switzerland: Springer International, 2017.

De Barros, Juanita. "Urban British Guiana, 1838–1924." In *Masters, Servants, and Magistrates in Britain and the Empire, 1562–1955,* edited by Douglas Hay and Paul Craven, 323–37. Chapel Hill: University of North Carolina Press, 2004.

Donoghue, John. "'Out of the Land of Bondage': The English Revolution and the Atlantic Origins of Abolition." *The American Historical Review* 115(4) (October 2010): 943–74.

Dressler, Nicole. "'Enimies to Mankind': Convict Servitude, Authority, and Humanitarianism in the British Atlantic World." *Early American Studies* 17(3): 343–76.

Dummett, Ann, and Andrew Nicol. *Subjects, Citizens, Aliens and Others.* London: Weidenfeld and Nicolson, 1990.

Dunn, Richard. *Sugar and Slaves: The Rise of the Planter Class in the English West Indies, 1624–1713.* Chapel Hill: University of North Carolina Press, 1972.

Ekirch, A. Roger. "Bound for America: A Profile of British Convicts Transported to the Colonies, 1718–1775." *William and Mary Quarterly,* 3rd Series, (1985): 184–200.

Elliott, John H. *Empires of the Atlantic World.* New Haven: Yale University Press, 2006.

Eltis, David. "Europeans and the Rise and Fall of African Slavery in the Americas." *American Historical Review* 98(5) (December 1993): 1399–1423.

– *The Rise of African Slavery in the Americas*. New York: Cambridge University Press, 2000.

Erikson, Amy Louise. *Women and Property in Early Modern England*. London: Routledge, 1993.

Ethridge, Robbie, and Sheri M. Shuck-Hall, eds. *Mapping the Mississippian Shatter Zone: The Colonial Indian Slave Trade and Regional Instability in the American South*. Lincoln: University of Nebraska Press, 2009.

Ewen, Misha. "'Poore Soules' Migration, Labor, and Visions for Commonwealth in Virginia." In *Virginia 1619: Slavery and Freedom in the Making of English America*, edited by Paul Musselwhite, Peter Mancall, and James Horn, 133–49. Chapel Hill: University of North Carolina Press, 2019.

Fildes, Valerie. *Breasts, Bottles and Babies: A History of Infant Feeding*. Edinburgh: Edinburgh University Press, 1986.

Fisher, Linford D. "'Why Shall Wee Have Peace to Bee Made Slaves': Indian Surrenderers during and after King Philip's War." *Ethnohistory* 64(1) (1 January 2017): 91–114.

Fitzmaurice, Andrew. "The Company-Commonwealth." In *Virginia 1619*, edited by Paul Musselwhite, Peter Mancall, and James Horn, 193–214. Chapel Hill: University of North Carolina Press, 2019.

Fogleman, Aaron. "From Slaves, Convicts, and Servants to Free Passengers: The Transformation of Immigration in the Era of the American Revolution." *The Journal of American History* 85(1) (June 1998): 43–76.

– "Migrations to the Thirteen British North American Colonies." *Journal of Interdisciplinary History* 22(4) (Spring 1992): 691–709.

Foner, Eric. *Give Me Liberty!: An American History*. New York: W.W. Norton & Company, 2009.

Fontaine, Laurence, ed. *Alternative Exchanges: Second-Hand Circulations from the Sixteenth Century to the Present*. Oxford: Berghahn Books, 2008.

Foxley, Rachel. *The Levellers: Radical Political Thought in the English Revolution*. New York: Manchester University Press, 2013.

Franklin, John Hope. *Runaway Slaves: Rebels on the Plantations*. Oxford: Oxford University Press, 1999.

Franks, Mary Anne. "Real Men Advance, Real Women Retreat: Stand Your Ground, Battered Women's Syndrome, and Violence as Male Privilege." *University of Miami Law Review* 68(4) (2014): 1099–128.

Fumerton, Patricia. *Unsettled: The Culture of Mobility and the Working Poor in Early Modern England*. Chicago: University of Chicago Press, 2006.

Galenson, David. "The Market Evaluation of Human Capital: The Case of

Indentured Servitude." *Journal of Political Economy* 89(3) (June 1981):
446–67.
– "The Rise and Fall of Indentured Servitude in the Americas: An Economic
Analysis." *Journal of Economic History* 44(1) (March 1984): 1–26.
– *White Servitude in Colonial America*. Cambridge: Cambridge University
Press, 1981.
Gallay, Alan. *The Indian Slave Trade: The Rise of the English Empire in the
American South, 1670–1717*. New Haven: Yale University Press, 2002.
Gallay, Alan, ed. *Indian Slavery in Colonial America*. Lincoln: University of
Nebraska Press, 2009.
Games, Alison. "Migration." In *The British Atlantic World, 1500–1800*, edited
by David Armitage and Michael Braddick, 31–50. New York: Palgrave,
2002.
Gardiner, Samuel Rawson. *History of the Commonwealth and Protectorate:
1649–1656*, v. 4: 1655–1656. Gloucestershire: Windrush, 1989 (1903).
Gardner, Carol. *The Involuntary American: A Scottish Prisoner's Journey to the
New World*. Yardley, PA: Westholme Publishing, 2019.
Gaskill, Malcolm. *Crime and Mentalities in Early Modern England*. Cam-
bridge: Cambridge University Press, 2000.
– "Reporting Murder: Fiction in the Archives in Early Modern Eng-
land." *Social History* 23(1) (1998): 1–30.
Gerrard, Christopher, Pam Graves, Andrew Millard, Richard Annis, and
Anwen Caffell. *Lost Lives, New Voices: Unlocking the Stories of the Scottish
Soldiers at the Battle of Dunbar, 1650*. Oxford: Oxbow Books, 2018.
Goldie, Mark. "The Unacknowledged Republic: Officeholding in Early
Modern England." In *The Politics of the Excluded, c. 1500–1850*, edited by
Tim Harris, 153–94. New York: Palgrave, 2001.
Gowing, Laura. *Domestic Dangers: Women, Words, and Sex in Early Modern
London*. Oxford: Clarendon Press, 1998.
– *Gender Relations in Early Modern England*. London: Routledge, 2012)
– "Girls on Forms: Apprenticing Young Women in Seventeenth-Century
London." *Journal of British Studies* 55 (July 2016): 447–73.
– "Language, Power and the Law: women's Slander Litigation in Early
Modern London." In *Women, Crime and the Courts in Early Modern Eng-
land*, edited by Jennifer Kermode and Garthine Walker, 26–47. Chapel
Hill: University of North Carolina Press, 1994.
Griffiths, Paul. *Lost Londons: Change Crime, and Control in the Capital City,
1550–1660*. Cambridge: Cambridge University Press, 2008.
– "Masterless Young People in Norwich, 1560–1645." In *The Experience of*

Authority in Early Modern England, edited by Paul Griffiths, Adam Fox, and Steve Hindle, 146–86. New York: St Martin's Press, 1996.

Griffiths, Paul, Adam Fox, and Steve Hindle, eds. *The Experience of Authority in Early Modern England*. New York: St Martin's, 1996.

Grubb, Farley. "The Auction of Redemptioner Servants, Philadephia, 1771–1804." *Journal of Economic History* 48(3) (September 1988): 583–603.

– "Fatherless and Friendless: Factors Influencing the Flow of English Emigrant Servants." *The Journal of Economic History* 52(1) (1992): 85–108.

– "The Market Evaluation of Criminality: Evidence from the Auction of British Convict Labor in America, 1767–1775." *The American Economic Review* 91(1) (March 2001): 295–304.

– "The Market Structure of Shipping German Immigrants to Colonial America." *Pennsylvania Magazine of History and Biography* 11(1) (January 1987): 27–48.

– "Redemptioner Immigration to Pennsylvania." *Journal of Economic History* 46(2) (June 1986): 407–18.

– "Servant Auction Records and Immigration into the Delaware Valley, 1745–1831: The Proportion of Females among Immigrant Servants." *Proceedings of the American Philosophical Society* 133(2) (1989): 154–69.

– "The Transatlantic Market for British Convict Labor." *Journal of Economic History* 60(1) (March 2000): 94–122.

Gwynn, Aubrey. "Cromwell's Policy of Transportation, Part I." *Studies: An Irish Quarterly Review of Letters, Philosophy & Science* 19 (1930): 607–23.

Hajnal, John. "European Marriage Patterns in Perspective." In *Population in History: Essays in Historical Demography,* edited by D.V. Glass and D.E.C. Eversley, chapter 6. London: Edward Arnold, 1965.

– "Two Kinds of Preindustrial Household Formation Systems." *Population and Development Review* 8 (1982): 449–94.

Halliday, Paul. "Brase's Case Making Slave Law as Customary Law in Virginia's General Court, 1619–1625." In *Virginia 1619*, edited by Paul Musselwhite, Peter Mancall, and James Horn, 236–55. Chapel Hill: University of North Carolina Press, 2019.

Handler, Jerome. "Custom and Law: The Status of Enslaved African Seventeenth-Century Barbados." *Slavery & Abolition* 37(2) (January 2016): 233–55.

– "An Early Edict on Slavery in English America." *Journal of the Barbados Museum and Historical Society* 65: 22–43.

– "Slave Revolts and Conspiracies in Seventeenth-Century Barbadoes." *New West Indian Guide* 56 (1982): 5–42.

Handler, Jerome, and Matthew Reilly. "Contesting 'White Slavery' in the

Caribbean: Enslaved Africans and European Indentured Servants in Seventeenth-Century Barbados." *New West Indian Guide* 91 (2017): 30–55.

– "Father Antoine Biet's Account Revisited: Irish Catholics in Mid-Seventeenth Century Barbados." In *Caribbean Irish Connections*, edited by A. Donnell, M. McGarrity, and E. O'Callaghan, 33–46. Mona, Jamaica: University of the West Indies Press, 2015.

Harding, Christopher. *Imprisonment in England and Wales.* London: Croom Helm, 1985.

Harding, Vanessa. "Families in Later Medieval London: Sex, Marriage and Mortality." In *Medieval Londoners*, edited by Elizabeth New and Christian Steer, 11–36. London: University of London Press, 2019.

Harris, Tim, ed. *The Politics of the Excluded, c. 1500–1850.* New York: Palgrave, 2001.

Haskell, Alexander. "A Part of That Commonwealth Hetherto Too Much Neglected." In *Virginia 1619*, edited by Paul Musselwhite, Peter Mancall, and James Horn, 173–92. Chapel Hill: University of North Carolina Press, 2019.

Hay, Douglas, "England, 1562–1875," In *Masters, Servants, and Magistrates in Britain and the Empire, 1562–1955*, edited by Douglas Hay and Paul Craven, 59–116. Chapel Hill: University of North Carolina Press, 2004.

Herndon, Ruth Wallis, and John Murray, eds. *Children Bound to Labor: The Pauper Apprentice System in Early America.* Ithaca, NY: Cornell University Press, 2009.

Herrup, Cynthia. *The Common Peace: Participation and the Criminal Law in Seventeenth-Century England.* Cambridge: Cambridge University Press, 1987.

Hindle, Steve. *On the Parish? The Micro-Politics of Poor Relief in Rural England c. 1550–1750.* Oxford: Oxford University Press, 2004.

– *The State and Social Change in Early Modern England, c. 1550–1640.* London: St Martin's, 2000.

– "'Waste' Children? Pauper Apprenticeship under the Elizabethan Poor Laws." In *Women, Work, and Wages in England, 1600–1850*, edited by Penelope Lane and Neil Raven, 15–46. Woodbridge, Suffolk: Boydell Press, 2004.

Hindle, Steve, and John E. Murray. "Recreating Proper Families in England and North America." In *Children Bound to Labor: The Pauper Apprentice System in Early America*, edited by Ruth Wallis Herndon, and John Murray. Ithaca, NY: Cornell University Press, 2009.

Hoff, Joan. *Law, Gender, and Injustice: A Legal History of US Women.* New York: New York University Press, 1991.

Hodes, Martha. *White Women, Black Men: Illicit Sex in the Nineteenth-Century South.* New Haven: Yale University Press, 1999.

Houlbrooke, Ralph. *The English Family, 1450–1700.* London: Routledge, 1984.

Hui, Ong Jin. "Chinese Indentured Labour: Coolies and Colonies." In *The Cambridge Survey of World Migration*, edited by Robin Cohen, 51–56. Cambridge, UK: Cambridge University Press, 1995.

Hulsebosch, Daniel. "The Ancient Constitution and the Expanding Empire: Sir Edward Coke's British Jurisprudence." *Law and History Review* 21(3) (Autumn 2003): 439–82.

Humphries, Jennett. "Mary Carleton." In *Dictionary of National Biography*, v. 9, edited by Leslie Stephen. London: Smith, Elder & Co., 1887.

Ibbetson, David. "Sixteenth Century Contract Law: Slade's Case in Context." *Oxford Journal of Legal Studies* 4(3) (1984): 295–317.

Jennings, John Melville. "The Poor Unhappy Transported Felon's Sorrowful Account." *The Virginia Magazine of History and Biography* 56(2) (April 1948): 180–94.

Johnson, Robert C. "The Transportation of Vagrant Children from London to Virginia, 1618–22." In *Early Stuart Studies*, edited by Howard S. Reinmuth Jr, 137–51. Minneapolis: University of Minnesota Press, 1970.

Jordan, Winthrop. *White over Black: American Attitudes toward the Negro, 1550–1812*, 2nd ed. Chapel Hill: University of North Carolina Press, 2012.

Kahn, Victoria. *Wayward Contracts: The Crisis of Political Obligation in England, 1640–1674.* Princeton: Princeton University Press, 2004.

Kesselring, Krista. *Mercy and Authority in the Tudor State.* Cambridge: Cambridge University Press, 2003.

– "No Greater Provocation? Adultery and the Mitigation of Murder in English Law." *Law and History Review* 34(1) (2016): 199–225.

Kettner, James H. *The Development of American Citizenship, 1608–1870.* Chapel Hill: University of North Carolina Press, 1978.

Kussmaul, Ann. *Servants in Husbandry in Early Modern England.* Cambridge: Cambridge University Press, 1981.

Lai, Walton Look. *The Chinese in the West Indies, 1806–1995.* Kingston, Jamaica: University of the West Indies Press, 1998.

Lashua, Kristen. "Children at the Birth of Empire, c. 1600–1760." PhD dissertation, University of Virginia, 2015.

Laslett, Peter. "Size and Structure of the Household in England over Three Centuries." *Population Studies* 23 (1969): 199–223.

MacFarlane, Alan. *Marriage and Love in England, 1300–1840.* Oxford: Blackwell, 1986.

Mair, Lucille. *A Historical Study of Women in Jamaica, 1655–1844.*
   Barbados: University of the West Indies Press, 2006.
McLaren, Dorothy. "Marital Fertility and Lactation, 1570–1720." In *Women in English Society 1500–1800*, edited by Mary Prior, 22–53. New York: Methen & Co., 1985.
Meldrum, Tim. *Domestic Service and Gender, 1660–1750: Life and Word in the London Household.* Cambridge: Cambridge University Press, 1999.
– "London Domestic Servants from Depositional Evidence, 1660–1750." In *Chronicling Poverty, the Voices and Strategies of the English Poor, 1640–1840*, edited by Tim Hitchcock, Pamela Sharpe, and Peter King, 47–69 (New York: St Martin's Press, 1997).
Menard, Russell. "From Servant to Freeholder: Status Mobility and Property Accumulation in Seventeenth-Century Maryland." *The William and Mary Quarterly* 30(1) (1973): 37–64.
– "Making a 'Popular Slave Society' in Colonial British America." *The Journal of Interdisciplinary History* 43(3) (2013): 377–95.
– *Migrants, Servants, and Slaves: Unfree Labor in Colonial British America.* Aldershot: Ashgate, 2001.
– *Sweet Negotiations: Sugar, Slavery, and Plantation Agriculture in Early Barbados.* Charlottesville: University of Virginia Press, 2014.
Mendelson, Sara, and Patricia Crawford. *Women in Early Modern England, 1550–1720.* Oxford: Oxford University Press, 1998.
Mohapatra, Prabhu. "Assam and the West Indies, 1860–1920." In *Masters, Servants, and Magistrates in Britain and the Empire, 1562–1955*, edited by Douglas Hay and Paul Craven, 455–80. Chapel Hill: University of North Carolina Press, 2004.
Morgan, Edmund. *American Slavery, American Freedom.* New York: Norton, 1975.
– *Inventing the People: the Rise of Popular Sovereignty in England and America.* New York: Norton, 1988.
Morgan, Gwenda. "Law and Social Change in Colonial Virginia: The Role of the Grand Jury in Richmond County, 1692–1776." *The Virginia Magazine of History and Biography* 95(4) (October 1987): 453–80.
Morgan, Gwenda, and Peter Rushton. *Banishment in the Early Atlantic World: Convicts, Rebels, and Slaves.* London: Bloomsbury, 2013.
– *Eighteenth Century Criminal Transportation: The Formation of the Criminal Atlantic.* New York: Palgrave, 2004.
– "Print Culture, Crime, and Transportation in the Criminal Atlantic." *Continuity and Change* 22(1) (2007): 49–71.

- "Running Away and Returning Home: The Fate of English Convicts in the American Colonies." *Crime, History, & Societies* 7(2) (2003): 61–80.

Morgan, Kenneth. "Convict Runaways in Maryland, 1745–74." *Journal of American Studies* 23 (1989): 253–68.

- "English and American Attitudes towards Convict Transportation 1718–1775." *History*, 72(236) (October 1987): 416–31.

- *Slavery and the British Empire*. Oxford: Oxford University Press, 2007.

- *Slavery and Servitude in North America, 1607–1800*. Edinburgh: Edinburgh University Press, 2000.

Morgan, Philip. "Virginia Slavery in Atlantic Context, 1550 to 1650." In *Virginia 1619*, edited by Paul Musselwhite, Peter Mancall, and James Horn, 85–107. Chapel Hill: University of North Carolina Press, 2019.

Muller, Hannah Weiss. *Subjects and Sovereign: Bonds of Belonging in the Eighteenth-Century British Empire*. New York: Oxford University Press, 2017.

Murphy, Justin. "Are 'Stand Your Ground' Laws Racist and Sexist? A Statistical Analysis of Cases in Florida, 2005–2013." *Social Science Quarterly* 99(1) (2013): 439–45.

Nash, Gary. *Red, White & Black*, 4th ed. Upper Saddle River, NJ: Prentice Hall, 2000.

Newman, Simon P. *A New World of Labor: The Development of Plantation Slavery in the British Atlantic*. Philadelphia: University of Pennsylvania Press, 2013.

Newton, Arthur Percival. *The Colonizing Activities of the English Puritans*. New Haven: Yale University Press, 1914.

Northrup, David. *Indentured Labor in the Age of Imperialism, 1834–1922*. Cambridge: Cambridge University Press, 1995.

Norton, Mary Beth. "'Either Married or to Be Married': Women's Legal Inequality in Early America." In *Inequality in Early America*, edited by Carla Pestana and Sharon Salinger, 25–45. Hanover, NH: University Press of New England, 1999.

Offutt Jr, William M. "The Limits of Authority Courts, Ethnicity, and Gender in the Middle Colonies, 1670–1710." In *The Many Legalities of Early America*, edited by Christopher Tomlins and Bruce Mann, 356–87. Chapel Hill: University of North Carolina Press, 2001.

Oldham, J.C. "On Pleading the Belly: A History of the Jury of Matrons." *Criminal Justice History* 6 (1985): 1–64.

O'Malley, Gregory. *Final Passages: The Intercolonial Slave Trade of British America, 1619–1807*. Chapel Hill: University of North Carolina Press, 2014.

Ozment, Stephen. *When Fathers Ruled: Family Life in Reformation Europe*. Cambridge, MA: Harvard University Press, 1983.

Pagan, John. *Anne Orthwood's Bastard: Sex and Law in Early Virginia*. Oxford: Oxford University Press, 2003.

Pagden, Anthony. "Human Rights, Natural Rights, and Europe's Imperial Legacy." *Political Theory* 31(2) (2003): 171–99.

Patterson, Orlando. *Slavery and Social Death: A Comparative Study*. Cambridge, MA: Harvard University Press, 1982.

Peltonen, Markku. "Citizenship and Republicanism in Elizabethan England." In *Republicanism: A Shared European Heritage*, v. 1, edited by Martin van Gelderen and Quentin Skinner, 85–106. Cambridge: Cambridge University Press, 2002.

– *Classical Humanism and Republicanism in English Political Thought, 1570–1640*. Cambridge: Cambridge University Press, 1995.

Pendry, E.D. *Elizabethan Prisons and Prison Scenes*. Salzburg: Institut für Englische Sprache und Literatur, 1974.

Pestana, Carla Gardina. *The English Atlantic in an Age of Revolution, 1640–1661*. Cambridge, MA: Harvard University Press, 2004.

Peyrol-Kleiber, Elodie. "Starting Afresh: Freedom Dues vs Reality in 17th Century Chesapeake." *Mémoire(s), identité(s), marginalité(s) dans le monde occidental contemporain* 19 (2018): n.p.

Pollock, Linda. *Forgotten Children: Parent-Child Relations from 1500–1900*. Cambridge: Cambridge University Press, 1983.

Pound, John. *Poverty and Vagrancy in Tudor England*, 2nd ed. London: Longman, 1986.

Prendergast, John. *The Cromwellian Settlement of Ireland*. New York: P.M. Haverty, 1868.

Price, Polly J. "Natural Law and Birthright Citizenship in Calvin's Case (1608)." *Journal of Law and the Humanities* 9(1) (1997): 73–145.

"Purchasing Power of British Pounds from 1270 to Present." Measuring-Worth, 2020. www.measuringworth.com/ppoweruk/.

Quinlan, Michael. "Australia, 1788–1902." In *Masters, Servants, and Magistrates in Britain and the Empire, 1562–1955*, edited by Douglas Hay and Paul Craven, 219–50. Chapel Hill: University of North Carolina Press, 2004.

Rabb, Theodore K. *Jacobean Gentleman: Sir Edwin Sandys, 1561–1629*. Princeton: Princeton University Press, 1998.

Rackrow, Felix. "The Right to Counsel: English and American Precedents." *The William and Mary Quarterly* 11(1) (January 1954): 3–27.

Ransome, David. "Wives for Virginia." *The William and Mary Quarterly*, 3rd Series, 48(1) (1991): 3–18.

Rediker, Marcus. *The Slave Ship: A Human History*. New York: Viking, 2007.

Rediker, Marcus, Cassandra Pybus, and Emma Christopher, eds. *Many Middle Passages: Forced Migration and the Making of the Modern World*. Berkeley: University of California Press, 2007.

Reinke-Williams, Tim. "Women's Clothes and Female Honour in Early Modern London." *Continuity and Change* 26(1) (2011): 69–88.

Reséndez, Andrés. *The Other Slavery: The Uncovered Story of Indian Enslavement in America*. Boston: Houghton Mifflin, 2017.

Rice, James D. *Tales from a Revolution, Bacon's Rebellion and the Transformation of Early America*. Oxford: Oxford University Press, 2012.

Riesenberg, Peter. *Citizenship in the Western Tradition*. Chapel Hill: University of North Carolina Press, 1992.

[no author]. "The Right to Counsel in Civil Litigation." *Columbia Law Review* 66(7) (1966): 1326–8.

Rogers, Nini. *Ireland, Slavery and Anti-Slavery*. New York: Palgrave, 2001.

Roopnarine, Lomarsh. *Indo-Caribbean Indenture: Resistance and Accommodation, 1838–1920*. Kingston, Jamaica: University of the West Indies Press, 2007.

Rosenthal, Margaret. "Cultures of Clothing in Late Medieval and Early Modern Europe." *Journal of Medieval and Early Modern Studies* 39(3) (2009): 459–81.

Rountree, Helen. *Pocahontas's People: The Powhatan Indians of Virginia through Four Centuries*. Norman: University of Oklahoma Press, 1990.

Rugemar, Edward. "The Development of Mastery and Race in the Comprehensive Slave Codes of the Greater Caribbean during the Seventeenth Century." *William and Mary Quarterly* 70(3) (July 2013): 429–58.

Russo, Jean, and Elliot Russo. "Responsive Justices." In *Children Bound to Labor: The Pauper Apprentice System in Early America*, edited by Ruth Wallis Herndon and John Murray. Ithaca, NY: Cornell University Press, 2009.

Salinger, Sharon. "'Send No More Women': Female Servants in Eighteenth-Century Philadelphia." *The Pennsylvania Magazine of History and Biography* 107(1) (1983): 29–48.

– *To Serve Well and Faithfully: Labor and Indentured Servants in Pennsylvania, 1682–1800*. Cambridge: Cambridge University Press, 1987.

Salmon, Marylynn. *Women and the Law of Property in Early America*. Chapel Hill: University of North Carolina Press, 1986.

Sharpe, J.A. *Crime in Early Modern England 1550–1750*. London: Longman, 1984.

- *Defamation and Sexual Slander in Early Modern England.* York: Borthwick Institute of Historical Research, 1980.
- "Domestic Homicide in Early Modern England." *The Historical Journal* 24(1) (March 1981): 29–48.

Shaw, Jenny. *Everyday Life in the Early English Caribbean: Irish, Africans, and the Construction of Difference.* Athens, GA: University of Georgia Press, 2013.

Sheppard, Jill. *The "Redlegs" of Barbados: Their Origins and History.* Millwood, NY: KTO Press, 1977.

Sheridan, Richard B. *Sugar and Slavery: An Economic History of the British West Indies, 1623–1775.* Kingston: Canoe Press, 2000.

Skinner, Quentin. "Classical Liberty and the Coming of the English Civil War." In *Republicanism: A Shared European Heritage,* edited by Martin van Gelderen and Quentin Skinner, v. 2, 9–28. Cambridge: Cambridge University Press, 2002.

Slack, Paul. *The English Poor Law, 1531–1782.* Cambridge: Cambridge University Press, 1995.
- *The Impact of Plague in Tudor and Stuart England.* Routledge: London, 1983.
- *From Reformation to Improvement: Public Welfare in Early Modern England.* Oxford: Clarendon Press, 1998.
- *Poverty and Policy in Tudor and Stuart England.* London: Longman, 1988.

Smallwood, Stephanie. *Saltwater Slavery: A Middle Passage from Africa to American Diaspora.* Cambridge, MA: Harvard University Press, 2008.

Smith, Abbot Emerson. *Colonists in Bondage: White Servitude and Convict Labor in America, 1607–1776.* Chapel Hill: University of North Carolina Press, 1947.
- "The Transportation of Convicts to the American Colonies in the Seventeenth Century." *American Historical Review* 39(2) (January 1934): 232–49.

Somers, Margaret R. "Citizenship and the Place of the Public Sphere: Law, Community and Political Culture in the Transition to Democracy." *American Sociological Review* 58(5) (October 1993): 587–620.
- "Rights, Relationality and Membership: Rethinking the Making and Meaning of Citizenship." *Law & Social Inquiry* 19(1) (1994): 63–112.

Spence, Cathryn. *Women, Credit, and Debt in Early Modern Scotland.* Manchester: Manchester University Press, 2016.

Stone, Lawrence. *The Family, Sex, and Marriage in England, 1500–1800*. New York: Harper & Row, 1977.

Sturtz, Linda. "'As Though I My Self Was Pr[e]sent': Virginia Women with Power of Attorney." In *The Many Legalities of Early America*, edited by Christopher Tomlins and Bruce Mann, 250–71. Chapel Hill: University of North Carolina Press, 2001.

Suranyi, Anna. "Indenture, Transportation, and Spiriting: Seventeenth-Century English Penal Policy and 'Superfluous' Populations." In *Building the Atlantic Empires*, edited by John Donoghue and Evelyn Jennings, 133–59. Leiden, The Netherlands: Brill, 2015.

– "'Willing to Go if They Had Their Clothes': Early Modern Women and Indentured Servitude." In *Challenging Orthodoxies: The Social and Cultural Worlds of Early Modern Women*, edited by Melinda Zook and Sigrun Haude, 193–210. Farnham, UK: Ashgate, 2014.

Thirsk, Joan, ed. *The Agrarian History of England and Wales, v. 4, 1500–1640*. Cambridge: Cambridge University Press, 1967.

Tomlins, Christopher. "Early British America, 1585–1830." In *Masters, Servants, and Magistrates in Britain and the Empire, 1562–1955*, edited by Douglas Hay and Paul Craven, 117–52 (Chapel Hill: University of North Carolina Press, 2004).

– *Freedom Bound: Law, Labor, and Civic Identity in Colonizing English America, 1580–1865*. New York: Cambridge University Press, 2010.

Treckel, Paula A. "Breastfeeding and Maternal Sexuality in Colonial America." *The Journal of Interdisciplinary History* 20(1) (1989): 25–51.

Ulrich, Laurel. *Good Wives: Images and Reality in the Lives of Women in Northern New England*. New York: Knopf, 1982.

Van Den Boogaart, Ernst. "The Servant Migration to New Netherland, 1624–1664." In *Colonialism and Migration: Indentured Labour Before and After Slavery*, edited by P.C. Emmer, 55–82. Hingham, MA: Martinus Nijhoff, 1986.

Van Gelderen, Martin, and Quentin Skinner, eds. "Introduction." In *Republicanism: A Shared European Heritage*, v. 2, 1–8. Cambridge: Cambridge University Press, 2002.

Walker, Garthine. *Crime, Gender, and Social Order in Early Modern England*. Cambridge: Cambridge University Press, 2003.

– "Women, Theft, and the World of Stolen Goods." In *Women, Crime, and the Courts in Early Modern England*, edited by Jennifer Kermode and Garthine Walker, 81–112. Chapel Hill: University of North Carolina Press, 1994.

Walvin, James. *Black Ivory: Slavery in the British Empire.* Oxford: Blackwell, 2001.

Wareing, John. *Indentured Migration and the Servant Trade from London to America, 1618–1718: 'There is Great Want of Servants'.* Oxford: Oxford University Press, 2017.

Wells, Charlotte C. *Law and Citizenship in Early Modern France.* Baltimore: Johns Hopkins University Press, 1995.

Wells, Robert. *The Population of the British Colonies in America before 1776.* Princeton: Princeton University Press, 1975.

Wheeler, Harvey. "Calvin's Case (1608) and the McIlwaine-Schuyler Debate." *The American Historical Review* 61(3) (April 1956): 587–97.

Whittle, Jane. "Housewives and Servants in Rural England, 1440–1650." *Transactions of the Royal Historical Society* 15 (2005): 51–74.

Willen, Diane. "Women in the Public Sphere in Early Modern England: The Case of the Urban Working Poor." *The Sixteenth Century Journal* 19(4) (1988): 559–75.

Withington, Phil. *The Politics of Commonwealth: Citizens and Freemen in Early Modern England.* Cambridge: Cambridge University Press, 2009.

Wolfe, Brendan. "Gloucester County Conspiracy (1663)." *Encyclopedia Virginia,* Virginia Humanities. www.encyclopediavirginia.org/Gloucester_County_Conspiracy_1663#start_entry.

Wood, Betty. *The Origins of American Slavery: Freedom and Bondage in the English Colonies.* New York: Hill and Wang, 1997.

– "Servant Women and Sex in the Seventeenth-Century Chesapeake." In *Women in Early America,* edited by Thomas Foster, Jennifer Morgan, and Carol Berkin, 95–117. New York: NYU Press, 2015.

Woodbridge, Linda. *Vagrancy, Homelessness, and English Renaissance Literature.* Urbana: University of Illinois Press, 2001.

Worden, Blair. "Republicanism, Regicide and Republic: The English Experience." In *Republicanism: A Shared European Heritage,* edited by Martin van Gelderen and Quentin Skinner, v. 1, 307–27. Cambridge: Cambridge University Press, 2002.

Wrightson, Keith. "Two Concepts of Order: Justices, Constables, and Jurymen in Seventeenth-Century England." In *An Ungovernable People: The English and Their Law in the Seventeenth and Eighteenth Centuries,* edited by John Brewer and John Styles, 21–46. London: Hutchinson, 1980.

Wrigley, E.A., R.S. Davies, J.E. Oppen, and R.S. Schofield. *English Population History from Family Reconstitution, 1580–1837.* Cambridge: Cambridge University Press, 1997.

Wrigley, E.A., and R.S. Schofield. *The Population History of England.* Cambridge: Cambridge University Press, 1989.

Zacek, Natalie. "John Nickson (fl. 1687)." *Encyclopedia Virginia,* Virginia Humanities. www.encyclopediavirginia.org/Nickson_John_fl_1687#start_entry.

Zaller, Robert. "The Debate on Capital Punishment during the English Revolution." *The American Journal of Legal History* 31(2) (1987): 126–44.

Index